An Anthology Of Mysticism And Mystical Philosophy

William Kingsland

AN ANTHOLOGY OF MYSTICISM
AND MYSTICAL PHILOSOPHY

AN ANTHOLOGY OF MYSTICISM AND MYSTICAL PHILOSOPHY

WITH NOTES BY THE COMPILER
WILLIAM KINGSLAND

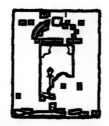

METHUEN & CO. LTD.
36 ESSEX STREET W.C.
LONDON

First Published in 1927

PRINTED IN GREAT BRITAIN

PREFACE

THIS collection of quotations can make no claim to be either comprehensive of the subject of Mysticism in general, or even of the special aspects to which it is mainly devoted. How, indeed, could this be otherwise, seeing that there is such a glorious wealth of mystical literature to draw upon. The work is put forward more or less tentatively ; and should it meet with sufficient favour, it may possibly be enlarged in a future edition.

The quotations herein given, however, have not been selected haphazard. There are some definite and fundamental principles which they are intended to illustrate. These principles have been presented in detail in my two works *Scientific Idealism*, and *Rational Mysticism* ; and also in a more condensed form in *Our Infinite Life*. This Volume may therefore be considered to be more or less of a Supplement to these works.

That which has gradually emerged in my mind as the result of a life-long study of the problems of life, and of mystical and philosophical literature in general, has been a profound conviction that there are certain principles which, in some form or another, have obtained recognition by the wisest and the best in all ages. These principles have been formulated and re-formulated from time to time, from age to age, in divers manners : sometimes in myth and allegory, sometimes as philosophy, sometimes as religion, sometimes as science. I would go even further than that, and say that I am profoundly convinced that underlying all these various forms and modes of presentation there has always existed in the world a real *Gnôsis*, a most profound knowledge of the true nature of *Man*, and of his relation to the world in which he lives and to the greater Universe. But to attain to this knowledge the individual must have special qualifications which have been more or less clearly indicated at various times, and which some of the quotations herein given are intended to set forth.

The present age is one in which great re-adjustments of thought are taking place. The old age-long principles which were almost totally obscured and suppressed by the dogmas and temporal power of ecclesiastical Christianity, are reappearing, and require to be brought into line with our great advance in scientific knowledge, and our resultant philosophical concepts. That this can be done I have endeavoured to show in the three works mentioned above ; and in the present Volume I have prefaced some of the quotations with a short introductory note where this appeared to be necessary or useful. In other cases the quotations speak for themselves.

Without endorsing specifically the idea, or ideas, expressed in any particular quotation, I may say that there is hardly one which has not been to me either profoundly illuminating or greatly inspiring. It is certain that this will also be the case with many readers ; but to what extent must be left for the future to disclose. Meanwhile I may at least dedicate the work to those whose mystical intuition and faculty has been sufficiently developed to enable them to discern that " ONE in the Many, and Many in the ONE " which is the goal of mystical experience and the summation of mystical philosophy.

Mysticism is essentially the exercise of a supernormal faculty transcending intellect, whereby the individual obtains a vital and conscious experience in his inmost being of his oneness with what has been variously termed the Absolute, or Reality, or the Intelligible world, or the Infinite, or God—a sense of *union* with the transcendent yet immanent Root and Source of all Being and all Becoming.

The principles, therefore, which I have endeavoured more particularly to illustrate may be stated as follows :

1. The limits of the intellect, and the intellectual unknowableness of the Absolute.
2. The nature and method of the exercise of the mystical faculty transcending intellect.
3. The Unity of the Universe, and of Man therewith, in every part of his nature. This carries with it by implication *the Divine Nature of Man*.

There are two main aspects of Mysticism, the philosophical or rational, and the emotional or devotional. Following the line of thought developed in my work on *Rational Mysticism*, it is the former of these to which I have given most prominence in this Anthology ; but the latter cannot altogether escape, or be treated as a separate thing. At root, Rational Mysticism is only the ground which we find in our rational faculty or intellect for our emotional states, or deep inner convictions ; or for that *faith* from whence springs the deepest motives of our life, and which lies wholly in a super-rational region, or, in one word, in the *mystical* region of the total content of the SELF.

For the rest, a careful study of the excerpts herein given will, I think, be in itself a liberal education in the philosophy of life, whole and complete.

It remains to add that I desire to tender my warmest thanks to those Authors and Publishers who have freely granted me permission to quote from their works. A complete list of the works referred to in this Anthology is given in the Bibliographical Index ; and to avoid unnecessary repetition of names of books, authors, and publishers, I have there made my acknowledgments individually and severally in connection with each work.

W.K.

RYDE, I.W.
January, 1927

CONTENTS

CONTENTS

BIBLIOGRAPHY

The letters and numbers given after each quotation in this work refer to this Bibliography.

I have also in this indicated my acknowledgme~ to the various Authors and Publishers from whom ₴r- mission to quote from their works has been obtained.

BIOGRAPHICAL NOTES AND INDEX

This contains a short note giving particulars of each ᵛf the Authors herein quoted, together with the page referenc᷄ on which their quotations will be found.

AN ANTHOLOGY OF MYSTICISM
AND MYSTICAL PHILOSOPHY

THE ABSOLUTE

NOTE ON THE ABSOLUTE

THE Absolute is by definition that which has nothing relative to it, and is therefore unitary or all-comprehensive in its nature. And yet not merely do we live in a universe in which everything has the appearance of relativity and multiplicity, but the mind itself refuses to overpass an inherent duality, while at the same time apprehending, but not comprehending, a fundamental unity.

That is the great paradox of metaphysics, the problem which the rational faculty or intellect vainly endeavours to solve—how, namely, to reconcile in one unitary concept, in one *Absolute*, all the *opposites* which are the great facts of our consciousness.

Perhaps, however, it would be better to say that our *present or normal consciousness* is one of relativity, and not of wholeness ; for it is an undoubted fact that in the *mystical consciousness* this relativity is transcended, and a sense of wholeness, completeness and union is achieved. This fact, as will be clearly seen from the quotations which I have given, has been recognised in the most ancient literature which we possess, and is fully endorsed at the present day.

That which emerges from the concept of the Absolute as

the all-inclusive *Life* or *Being* of the Universe, is in fact
this very *oneness* of the individual and the Absolute which
is the great mystical experience. It has nowhere been
more clearly stated than in the ancient *Upanishads*, where
it is summed up in the formula ' THAT ART THOU.'

It will further be seen from the following quotations how
definitely it has been recognised from the most ancient
times that nothing can be affirmed of the Absolute ; for
affirmation of any quality implies its opposite : something
which the Absolute is *not*. But if that opposite exists, it
clearly—by our very concept of the Absolute as being all-
inclusive—belongs to the Absolute as much as that which
we affirm.

All this stands in contradistinction to the popular or
dogmatic theology, which does not hesitate to affirm this,
that and the other of ' God ' as an alternative term for the
Absolute.

ABSOLUTE BEING

(*a*) " For to *be* truly, is never not to be, nor to be otherwise. But the former of these is to be invariably the
same ; and the latter is to be without diversity. Hence
it has not in any respect another and another. You must
not, therefore, conceive it to have interval, nor evolve, nor
extend it. Neither, therefore, must you admit that there
is anything of prior and posterior in it. Hence, if there is
neither prior nor posterior about it, but the *is*, is the truest
of all the things about it, and is itself, and this in such a
way as to be essence and life :—if this be the case, again
that which we call eternity will present itself to our view.
But when we say that it is always, and that it is not at one
time being, and at another time non-being, it is requisite to
think that we thus speak for the sake of perspicuity ; since
the term always, is perhaps not properly employed, but is
assumed for the purpose of manifesting its incorruptible

nature. And farther still, it signifies that it never fails. Perhaps, however, it would be better to call it only *being*. But though *being* is a name sufficient to essence, yet since some are of opinion that generation also is essence, it is requisite for the sake of discipline to add the term *always.*" Plotinus. Enn. III, V. (P. 1, p. 123.)

(*b*) " That which is perfect is a Being, who hath comprehended and included all things in Himself and His own Substance, and without whom, and beside whom, there is no true Substance, and in whom all things have their Substance. For He is the Substance of all things, and is in Himself unchangeable and immovable, and changeth and moveth all things else."

Theologia Germanica. (T. 1, p. 1.)

(*c*) " Nearly seven hundred years before the time when Christianity first came into large contact with Greek philosophy, the mind of a Greek thinker, outstripping the slow inferences of popular thought, had leapt to the conception of God as the Absolute Unity. He was the ultimate generalization of all things, expressed as the ultimate abstraction of number : He was not limited by parts or by bodily form ; ' all of Him is sight, all of Him is understanding, all of Him is hearing.' But it is probable that the conception in its first form was rather of a material than of an ideal unity : the basis of later metaphysics was first securely laid by a second form of the conception which succeeded the first half-a-century afterwards. The conception was that of Absolute Being. Only the One really *is* : it was not nor will be : it *is* now, and is everywhere entire, a continuous unity, a perfect sphere which fills all space, undying and immovable." E. Hatch. (H. 1, p. 240.)

(*d*) " We can find no province of the world so low but the Absolute inhabits it. Nowhere is there even a single fact so fragmentary and so poor that to the universe it does not matter. There is truth in every idea however false, there is reality in every existence however slight ; and, where we can point to reality or truth, there is the one undivided life of the Absolute."

F. H. Bradley.   (B. 30, p. 487.)

(e) " The separation (of the Absolute from the Word—Logos) is for us alone who, confined by the limits of our darksome dwelling, can conceive of absolute beings only successively and apart from one another ; but all faculties and all actions which thus seem successive and distinct are one, undivided and ever present to the eyes of that one Being who leads and directs them."

Saint-Martin.   (W. 2, p. 229.)

(f) "He who attributes least mystery to matter is furthest from truth, and he nighest who conjectures the Absolute to be present in fulness of being in the atom."

" A. E." (R. 5, p. 106.)

THE ABSOLUTE, NOT CONCEIVABLE

(a)   " Other, indeed, is IT than the known,
And moreover above the unknown,
—Thus have we heard of the ancients
Who to us have explained IT.

" That which is unexpressed with speech,
That with which speech is expressed—
That indeed know as Brahma,
Not this that people worship as this."
Kena Upanishad, 1, 3, 4. (U. 1, p. 335.)

(b) " For where there is a duality, as it were, there one sees another ; there one speaks to another ; there one hears another ; there one thinks of another ; there one touches another ; there one understands another. But where everything has become just one's own self, then whereby and whom would one see ? then whereby and whom would one smell ? then whereby and whom would one taste ? then whereby and to whom would one speak ? then whereby and whom would one hear ? then whereby and of whom would one think ? then whereby and whom would one touch ? then whereby and whom would one under- stand ? whereby would one understand him by means of whom one understands this All ?

That Soul (or Self, *Atman*) is not this, it is not that (*neti, neti*). It is unseizable, for it cannot be seized ; indestructible, for it cannot be destroyed ; unattached, for it does not attach itself ; is unbound, does not tremble, is not injured.

Lo, whereby would one understand the understander ? "
Brihad-āranyaka Upanishad, IV, 5, 15.   (U. 1, p. 147.)

(*c*) " To find the Father and Maker of this universe is a [great] work, and finding [Him] it is impossible to tell [Him] unto all."   Plato.   (M. 6, Vol. III, p. 217.)

(*d*) " To understand God is difficult, to speak [of Him] impossible. . . .   I have it in my mind, O. Tat, I have it in my mind, that what cannot be spoken of, is God."
                    Hermes.   (M. 6, Vol. III, p. 14.)

(*e*) " Hence, it [*the one*] is in reality ineffable. For of whatever you speak, you speak of a certain thing. But of that which is beyond all things, and which is beyond even most venerable intellect, it is alone true to assert that it has not any other name [than the ineffable], and that it is not some one of all things. Properly speaking, however, there is no name of it, because nothing can be asserted of it."   Plotinus. Enn. V. 3, 13.   (P. 2, p. 280.)

(*f*) " How, therefore, can we speak of it [true *being*] ? We are able, indeed, to say something *of* it, but we do not speak *it*. Nor have we either any knowledge, or intellectual perception of it. How, therefore, do we speak of it, if we do not possess it ? May we not say, that though we do not possess it by knowledge, yet we are not entirely deprived of the possession of it ; but we possess it in such a way that we can speak *of* it, but cannot speak *it* ? For we can say what it is not, but we cannot say what it is ; so that we speak *of* it from things posterior to it. We are not, however, prevented from possessing it, though we cannot say what it is."

Plotinus.   Enn. V. 3, 14.   (P. 2, p. 282.)

(*g*) " Hence there is something even beyond *the one*. The most sublime of the arcane dogmas of the Platonic Theology is this, that the ineffable principle of things is something even beyond *the one*, as is demonstrated by Proclus in his second book, ' On the Theology of Plato,' and particularly by Damascius in his MS. treatise ' On Principles.' . . . What then ? Shall we investigate something else beyond the ineffable ? Or, perhaps, indeed, Plato leads us ineffably through *the one* as a medium, to the ineffable beyond *the one* which is now the subject of discussion ; and this by an ablation of *the one*, in the same manner as he leads us to *the one* by an ablation of other things. But if having ascended as far as to *the one* he is silent, this also is becoming in Plato to be perfectly silent, after the manner of the ancients, concerning things in every respect unspeakable ; for the discourse was indeed most dangerous in consequence of falling on idiotical ears. Hence that which is beyond *the one* is to be honoured in the most perfect silence, and prior to this, by the most perfect ignorance, which despises all knowledge."

Thos. Taylor. *Notes on Plotinus*. (P. 2, pp. 339, 341.)

(*h*) " God, the Father and Fashioner of all things that are, He who is older than the sun, older than the sky, greater than time and lapse of time and the whole stream of nature, is unnamed by legislators, and unspoken by the voice and unseen by the eyes : and since we cannot apprehend His essence, we lean upon words and names and animals, and forms of gold and ivory and silver, and plants and rivers and mountain-peaks and springs of waters, longing for an intuition of Him, and in our inability naming by His name all things that are beautiful in this world of ours.

" It is of this Father and Begetter of the universe that Plato tells us : His name he does not tell us, for he knew it not ; nor does he tell us His colour, for he saw Him not ; nor His size, for he touched Him not. Colour and size are felt by the touch and seen by the sight : but the Deity Himself is unseen by the sight, unspoken by the voice, untouched by fleshly touch, unheard by the hearing, seen only—through its likeness to Him, and heard only—through its kinship with Him, by the noblest and purest and clearest-sighted and swiftest and oldest element of the soul."   Maximus of Tyre.   (H. I, p. 242.)

(*i*) " God is neither sonship nor fatherhood nor anything else known to us or to any other beings, either of the things that are or of the things that are not ; nor does anything that is, know Him as He is, nor does He know anything that is as it is ; He has neither word nor name nor knowledge ; He is neither darkness nor light nor truth nor error ; He can neither be affirmed nor denied ; nay, though we may affirm or deny the things that are beneath Him, we can neither affirm nor deny Him ; for the perfect and sole cause of all is above all affirmation, and that which transcends all is above all subtraction, absolutely separate, and beyond all that is." Dionysius. (S. 15, p. 223.)

(*j*) '' Now if any of you should think that he has learnt the doctrine concerning God from those of the philosophers who are mentioned among you as most ancient, let him give ear to Ammon and Hermes. For Ammon in the Words (*Logoi*) concerning himself calls God ' utterly hidden ' ; while Hermes clearly and plainly declares : To understand God is difficult ; to speak [of Him] impossible, even for one who can understand.''

Justin Martyr.   (M. 6, Vol. III, p. 215.)

(*k*) '' The things which are in part can be apprehended, known, and expressed ; but the Perfect cannot be apprehended, known, or expressed by any creature as creature. Therefore we do not give a name to the Perfect, for it is none of these.   The creature as creature cannot know nor apprehend it, name nor conceive it.''

Theologia Germanica.   (T. 1, p. 2.)

(*l*) '' Now mark ! God is nameless, for no one can know or say anything of him. Anent which a heathen philosopher observes that what we know or predicate about the First Cause is what we ourselves are rather than what the First Cause is, seeing that this transcends speech and knowledge.   If I say God is good, it is not true : I am good, God is not good.   I say more : I am better than God is, for what is good can be better, and what is better can be best.   Now since God is not good therefore he cannot be better : and since he cannot be better therefore he cannot be best.   These three : good, better, best, are remote from God for he is above all.

'' Again, if I say, God is wise, it is not true : I am wiser than he is.   And if I say, God is a being, it is not true : he is a transcendental essence, a super-essential nothingness. Anent which St. Augustine says : the finest thing a man can say of God is that he is silent from consciousness of interior fulness.   Therefore hold thy peace and prate not of God, for prating of him thou liest, committing sin. An thou wilt be without sin and perfect, babble not of God. Neither know anything of God for God is beyond knowing. One philosopher says : had I a God that could know I would have him for my God no longer. Know'st thou of him anything ? He is no such thing, and in that thou knowest of him anything at all thou dost lapse into ignorance, and from ignorance to the condition of a brute. For that which is ignorant in creatures is brutish. Art thou minded, therefore, not to become brutish, know nothing of the unuttered God.

" —What then shall I do ?

" Thou shalt lose thy *thyness* and dissolve in his *hisness* ; thy *thine* shall be his *mine*, so utterly one *mine* that thou in him shalt know eternalwise his *isness*, free from becoming : his nameless nothingness." Eckhart. (E. 1, p. 49.)

(*m*) " Thou shalt apprehend God without image, without semblance and without means.—But for me to know God thus, without means, I must be very he, he very me !

" I say : God must be very I, I very God, so consummately one that this he and this I are one *is*, in this *isness* working one work eternally ; but so long as this he and this I, to wit, God and the soul, are not one single *here*, one single *now*, this *I* cannot work with nor be one with that *he*."　　(*Ibid.*, p. 51.)

(*n*)　　" Think'st thou in temporal speech God's
　　　　Name may uttered be ?
　　It is unspeakable to all eternity."
　　　　　　Angelus Silesius.　(S. 4, p. 34.)

(*o*) " OM, AMITAYA ! measure not with words
　　　Th' Immeasurable ; nor sink the string of thought
　　Into the Fathomless.　Who asks doth err,
　　　Who answers, errs.　Say nought ! "
The Light of Asia.　Sir Edwin Arnold.　(A. 2, p. 214.)

(*p*) " Who dare express Him ?   And who profess Him, saying : ' I believe in Him ! '   Who, feeling, seeing, deny His being, saying : ' I believe Him not ! '   The All-enfolding, the All-upholding, folds and upholds He not thee, me, Himself ?   Arches not there the sky above us ? Lies not beneath us, firm, the earth ?   And rise not, on us shining, friendly, the everlasting stars ?   Look I not, eye to eye, on thee, and feel'st not, thronging to head and heart, the force, still weaving its eternal secret, invisible, visible, round thy life ?   Vast as it is, fill with that force thy heart, and when thou in the feeling wholly blessed art, call it, then, what thou wilt,—call it Bliss ! Heart ! Love ! God ! I have no name to give it ! Feeling is all in all : the name is sound and smoke, obscuring Heaven's clear glow."

Goethe. *Faust*, Scene XVI. (G. 1, Vol. I, p. 191.)

(*q*) " With the people, and especially with the clergy-men, who have Him daily upon their tongues, God becomes a phrase, a mere name, which they utter without any accompanying idea.   But if they were penetrated with His greatness, they would rather be dumb, and for very reverence would not dare to name Him."

Goethe. (G. 1, Vol. I, p. 325.)

(*r*) " The conception of the Absolute and Infinite, from whatever side we view it, appears encompassed with con-tradictions.   There is a contradiction in supposing such an object to exist, whether alone or in conjunction with others ; and there is a contradiction in supposing it not to exist.   There is a contradiction in conceiving it as one ; and there is a contradiction in conceiving it as many. There is a contradiction in conceiving it as personal ; and there is a contradiction in conceiving it as impersonal.   It cannot without contradiction be represented as active, nor without equal contradiction, be represented as inactive.

It cannot be conceived as the sum of all existence ; nor yet can it be conceived as a part of that sum.   A contradiction thus thoroughgoing, while it sufficiently shows the impotence of human reason as an *à priori* judge of all truth, yet is not in itself inconsistent with any form of religious belief."   Henry L. Mansel.   (M. 8, p. 41.)

(*s*) " By the *Absolute* is meant that which exists in and by itself, having no necessary relation to any other being."
(*Ibid.*, p. 75.)

(*t*) " That which is conceived as *absolute* and infinite must be conceived as containing within it the sum not only of all actual but of all possible modes of being."
(*Ibid.*, p. 76.)

(*u*) " Besides that *definite* consciousness of which Logic formulates the laws, there is also an *indefinite* consciousness which cannot be formulated.   Besides complete thoughts, and besides the thoughts which though incomplete admit of completion, there are thoughts which it is impossible to complete, and yet which are still real, in the sense that they are normal affections of the intellect. . . .   To say that we cannot know the Absolute, is, by implication, to affirm that there *is* an Absolute.   In the very denial of our power to learn *what* the Absolute is, there lies hidden the assumption *that* it is ; and the making of this assumption proves that the Absolute has been present to the mind, not as a nothing but as a something. . . .   The very demonstration that a *definite* consciousness of the Absolute is impossible to us, unavoidably presupposes an *indefinite* consciousness of it."
Herbert Spencer.   (S. 10, p. 88.)

(*v*) " We pass into mystical states from out of ordinary consciousness as from a less to a more, as from a smallness into a vastness, and at the same time as from an unrest to a rest. We feel them as reconciling, unifying states. They appeal to the yes-function more than to the no-function in us. In them the unlimited absorbs the limits and peacefully closes the account. Their very denial of every adjective you may propose as applicable to the ultimate truth,—He, the Self, the Atman, is to be described by ' No ! no ! ' only, say the Upanishads,—though it seems on the surface to be a no-function, is a denial made on behalf of a deeper yes. Whoso calls the Absolute anything in particular, or says that it is *this*, seems implicitly to shut it off from being *that*—it is as if he lessened it. So we deny the ' *this*,' negating the negation which it seems to us to imply, in the interests of the higher affirmative by which we are possessed. The fountain-head of Christian mysticism is Dionysius the Areopagite. He describes the absolute truth by negatives exclusively."

William James. (J. 5, p. 416.)

(*w*) " As, in a narrow isle, whatever path we follow it soon ends in the pathless sea, and all movements have one destiny ; so in our narrow life thought never travels far before it looks out on that which it cannot measure or define ; which was, and is, and is to come. This the Everlasting is the only Substance, of which all things are phenomena. This is the abiding Power of which the recurring sequences of natural law are fragmentary manifestations. This is the all-pervading Life which makes the heavens to smile, and the twinkling leaves to dance, and the clouds to frown, and the winds and the waves to sing their song which is wild and slow. In any scientific sense, nay, in any but the vaguest intellectual sense, that Being is Itself unknown, unknowable. Yet the inevitable fascination, with which it draws the dumb, pleading desire of all noblest souls, is a burning fact that shines through all the history of man, and which, were there no adequate significance within it, would convict the universe of vanity and lies."   J. A. Picton.   (P. 3, p. 126.)

(*x*) " An Omnipresent, Eternal, Boundless, and Immutable PRINCIPLE on which all speculation is impossible, since it transcends the power of human conception and could only be dwarfed by any human expression or similitude. It is beyond the range and reach of thought—in the words of Mandukya, ' unthinkable and unspeakable.' "

H. P. Blavatsky.   (B. 31, Vol. I, p. 14.)

THE METAPHYSICAL ABSOLUTE

(*a*) " The rational Absolute is nothing but the extreme point where we arbitrarily suspend causality, continuous and successive magnitude, nothing but an artifice to arrest the indefinite progression of our ideas."

E. Récéjac.   (R. 1, p. 38.)

(*b*) " The concept of the Absolute as it exists in the consciousness of the pure scholar or the pure logician, is the poorest of all in content. Not only is the idea of God fuller in the mystic consciousness, but it appears to develop facts of consciousness of a nature to demand special attention."   (*Ibid.*, p. 40.)

(*c*) " The Absolute, by this time, is no longer, in our eyes, an abstraction, or limit, as it were, with which to define verbally the bounds of the knowable ; it is the supreme Unity which implies substantially all first principles, and which is, in its wholly active essence, Life, Reason, and Freedom. It is the Absolute which creates us and all things with us."   (*Ibid.*, p. 236.)

(*d*) " Efforts to conceive the Absolute rationally tend to suppress imagination and feeling, rather than to heighten them ; and we have learned that they lead us to an Infinite which, qualitatively, is the most meagre of all our concepts. The mystic consciousness, on the contrary, is set in motion in every part of it by Desire ; representations pour in to render the absolute present and ' felt ' ; and if it comes to lose the sense of its own identity, it is through an excess of imagination desiring to express the Infinite by the most vivid synthesis of images, and not by slow elimination of concepts."   (*Ibid.*, p. 172.)

(*e*) " The Absolute is the universal and one idea, which, by an act of ' judgment,' particularises itself to the system of specific ideas ; which after all are constrained by their nature to come back to the one idea where their truth lies. As issued out of this ' judgment ' the Idea is *in the first place* only the one universal *substance* ; but its developed and genuine actuality is to be as a *subject* and in that way as mind."   Hegel.   (H. 9, p. 353.)

(*f*) " We have neither the vocabulary nor the imagination for a description of absolute properties as such.   All physical knowledge is relative to space and time partitions ; and to gain an understanding of the absolute it is necessary to approach it through the relative.   The absolute may be defined as a relative which is always the same no matter what it is relative to.   Although we think of it as self-existing, we cannot give it a place in our knowledge without setting up some dummy to relate it to."
          Profess. A. S. Eddington.   (E. 3, p. 82.)

THE MYSTICAL ABSOLUTE

(*a*) " He who knows the Tao, tells it not : he who tells it, knows it not."
          Lao Tsze.   *The Tâo Teh King.*   (L. 1, p. 12.)

(*b*) " To him who holds in his hands the Great Image

(of the invisible Tâo) the whole world repairs. Men resort to him, and receive no hurt, but (find) rest, peace, and the feeling of ease.

2. Music and dainties will make the passing guest stop (for a time). But though the Tâo as it comes from the mouth, seems insipid and has no flavour, though it seems not worth being looked at or listened to, the use of it is inexhaustible."

Lao Tsze. *The Tâo Teh King.* (S. 1, Vol. XXXIX, p. 77.)

(c) " The Absolute must then be ineffable, indescribable, *and yet not outside of the circle within which we at present are conscious.* It is no other than we are ; consciousness contains it just in so far as consciousness is a knowing. Yet, when we speak of the Absolute all our words must be : ' Neti, Neti,' ' It is not thus ; it is not thus.' So the sage Yâjnavalkya himself, more than once in these legends (*Upanishads*) teaches : To us, *it is as if* the Absolute, in its immediacy, were identical with Nothing. But once more : —Is the Absolute verily a *mere* nothing ? The Hindoo's answer to this question is in one sense precise enough. The Absolute is the very Opposite of a mere Nothing. For it is the fulfilment, attainment, peace, the goal of life, the object of desire, the end of knowledge. Why then does it stubbornly appear as indistinguishable from mere Nothing ? The answer is · *That is a part of our very illusion itself.* The light above the light is, to our deluded vision, darkness. It is our finite realm that is the falsity, the mere nothing. The Absolute is ALL TRUTH."

Josiah Royce. (R. 3, Vol. I, p. 170.)

(d) " This overcoming of all the usual barriers between the individual and the Absolute is the great mystic achievement. In mystic states we both become one with the Absolute and we become aware of our oneness. This is the everlasting and triumphant mystical tradition, hardly altered by differences of clime or creed. In Hinduism, in Neoplatonism, in Sufism, in Christian mysticism, in Whitmanism, we find the same recurring note, so that there is about mystical utterances an eternal unanimity which ought to make a critic stop and think, and which brings it about that the mystical classics have, as has been said, neither birthday nor native land. Perpetually telling of the unity of man with God, their speech antedates languages, and they do not grow old."

William James. (J. 5, p. 419.)

(e) " The mystic Absolute does not withdraw to the heights of the mind, but takes possession of the whole soul, and in that is its distinction from the rational Absolute."

Récéjac. (R. 4, p. 126.)

ADAM

NOTE ON ADAM AND THE FALL

The teaching of Jacob Böhme with regard to Adam and the Fall of Man is exceedingly instructive and mystical ; and yet at the same time, when the student of Bohme has become accustomed to his terminology, it will be found to accord with all that is best in modern science and philosophy.

The Garden of Eden story is allegorical and symbolical. Adam is Humanity, Man, the whole Human Race. Man was created originally " in Paradise to the life eternal in the image of God." [1] But this original spiritual nature of Man has " faded," has sunk into the background, and Man is now impotent in his divine nature because he has turned away from it, being wholly under the sway of the outward physical world, with its attractions, desires and lusts. This is his " Fall," whereby he has lost his original Paradisical state of purity, happiness, and control of all natural forces. " God knew very well that Man would not

[1] *Mysterium Magnum*, XVIII, 4.

stand but fall," says Böhme; thereby recognising that this was an inevitable part of the ordered scheme of the Universe. It is in fact a recognition that what we now call *evolution* is a part of the Divine order of things. In so far as evolution is the *return* of man to his Paradisical state, there must in the first instance necessarily have been an *involution*; and that involution is the "Fall." Evolution here, then, means something very much more than a mere development of physical forms. It means the recovery by Man of his faded spiritual nature; and this is accomplished by the coming to birth again *within* him of this inner divine nature from which he departed, and who (or which) is the Christ, the " second Adam "; but yet is Man himself in his original divine nature.

" Such a man, as Adam was before his Eve, shall arise and again enter into, and eternally possess Paradise." [1] Such is the destiny of the Race, of Man as a unitary whole. It is the World Process as we may very well understand it to-day in the light of science and philosophy. In Eastern philosophy it is represented as the outbreathing and inbreathing of Brahma. It will be found in symbolical language in all the World Scriptures.

ADAM

(*a*) " It is said, it was because Adam ate the apple that he was lost, or fell. I say, it was because of his claiming something for his own, and because of his I, Mine, Me, and the like. Had he eaten seven apples, and yet never claimed anything for his own, he would not have fallen : but as soon as he called something his own, he fell, and would have fallen if he had never touched an apple."

Theologia Germanica. (T. 1, p. 8.)

[1] *Ibid.*, XVIII, 3.

(*b*) " Whence Adam's imagination and earnest hunger did arise, that he should eat of the evil and good, and live in (his) own will.   That is, his will departed out of the equal concord into the multiplicity of the properties ; for he would prove, feel, taste, hear, smell and see them. . . . For the essence of the Tree of the Knowledge of Good and Evil, and the hunger of the desire in Adam, were alike ; what he desired was represented unto him by the Fiat ; Adam's imagination was the cause of it."

Jacob Böhme.   (B. 7, XVII, 37, 40.)

(*c*) " Thus hath Adam's spirit by the imagination brought a power into the earth, and so the matrix of nature gave him what he would have."

Jacob Böhme.   (B. 5.   Part I, Ch. V, 103.)

(*d*) " Now when Adam's hunger was set after the earthliness, it did, by its magnetic power, impress into his fair image the vanity of evil and good ; whereupon the heavenly image of the angelical world's essence did disappear ; as if a man should insinuate some strange matter into a burning and light-shining candle, whereby it should become dark, and at last wholly extinguish.   So it went also with Adam, for he brought his will and desire from God into selfhood and vanity, and broke himself off from God, viz. from the divine harmony."

Jacob Böhme.   (B. 7, XIX, 3.)

(*e*) " Therefore now we know, that we were not created to generate [that which is] earthly, but heavenly, out of the body of the pure element, which [body] *Adam* had before his sleep, and [before] his *Eve* [was], when he was neither man nor woman [male nor female], but one only image of God, full of chastity, out of the pure element. He should have generated an image again like himself ; but because he went into the spirit of this world, therefore his body became earthly, and so the heavenly birth was gone, and God must make the woman out of him, as is before mentioned. Now if we, the children of *Eve*, are to be helped, then there must come a new virgin, and bear us a Son, who should be God with us, and in us."

Jacob Böhme. (B. 2, XXII, 27.)

See also FALL OF MAN (p. 80).

ATTAINMENT, NATURE AND METHOD OF

(a) "Throw out of work the body's senses, and thy Divinity shall come to birth."

Hermes. (M. 6, Vol. II, p. 223.)

(b) " If, then, thou dost not make thyself like unto God, thou canst not know Him. For like is knowable to like [alone].

Make, [then], thyself to grow to the same stature as the Greatness which transcends all measure ; leap forth from every body ; transcend all Time ; become Eternity ; and [thus] shalt thou know God.

Conceiving nothing is impossible unto thyself, think thyself deathless and able to know all,—all arts, all sciences, the way of every life.

Become more lofty than all height, and lower than all depth. Collect into thyself all senses of [all] creatures,— of fire, [and] water, dry and moist. Think that thou art at the same time in every place,—in earth, in sea, in sky ; not yet begotten, in the womb, young, old, [and] dead, in after-death conditions.

And if thou knowest all these things at once,—times, places, doings, qualities, and quantities ; thou canst know God.

But if thou lockest up thy soul within thy body, and dost

debase it, saying : I nothing know ; I nothing can ; I fear the sea ; I cannot scale the sky ; I know not who I was, who I shall be ;—what is there [then] between [thy] God and thee ? " *(Ibid.*, p. 187.)

(c) " Thou knowest [now], my son, the manner of Rebirth. And when the Ten is come, my son, that driveth out the Twelve, the Birth in understanding is complete, and by this Birth we are made into Gods.

Who then doth by His mercy gain this Birth in God, abandoning the body's senses, knows himself [to be of Light and Life] and that he doth consist of these, and [thus] is filled with Bliss." *(Ibid.*, p. 226.)

(d) " The soul also proceeding to, and having now arrived at the desired end, and participating of deity, will know that the supplier of true life is then present. She will likewise then require nothing farther ; for on the contrary, it will be requisite to lay aside other things, to stop in this alone, and to become this alone, amputating every thing else with which she is surrounded. Hence, it is necessary to hasten our departure from hence, and to be indignant that we are bound in one part of our nature, in order that with the whole of our [true] selves, we may fold ourselves about divinity, and have no part void of contact with him. When this takes place, therefore, the soul will both see divinity and herself, as far as it is lawful for her to see him. And she will see herself indeed illuminated, and full of intelligible light ; or rather, she will perceive herself to be a pure light, unburthened, agile, and becoming to be a God, or rather being a God, and then shining forth as such to the view."

Plotinus. Enn. VI, 9. 9. (P. 1, p. 318.)

(e) " This, therefore, is the life of the Gods, and of

divine and happy men, a liberation from all terrene concerns, a life unaccompanied with human pleasures, and a flight of the alone to the alone."

Plotinus. Enn. VI, 9, 11. (P. 2, p. 322.)

(*f*) " But there is another principle of the soul, which is superior to all nature and generation, and through which we are capable of being united to the Gods, of transcending the mundane order, and of participating eternal life, and the energy of the supercelestial Gods. Through this principle, therefore, we are able to liberate ourselves from fate. For when the more exalted parts of us energise, and the soul is elevated to natures better than itself, then it is entirely separated from things which detain it in generation, departs from subordinate natures, exchanges the present for another life, and gives itself to another order of things, entirely abandoning the former order with which it was connected."

Jamblichus. (Sect. VIII, Chap. 7. J. 1, p. 309.)

(*g*) " By what path do we go forth to seek the Lord ? By the way of perfect likeness and fullest union. Every good deed, however small, if it be directed to God by simplicity of intention, increases in us the Divine likeness, and deepens in us the flow of eternal life. . . . Entering into and transcending itself, traversing all worlds of being, surpassing all creatures, the soul meets God in its own depths. . . . The whole life of the spirit and its activity consists solely in the Divine likeness and this simplicity of intention ; and the final peace abides on the heights in simplicity also, in simplicity of essence. Men possess virtues and the Divine likeness in differing measure ; in greater or lesser degree have they found their own essence in the depth of themselves, according to their dignity. But God fulfils all ; and each, clearer or fainter, according to the measure of his love, possesses the sense of God's presence in the depths of his own being. This contact is Christ's call to the spirit : ' Pass out of thyself, act in the depths.' It invites, attracts, and draws the spirit to that deepest point in its own interior life at which the creature is able to act. Then by the power of love the spirit passes beyond the region of effort into that unity out of whose midst sprang the living flame that touched it. But this contact makes its own demands : the intelligence shall know God in its light ; love shall enjoy God without intermediary. This is what the spirit desires supremely, naturally, and supernaturally. And as a result of the contact, by virtue of this interior discernment, the spirit withdraws into itself, and from its own abyss contemplates the sanctuary whence came this Divine impulse. Reason and human seeing fail on this threshold, for the supernal light, eternal and limitless, whence proceeded the touch, blinds all created light ; and human intelligence depending on created light is like an owl in the splendour of the sun. . . . Out of this contemplation there arises a supernal light that no eyes can look on without being seized and broken and blinded. . . . Those who by the completeness of this interior act have probed and searched the abyss within themselves to its final depths, wherein is found the doorway into eternal life, can feel the contact. None the less, this light of God burns with such an intensity that the spirit fails, and powerless to take another step, yields wholly, without effort or resistance, to the majesty of the Unknowable. Reason and intelligence halt at this door, but love that has also heard the call knows it as a command, and though blinded like the others, would go forward, for through all the blindness it has held to its desire to participate. At the limit of its strength and power the intelligence halts and remains outside, but love enters." Ruysbroeck. (H. 5, p. 9 ff.)

(h)
        " The nearest way to God
        Leads through love's open door ;
        The path of knowledge is
        Too slow for evermore."
                Angelus Silesius. (S. 3, p. 145.)

(i) " It is the Heart, and never the Reason, which leads us to the Absolute."   Récéjac. (R. 4, p. 185.)

(j) " The art of creation, like every other art, has to be learnt :
Slowly, slowly, through many years, thou buildest up thy body,
And the power that thou now hast (such as it is) to build up this present body, thou hast acquired in the past in other bodies ;
So in the future shalt thou use again the power that thou now acquirest.
But the power to build up the body includes all powers."
                Ed. Carpenter. (C. 2, p. 360.)

(k) " The full spiritual consciousness of the true mystic is developed not in one, but in two apparently opposite but really complementary directions : on the one hand he is intensely aware of, and knows himself to be at one with the active world of Becoming, that deep and primal life of the All, from which his own life takes its rise. Hence, though he has broken for ever with the bondage of the senses, he perceives in every manifestation of life a sacramental meaning ; a loveliness, a wonder, a heightened significance, which is hidden from other men. . . . On the other hand, the full mystic consciousness also attains to what is, I think, its really characteristic quality. It develops the power of apprehending the Absolute, Pure Being, the utterly Transcendent : or, as its possessor would say, can rise to ' passive union with God.' This all-round expansion of consciousness, with its dual power of knowing by communion the temporal and eternal, immanent and transcendent aspects of reality—the life of the All, vivid, flowing and changing, and the changeless, conditionless life of the One—is the peculiar mark, the *ultimo sigillo* of the great mystic, and must never be forgotten in studying his life and work."

> Evelyn Underhill. (U. 3, p. 42.)

(*l*) " As one who stands on yonder snowy horn
    Having nought o'er him but the boundless blue,
So, these sins being slain, the man is come
    NIRVANA'S verge unto.

" Him the Gods envy from their lower seats ;
    Him the Three Worlds in ruin should not shake ;
All life is lived for him, all deaths are dead ;
    Karma will no more make

" New houses.   Seeking nothing, he gains all ;
    Foregoing self, the Universe grows ' I ' :
If any teach NIRVANA is to cease,
    Say unto such they lie.

" If any teach NIRVANA is to live,
    Say unto such they err ; not knowing this,
Nor what light shines beyond their broken lamps,
    Nor lifeless, timeless, bliss."

> *The Light of Asia.* (A. 2, Book VIII)

(*m*) " Then he arose—radiant, rejoicing, strong—
    Beneath the Tree, and lifting high his voice
    Spake thus, in hearing of all Times and Worlds :—

" MANY A HOUSE OF LIFE
HATH HELD ME—SEEKING EVER HIM WHO WROUGHT
THESE PRISONS OF THE SENSES.   SORROW-FRAUGHT ;
    SORE WAS MY CEASELESS STRIFE !

" BUT NOW,
THOU BUILDER OF THIS TABERNACLE—THOU !
I KNOW THEE ! NEVER SHALT THOU BUILD AGAIN
    THESE WALLS OF PAIN,

" NOR RAISE THE ROOF-TREE OF DECEITS, NOR LAY
    FRESH RAFTERS ON THE CLAY ;
BROKEN THY HOUSE IS, AND THE RIDGE-POLE SPLIT !
    DELUSION FASHIONED IT !
SAFE PASS I THENCE—DELIVERANCE TO OBTAIN."
          The Light of Asia. (A. 2, Book VI.)

(*n*) " Know, Conqueror of Sins, once that a Sowanee hath cross'd the seventh Path, all Nature thrills with joyous awe and feels subdued. The silver star now twinkles out the news to the night-blossoms, the streamlet to the pebbles ripples on the tale ; dark ocean waves will roar it to the rocks surf-bound, scent-laden breezes sing it to the vales, and stately pines mysteriously whisper : ' A Master has arisen, a MASTER OF THE DAY ' (Manvantara).

" He standeth now like a white pillar to the west, upon whose face the rising Sun of thought eternal poureth forth its first most glorious waves. His mind, like a becalmed and boundless ocean, spreadeth out in shoreless space. He holdeth life and death in his strong hand.

" Yea, He is mighty. The living power made free in him, that power which is HIMSELF, can raise the tabernacle of illusion high above the gods, above great Brahm and Indra. *Now* he shall surely reach his great reward !

·   ·   ·   ·   ·

" Now bend thy head and listen well, O Bôdhisattva— Compassion speaks and saith : ' Can there be bliss when all that lives must suffer ? Shalt thou be saved and hear the whole world cry ? '

" Now thou hast heard that which was said.

" Thou shalt attain the seventh step and cross the gate of final knowledge but only to wed woe—if thou would'st be Tathâgata, follow upon thy predecessor's steps, remain unselfish till the endless end.

" Thou art enlightened—Choose thy way."

Note on the above :—

" The ' Buddhas of Compassion ' are those *Bôdhisattvas* who, having reached the rank of Arhat, refuse to pass into the Nirvânic state or ' don the *Dharmakâya* robe and cross to the other shore,' as it would then become beyond their power to assist men even so little as Karma permits.   They prefer to remain invisibly (in Spirit, so to speak) in the world, and contribute to man's salvation by influencing them to follow the Good Law.

The three Buddhic bodies or forms are styled :

1. *Nirmânakâya.*
2. *Sambhogakâya.*
3. *Dharmakâya.*

The first is that ethereal form which one would assume when leaving his physical he would appear in his astral body—having in addition all the knowledge of an Adept. The *Bôdhisattva* develops it in himself as he proceeds on the Path.   Having reached the goal and refused its fruition, he remains on Earth, as an Adept ; and when he dies, instead of going into Nirvâna, he remains in that glorious body he has woven for himself, *invisible* to uninitiated mankind, to watch over and protect it.

Sambhogakâya is the same, but with the additional lustre of ' three perfections,' one of which is entire obliteration of all earthly concerns.

The *Dharmakâya* body is that of a complete Buddha, *i.e.*, no body at all, but an ideal breath : Consciousness merged in the Universal Consciousness, or Soul devoid of every attribute. Once a Dharmakâya, an Adept or Buddha leaves behind every possible relation with, or thought for this earth. Thus, to be enabled to help humanity, an Adept who has won the right to Nirvâna, ' renounces the *Dharmakâya* body ' in mystic parlance ; keeps, of the *Sambhogakâya*, only the great and complete knowledge, and remains in his *Nirmânâkaya* body."

> H. P. Blavatsky. *The Voice of the Silence.*
> (B. 32, pp. 65, 71, 95, 96.)

(*o*) " The human being,—simply because he is himself fragmentary and incomplete,—has always this urge within himself to seek other and greater than himself. It is this that drives him back to the centre of his being, and it is this that forces him to take the path of return to the All-Self. Ever, throughout the æons, does the Prodigal Son arise and go to his Father, and always latent within him is the memory of the Father's home and the glory there to be found. But the human mind is so constituted that the search for light and for the ideal is necessarily long and difficult. ' Now we see through a glass darkly, but then face to face.' Now we catch glimpses through the occasional windows we pass in our ascension of the ladder, of other and greater Beings than ourselves. They hold out to us helping hands, and call to us in clarion tones to struggle bravely on if we hope to stand where They are now standing.

We sense beauties and glories surrounding us that as yet we cannot revel in ; they flit into our vision, and we touch the glory at a lofty moment only again to lose the contact and sink back again into the murky gloom that envelops. But we *know* that outside and further on is something to be desired ; we learn also the mystery that that external wonder can only be contacted by withdrawing within, till the centre of consciousness is found that vibrates in tune with those dimly realised wonders, and with those radiant Souls Who call Themselves our Elder Brothers. Only by trampling on the external sheaths that veil and hide the inner centre do we achieve the goal, and find the Ones we seek. Only by the domination of all forms, and the bringing of those forms under the rule of the God within, can we find the God in all ; for it is only the sheaths in which we move upon the plane of being that hide from us our inner God, and that shut us off from Those in Whom the God transcends all outer forms."

Alice A. Bailey.   (B. 40, p. 253.)

ATTAINMENT,   MYSTICAL

(a) " The Self (Ātman) which is free from evil, ageless, deathless, sorrowless, hungerless, thirstless, whose desire is the Real, whose conception is the Real—He should be searched out, Him should one desire to understand. He obtains all worlds and all desires who has found out and who understands that Self."

Chāndogya Upanishad, VIII, 7, 1.   (U. 1, p. 268.)

(b) " As the flowing rivers in the ocean
    Disappear, quitting name and form,
    So the knower, being liberated from name and
        form,
    Goes unto the heavenly Person, higher than the
        high."
Mundaka Upanishad, III, 2, 8.   (U. 1, p. 376.)

(c) " From the unreal (*asat*) lead me to the real (*sat*) !
    From darkness lead me to light !
    From death lead me to immortality ! "
Brihad-āranyaka Upanishad, I, 3, 28.   (U. 1, p. 80.)

(d) " And when this power also within me found itself

changeable, it lifted itself up to its own intelligence, and withdrew its thoughts from experience, abstracting itself from the contradictory throng of sensuous images, that it might find out what that light was wherein it was bathed, when it cried out that beyond doubt the unchangeable was better than the changeable, and how it came to know the unchangeable, which it must have known in some way or another, for otherwise it could not have preferred it so confidently to the changeable. And thus, with the flash of one hurried glance, it attained to the vision of THAT WHICH IS. And then at last I saw Thy invisible things understood by means of the things that are made, but I could not sustain my gaze; my weakness was dashed back, and I was relegated to my ordinary experience, bearing with me nothing but a loving remembrance, cherishing, as it were, the fragrance of those viands which I was not yet able to feed upon." (Chap. XVII.)

St. Augustine. (S. 2, p. 244.)

(e) " And so we came to our own minds, and passed beyond them into the region of unfailing plenty, where Thou feedest Israel for ever with the food of truth, where Life is Wisdom by which all these things come to be ; and the Life itself never comes to be, but is, as it was and shall be evermore, because in it is neither past nor future but present only, for it is eternal ; for past and future are not eternal. And as we talked and yearned after it, we touched it for an instant with the whole force of our hearts. And we sighed, and left there impawned the first-fruits of the spirit, and heard again the babble of our own tongues, wherein each word has a beginning and an ending. Far unlike Thy Word, our Lord, who abideth in Himself, never growing old and making all things new." (Chap. X.)

(*Ibid.*, p. 321.)

(f) " He to whom all things are one, he who reduceth

all things to one, and seeth all things in one, may enjoy a quiet mind, and remain peaceable in God."

Thomas à Kempis. (K. 1, Book 1, Chap. 3, p. 6.)

(g) " Hence she (the soul) neither sees, nor heeds, nor understands, nor perceives all the time she is in this state, and this time is short ; and, indeed, it seems to her shorter than it is. God so fixes Himself in the interior of this soul, that when she comes to herself she cannot but believe she was in God and that God was in her. The truth is so deeply rooted in her, that though many years may pass away before God bestows the like favour upon her, she never forgets it." St. Theresa. (S. 6, p. 69.)

(h)　　" When the mind's very being is gone,
　　　　Sunk in a conscious sleep,
　　　　In a rapture divine and deep,
　　　Itself in the Godhead lost—
　　It is conquered, ravished and won !
　　　　Set in Eternitie's sweep,
　　　　Gazing back on the steep,
　　　Knowing not how it was crossed—
　　To a new world now it is tossed,
　　　　Drawn from its former state,
　　　　To another, measureless, great—
　　　　Where Love is drowned in the sea.

　" It welcometh any fate :
　　　　Transformed so wondrously
　　　　By union profound and free,
　　　It whispereth ' all is mine ! '
　　Wide open standeth the gate—
　　　　The soul is joined to Thee,
　　　　Endlessly, utterly,
　　Possessing all that is Thine.

It feels what it cannot divine,
   Sees what it may not discern,
   Grasps more than faith can learn,
Tastes God unknowingly.

" It hath found the measureless way
   Itself to lose and to spend,
   And so it can comprehend
The Immeasurable Height :
And purifying its clay
   From all alloy or blend,
   It drinks without pause or end
Ineffable Delight.
Loosing, yet holding tight,
   No longer the soul doth seek
   Power to tell and to speak,
Transformed so utterly.

" To lose and yet to keep,
   To love, and in joy to wait,
   To gaze and to contemplate,
This is the True and the Real.
To possess in certainty deep ;
   To float in that blessed state,
   Anchored, yet early and late,
Nearer, nearer to steal—
Deeper than woe or weal
   Is the Act of Heavenly Love,
   And the Light of Truth from above,
Strong, eternal and free."

Jacopone da Todi.   Lauda XCI.   (U. 2, pp. 477, 479.)

(i) " If every earthly pleasure were melted into a single
experience and bestowed upon one man it would be as
nothing when measured by the joy of which I write ; for

here it is God who passes into the depths of us in all His purity, and the soul is not only filled but overflowing. This experience is that light that makes manifest to the soul the terrible desolation of such as live divorced from love ; it melts the man utterly ; he is no longer master of his joy. Such possession produces intoxication, the state of the spirit in which its bliss transcends the uttermost bounds of anticipation or desire. Sometimes the ecstasy pours forth in song, sometimes in tears : at one moment it finds expression in movement, at others in the intense stillness of burning, voiceless feeling. Some men knowing this bliss wonder if others feel God as they do ; some are assured that no living creature has ever had such experiences as theirs ; there are those who wonder that the world is not set aflame by this joy ; and there are others who marvel at its nature, asking whence it comes, and what it is. The body itself can know no greater pleasure upon earth than to participate in it ; and there are moments when the soul feels that it must shiver to fragments in the poignancy of this experience." Ruysbroeck. (H. 5, p. 19.)

(*j*) " That [entity] in the absolute sense real, highest of all, eternal, all-penetrating like the ether, exempt from all change, all-sufficing, undivided, whose nature is to be its own light, in which neither good nor evil has any place, nor effect, nor past, nor present, nor future,—this incorporeal [entity] is called *Liberation*." Sankara.

" As may be seen from this passage, the conception of *Liberation* contains the same characteristics as serve as a rule to define Brahman ; and indeed Brahman and the state of liberation are identical terms ; for liberation is nothing else than *the becoming one with Brahman*, or rather, since the identity of the Soul with Brahman has always subsisted and has only been hidden from it by an illusion, liberation is nothing else but the *awakening of the consciousness* that our own Self is identical with Brahman. Accordingly, in liberation there is no question of becoming something which does not already exist, but only the attainment of the knowledge of what has existed from all eternity. It is because of this, that liberation is not accomplished through any sort of work, nor through moral improvement, but by knowledge alone (as the Christian redemption is by faith alone, *sola fide*, which comes very near to the metaphysical knowledge here spoken of)."

Paul Deussen. (D. 4, p. 401.)

(*k*) " According to the system of the Vedânta, one thing alone is possible (for the attainment of liberation) : the awakening to perfect knowledge, in consequence of which the Soul recognises itself as identical with Brahman, and Brahman as the only Being ; and thus recognises the whole empirical reality, the *Samsâra* (cycle of migration, birth, and death) included, as an illusion.

" He who has reached this esoteric knowledge of the attributeless Brahman, is at his goal ; he knows all that is manifold, the world as well as his own body with all its organs, as non-Ego, non-Ātman, non-Existent,—for him death means only the cessation of an illusion, which has already been recognised as illusory, and as unreal, as nothing.

" With the exoteric knowledge it is otherwise : he who has by this recognised Brahman as having attributes, as a personal God, and has worshipped him according to this theological form of knowledge, after death mounts upwards on the *Devayâna* (path of the Gods) to the lower Brahman, and there at last gains the perfect knowledge, and therewith liberation. This mediate liberation by the path of *Devayâna* is called *Kramamukti*, ' progressive liberation,' because it is attained by progress towards Brahman, or ' liberation by steps,' because it is attained by the intermediate step of exoteric felicity." Paul Deussen. (D. 4, p. 398.)

3

(*l*) " How can a contact with God in any way be described ? It is not seeing, but meeting and fusion with awareness. The soul retaining her own individuality and consciousness to an intense degree, but imbued with and fused into a life of incredible intensity, which passes through the soul vitalities and emotions of a life so new, so vivid, so amazing, that she knows not whether she has been embraced by love or by fire, by joy or by anguish : for so fearful is her joy that she is almost unable to endure the might of it." (p. 41.)

" Of other forms of contact we have a swift, unexpected, even unsought-for attainment, which is entirely of His (God's) volition ; that sudden condescension to the soul, in which in unspeakable rapture she is caught up to her holy lover. These are the topmost heights which the creature dare recall, though to the soul they remain in memory as life itself. The variations of these forms of contact are infinite, for God would seem to will to be both eternal changelessness and variation in infinitude." (p. 91.)

" But the most wonderful flights of the soul are made during a high adoring contemplation of God. We are in high contemplation when the heart, mind, and soul, having dropped consciousness of all earthly matters, have been brought to a full concentration upon God—God totally invisible, totally unimaged, *and yet focussed to a centre point by the great power of love*. The soul, whilst she is able to maintain this most difficult height of contemplation, may be visited by an intensely vivid perception, inward vision, and knowledge of God's attributes or perfections, very brief ; and this *as a gift*, for she is not able to will such a felicity to herself, but being given such she is instantly consumed with adoration, and *enters ecstasy*." (p. 100.)

" In the highest rapture I ever was in, my soul passed into a fearful extremity of experience : she was burned with so terrible an excess of bliss that she was in great fear

and anguish because of this excess. Indeed, she was so
overcome by this too great realisation of the strength of
God that she was in terror of both God and joy. It was
three days before she recovered any peace, and more than
a year before I dared recall one instant of it to mind. I
am not able to think that even in Heaven the soul could
endure such heights for more than a period. These heights
are incomparably, unutterably beyond vision and union.
They are the utmost extremity of that which can be endured
by the soul, at least until she has re-risen to great altitudes
of holiness in ages to come." (p. 137.)

The Golden Fountain. (G. 7.)

(m) " And now thy *Self* is lost in SELF, *thyself* unto
THYSELF, merged in THAT SELF from which thou first
didst radiate. . . . Behold ! thou hast become the light,
thou hast become the Sound, thou art thy Master and thy
God. Thou art THYSELF the object of thy search : the
VOICE unbroken, that resounds throughout eternities,
exempt from change, from sin exempt, the seven sounds in
one, the VOICE OF THE SILENCE."

H. P. Blavatsky. (B. 32, pp. 20, 21.)

ART

(a) " Indeed, the divine wisdom standeth not in art and
reason, but it showeth art the way, what it should do and
how it should seek. Art is really the tool or instrument of
God wherewith the divine wisdom worketh or laboureth ;
why should I despise it ? . . . All profitable arts are
revealed out of God's wisdom ; *not* that they are that by
which man cometh to God, but for the government of the
outward life, and for the glorious manifestation of divine
wisdom and omnipotence."

Jacob Böhme. (B. 10, Text IV, III, 77.)

CONSCIOUSNESS

(*a*) " WE do not prove and we never shall prove by any reasoning that the psychic fact is fatally determined by the molecular movement. For in a movement we may find the reason of another movement, but not the reason of a conscious state : only observation can prove that the latter accompanies the former."

Henri Bergson. (B. 26, p. 148.)

(*b*) " No less inscrutable is this complex consciousness which has slowly evolved out of infantine vacuity—consciousness which, during the development of every creature, makes its appearance out of what seems unconscious matter ; suggesting the thought that consciousness in some rudimentary form is omnipresent."

Herbert Spencer. (S. 11, Vol. II, p. 470.)

(*c*) " It seems to me pretty plain that there is a third thing in the universe, to wit, consciousness, which, in the hardness of my heart or head, I cannot see to be matter, or force, or any conceivable modification of either, however intimately the manifestations of the phenomena of consciousness may be connected with the phenomena known as matter and force. The arguments used by Descartes and Berkeley to show that our certain knowledge does not extend beyond our states of consciousness, appear to me to be as irrefragable now as they did when I first became acquainted with them some half century ago. All the materialistic writers that I know of who have tried to bite that file have simply broken their teeth."

T. H. Huxley. (H. 2, p. 130.)

(d) " Nobody, I imagine, will credit me with a desire to limit the empire of physical science, but I really feel bound to confess that a great many very familiar and, at the same time, extremely important phenomena lie quite beyond its legitimate limits. I cannot conceive, for example, how the phenomena of consciousness, as such and apart from the physical process by which they are called into existence, are to be brought within the bounds of physical science. Take the simplest possible example, the feeling of redness. Physical science tells us that it commonly arises as a consequence of molecular changes propagated from the eye to a certain part of the substance of the brain, when vibrations of the luminiferous ether of a certain character fall upon the retina. Let us suppose the process of physical analysis pushed so far that one could view the last link of this chain of molecules, watch their movements as if they were billiard balls, weigh them, measure them, and know all that is physically knowable about them. Well, even in that case, we should be just as far from being able to include the resulting phenomenon of consciousness, the feeling of redness, within the bounds of physical science, as we are at present. It would remain as unlike the phenomena we know under the names of matter and motion as it is now. If there is any plain truth upon which I have made it my business to insist over and over again it is this." (*Ibid.*, p. 122.)

(e) " Looking at the matter from the most rigidly scientific point of view, the assumption that, amidst the myriads of worlds scattered through endless space, there can be no intelligence as much greater than man's as his is greater than a blackbeetle's ; no being endowed with powers of influencing the course of nature as much greater than his as his is greater than a snail's, seems to me not merely baseless, but impertinent. Without stepping beyond the analogy of that which is known, it is easy to people the cosmos with entities, in ascending scale, until we reach something practically indistinguishable from omnipotence, omnipresence, and omniscience. If our intelligence can, in some matters, surely reproduce the past of thousands of years ago, and anticipate the future of thousands of years hence, it is clearly within the limits of possibility that some greater intellect, even of the same order, may be able to mirror the whole past and the whole future."

Thomas Henry Huxley. (H. 3, p. 36.)

(f) " One conclusion, forced upon my mind . . . has ever since remained unshaken. It is that our normal waking consciousness, rational consciousness as we call it, is but one special type of consciousness, whilst all about it, parted from it by the filmiest of screens, there lie potential forms of consciousness entirely different. We may go through life without suspecting their existence ; but apply the requisite stimulus, and at a touch they are there in all their completeness, definite types of mentality which probably somewhere have their field of application and adaptation. No account of the universe in its totality can be final which leaves these other forms of consciousness quite disregarded. How to regard them is the question, —for they are so discontinuous with ordinary consciousness. Yet they may determine attitudes though they cannot furnish formulas, and open a region though they fail to give a map. At any rate, they forbid a premature closing of our accounts with reality. Looking back on my own experiences, they all converge towards a kind of insight to which I cannot help ascribing some metaphysical significance. The keynote of it is invariably a reconciliation. It is as if the opposites of the world, whose contradictoriness and conflict make all our difficulties and troubles, were melted into unity. Not only do they, as contrasted species, belong to one and the same genus, but *one of the species*, the nobler and better one, *is itself the genus, and so soaks up and absorbs its opposite into itself.* This is a dark saying, I know, when thus expressed in terms of common logic, but I cannot wholly escape from its authority. I feel as if it must mean something, something like what the hegelian philosophy means, if one could only lay hold of it more clearly. Those who have ears to hear, let them hear ; to me the living sense of its reality only comes in the artificial mystic state of mind.

" What reader of Hegel can doubt that that sense of a perfected Being with all its otherness soaked up into itself, which dominates his whole philosophy, must have come from the prominence in his consciousness of mystical moods like this, in most persons kept subliminal ? The notion is thoroughly characteristic of the mystical level, and the *Aufgabe* of making it articulate was surely set to Hegel's intellect by mystical feeling."

William James. (J. 5, p. 388.)

(g) " It will be found, we believe . . . that in the growth of our experience, in the process of our learning to know the world, an animal organism, which has its history in time, gradually becomes the vehicle of an eternally complete consciousness. What we call our mental history is not a history of this consciousness, which in itself can have no history, but a history of the process by which the animal organism becomes its vehicle. ' Our consciousness ' may mean either of two things ; either a function of the animal organism, which is being made, gradually and with interruptions, a vehicle of the eternal consciousness ; or that eternal consciousness itself, as making the animal organism its vehicle, and subject to certain limitations in so doing, but retaining its essential characteristic as independent of time, as the determinant of becoming, which has not and does not itself become."

T. H. Green. (G. 4, pp. 72, 73.)

(h) " In contact with the flux of cosmic consciousness all religions known and named to-day will be melted down. The human soul will be revolutionized. Religion will absolutely dominate the race. It will not depend on tradition. It will not be believed and disbelieved. It will not be a part of life, belonging to certain hours, times, occasions. It will not be in sacred books nor in the mouths of priests. It will not dwell in churches and meetings and forms and days. Its life will not be in prayers, hymns nor discourses. It will not depend on special revelations, on the words of gods who came down to teach, nor on any bible or bibles. It will have no mission to save men from their sins or to secure them entrance to heaven. It will not teach a future immortality nor future glories, for immortality and glory will exist in the here and now. The evidence of immortality will live in every heart as sight in every eye. Doubt of God and of eternal life will be as impossible as is now doubt of existence ; the evidence of each will be the same. Religion will govern every minute of every day of all life. Churches, priests, forms, creeds, prayers, all agents, all intermediaries between the individual man and God will be permanently replaced by direct unmistakable intercourse. Sin will no longer exist nor will salvation be desired. Men will not worry about death or a future, about the kingdom of heaven, about what may come with and after the cessation of the life of the present body. Each soul will feel and know itself to be immortal, will feel and know that the entire universe with all its good and with all its beauty is for it and belongs to it forever. The world peopled by men possessing cosmic consciousness will be as far removed from the world of to-day as

this is from the world as it was before the advent of self-
consciousness."   Dr. R. M. Bucke.   (B. 35, p. 4.)

CAUSE AND EFFECT

(*a*) " Beneath these deceptive appearances a more atten-
tive psychology sometimes reveals to us effects which
precede their causes, and phenomena of psychic attraction
which elude the known laws of the association of ideas."
          Henri Bergson.   (B. 26, p. 158.)

(*b*) " If there is anything in the world which I do firmly
believe in, it is the universal validity of the law of causa-
tion ; but that universality cannot be proved by any
amount of experience, let alone that which comes to us
through the senses."   T. H. Huxley.   (H. 2, p. 121.)

(*c*) " However natural it may be to mankind, to conceive
the relationship between Being-in-itself and the phenomenal
world from the point of view of causality, and so to regard
God as cause and the world as effect,—nevertheless this
view is false. For causality, which has its root in the
organisation of our intellect, and nowhere else, is the bond
which binds all the phenomena of the phenomenal world
together, but it does not bind the phenomenal world with
that which manifests itself through it. For between
Being-in-itself and the phenomenal world there is no
causality but identity : the world is the Thing-in-itself (das
Ding an sich) as it displays itself in the forms of our intellect.—This truth has been correctly grasped by the
Vedânta, which cannot free itself, however, from the old
error of looking upon God as the cause of the world, and
seeks to reconcile the two by interpreting the idea of
causality as that of identity. To this end it forms too
wide a concept of causality, in that it not only comprehends under this idea the bond of variations which only

have to do with the qualities, forms, and conditions of substance, but also the bond between substance and qualities, and also between substance and substance. *The continuity of substance* forms the chief argument in these discussions."   Paul Deussen.   (D. 4, p. 255.)

" CHRIST IN YOU "

NOTE ON " CHRIST IN YOU "

At the present time, when so much of the old theology is in the melting pot, and the very existence of an historical Christ as narrated in the Gospels is called in question : we may, and indeed *must*, fall back upon the mystical interpretation of the Scriptures if we are in any way to retain them as an explanation of Man's origin, present state, and destiny in a manner which shall not conflict with our present historical, scientific and philosophical knowledge.

In this connection nothing is clearer in the Mystics than that *Christ* stands for man's own inner divine nature, which must be " brought to birth "—as St. Paul so clearly taught—*in* each individual if he is in any sense to be " saved " ; that is to say, to achieve his immortality through the conquest of sin and death to which he is now subject in his lower nature. He must accomplish this in the power of his higher nature, the Christ *in him*.

Christ is the *divine spark* in each one of us : buried, obscured, " crucified " because of our lower, sinful nature. He must " rise again from the dead " in each one of us ; and it is only as this resurrection is accomplished, only as we realise the " Christ in us " as the active principle of our lives, that we can free ourselves from the " bondage of the flesh," obtain a mastery over physical conditions, and hope for immortality either here or hereafter.

How far a personal Jesus of Nazareth accomplished this,

and how far His life is mainly taken as the basis of this mystical knowledge—which certainly existed in the world and was taught before Christianity " began to be called Christianity "—must be left for each individual to decide for himself, according to his needs.

" CHRIST IN YOU "

(a)   " Though Christ our Lord a thousand times
          in Bethlehem be born,
       And not in thee, thy soul remains
          eternally forlorn.

       " The Cross on Calvary can never save
          thee from thy sin
       Unless it is upraised again thy very
          soul within."

Angelus Silesius.   (S. 4, p. 40.)

(b) " The most inward ground in man is Christus ; not according to the nature of man, but according to the Divine property in the heavenly substance, which he hath generated anew."   Jacob Bohme.   (B. 14, VII, 98.)

(c) " Seeing that Christ the Son of God hath generated us again to the paradisical image, we should not be so remiss as to rely upon art and earthly reason ; for so we find not paradise and Christ, who must become man *in us* if we will ever see God : in our reason it is all but dead and blind."   Jacob Böhme.   (B. 5, Part I, ch. IV, 6, 8.)

(d) " For that same image which died in Adam, from the heavenly world's essence, as the right Paradisical One, dwelleth not in the four elements ; its essence and life standeth not in this world, but in heaven (which becometh revealed by Christ in us) *viz.* in one pure holy element, whereout the four elements in the beginning of time, are sprung, and that same inward spiritual man eateth Christ's

flesh and blood ; for he is, and liveth in Christ, Christ is his stock, and he is the branch on the stock."
Jacob Böhme. (B. 17, *Life of a true Christian*, para. 17.)

(*e*) " Justification is effected in the blood of Christ *in man*, in the soul itself ; not through an outward, imputed, accounted strange show." Jacob Böhme. (B. 14, X, 119.)

(*f*) " It is said to thee, thou titulary and verbal Christendom, in the zeal of God, that thou, in thy tattling mouth, *without* Christ's Spirit, flesh and blood in thee, art as fully heathenish and a foreigner in the presence of God as they (the heathen) themselves. Thy supposed election, special acceptation, filiation and adoption *without* the new birth is thy snare and fall."
Jacob Böhme. (B. 14, X, 150, 151.)

(*g*) " At each moment of time in the fullest meaning of the word *now* Christ is born in us and the Holy Ghost proceeds, bearing all Its gifts. May we offer to the adornment of these gifts of the Holy Ghost the likeness of Him in ourselves, but to His Divinely regenerating power may we offer the sacred unity of our essence."
Ruysbroeck. (R. 4, p. 27.)

(*h*) " Here in time we make holiday because the eternal birth which God the Father bore and bears unceasingly in eternity is now born in time, in human nature. St. Augustine says this birth is always happening. But if it happen not in me what does it profit me ? What matters is that it shall happen in me." Eckhart. (E. 1, p. 37.)

(*i*) " When the Will is so united that it becometh a One in oneness, then doth the Heavenly Father produce his only-begotten Son in Himself and in me. Wherefore in Himself and in me ? I am one with Him—He cannot exclude me. In the self-same operation doth the Holy Ghost receive his existence, and proceeds from me as from

God. Wherefore ? I am in God, and if the Holy Ghost deriveth not his being from me, He deriveth it not from God. I am in nowise excluded.''

Eckhart. (V. 1, Vol. 1, p. 190.)

(*j*) " The second Distinction is a *twofold* consideration of man : *one*, as he is in *God* ; the *other* as he is *in himself*. As man is in *God*, so he may be owned, and acknowledged for a *Father*, or *Master* in Spiritual things themselves. *Saint Paul* attributes so much to himself ; but marke, how he doth it. . . . Saint Paul hedgeth in his expression on both sides, with *Christ*, and the Gospell ; that the glory might be all given to God. *In Jesus Christ I have begotten you thorow the Gospell.* I as I am, not in myself, *but comprehended in one Spirit with Christ, in one Mystical Person, which is Christ : thorow the Gospell*, that is, *thorow the presence, power, and appearance of Christ Jesus in me.*"

Peter Sterry. (S. 8, p. 4.)

(*k*) " The discovery of the Mystic Christ in you is being ' born from above.' This knowledge is of the utmost importance to human victory over the lower self :

 ' Though Christ a thousand times in Bethlehem be
   born,
   If He be not born in thee thy soul is still forlorn.'

" The first symptom of this discovery is that you will find yourself thinking differently of God and of man. The wrong sense of separateness from God passes away. God is no longer a law-giver to be obeyed but a Presence to be loved. You will think differently of your fellow-man. You will see others after the spirit and not after the flesh. You will see only the good in others.

 ' Two men looked from the prison bars,
   One saw the mud, the other saw the stars.'

" He who knows ' the mystery of Christ ' will always see the ' stars,' and not the ' mud ' in others."
Archdeacon Wilberforce.   (W. 7, p. 5.)

(*l*) " A recognition of the fact that the real *ego* in every man is Divine would be the golden key which would unlock the most puzzling of the social problems of the age.   The prominent evils which degrade humanity would pass away before it, and in private life love would reign instead of harsh criticism. . . . The universality of the Divine impress, the certainty that every individual life-centre is a manifestation of God, should convince us that ' one is our Father and all we are brethren.' "
Archdeacon Wilberforce.   (W. 7, p. 27.)

(*m*) " He who standeth at all times in a present Now, in him doth God the Father bring forth his Son without ceasing."   Eckhart.   (VI, Vol. I, p. 189.)

(*n*) " The Incarnation, which is for popular Christianity synonymous with the historical birth and earthly life of Christ, is for the mystic not only this but also a perpetual Cosmic and personal process.   It is an everlasting bringing forth, in the universe and also in the individual ascending soul, of the divine and perfect Life, the pure character of God, of which the one historical life dramatized the essential constituents.   Hence the soul, like the physical embryo, resumes in its upward progress the spiritual life-history of the race. ' The one secret, the greatest of all,' says Patmore, ' is the doctrine of the Incarnation, regarded not as an historical event which occurred two thousand years ago, but as an event which is renewed in the body of every one who is in the way to the fulfilment of his original destiny.' "
Evelyn Underhill.   (U. 1, p. 141.)

(*o*) " The Saviour of man is Cosmic Consciousness—in Paul's language—the Christ.   The cosmic sense (in whatever mind it appears) crushes the serpent's head—destroys sin, shame, the sense of good and evil as contrasted one with the other, and will annihilate labour, though not human activity." Dr. R. M. Bucke. (B. 35, p. 5.)

(*p*) " Christ the Son of God in the heart of humanity reaches out to man until he awakes to divine consciousness. The seven acts of Christ become actual to man, instead of belonging to a past period. He experiences the birth, the awakening in the Temple, the anointing, the temptation, the crucifixion, the resurrection, and the ascension. Christ must be in you ; nothing avails man from the outside, all is from within. Thank God for Jesus Christ, ' the unspeakable gift of God.' The evolution of one soul exalts the whole race. ' That they all may be one.' "

" Christ in You." (C. 10, p. 101.)

(*q*) " The ways of God are perfect, and the soul that is conscious of the living Christ, lifted into unity with the Father, becomes one with the work of redemption, lifting the whole race." (*Ibid.*, p. 46.)

CONTEMPLATION

(*a*) " Contemplation is an understanding transcending the ways of knowledge, a science above the methods of learning. It is beyond the reason, whose efforts to fathom fall short, whose strongest flights fail to reach to this contemplation in its own sphere. It is a luminous ignorance, a glorious mirror into which shines the eternal splendour of God ; it is illimitable and the steps of reason will never lead us to it. . . . This luminous ignorance though in itself beyond reason, is yet not alien from it for it holds all things within its view, knowing no wonder or surprise. It beholds something : but what is it ? We do not know. It is an excellence surpassing all else ; it is not this, not that." Ruysbroeck. (H. 5, p. 60.)

(b) " And what is this light save limitless contemplation and ever active intuition. We contemplate what we are and we are what we contemplate, since our essence losing nothing of its distinctive individuality is united to that Divine truth that respects diversity."   (*Ibid.*, p. 77.)

(c) " For the higher we soar in contemplation the more limited becomes our expressions of that which is purely intelligible ; even as now, when plunging into the Darkness which is above the intellect, we pass not merely into brevity of speech, but even into absolute Silence, of thoughts as well as of words."   Dionysius. (D. 1, p. 9.)

(d) " For [only] then wilt thou upon It [Supreme Beauty] gaze when thou canst say no word concerning It. For Gnosis of the Good is holy silence and a giving holiday to every sense. For neither can he who perceiveth It, per-ceive aught else ; nor can he who gazeth on It, gaze on aught else ; nor hear aught else, nor stir his body any way. Staying his body's every sense and every motion he stayeth still. And shining then round his mind, It shines through his whole soul, and draws it out of body, transforming all of him to essence. For it is possible, my son, that a man's soul should be made like to God, e'en while it still is in a body, if it doth contemplate the Beauty of the Good."
Hermes. (M. 6, Vol. II, p. 144.)

(e) " Let us now, if ever, remove from ourselves multi-form knowledge, exterminate all the variety of life, and in perfect quiet approach near to the cause of all things. For this purpose, let not only opinion and phantasy be at rest, nor the passions alone which impede our anagogic impulse to *the first* be at peace ; but let the air be still, and the universe itself be still. And let all things extend us with a tranquil power to communion with the ineffable. . . . And let us as it were celebrate him, not as establishing the earth and the heavens, nor as giving subsistence to souls, and the generations of all animals ; for he produced these indeed, but among the last of things. But, prior to these, let us celebrate him, as unfolding into light the whole intelligible and intellectual genus of the gods, together with all the supermundane and mundane divinities—as the god of all gods, the unity of all unities, and beyond the first adyta,—as more ineffable than all silence, and more un-known than all essence,—as holy among the holies, and concealed in the intelligible gods." Proclus. (P. 2, p. 164.)

(f) " Invoking God himself, not with external speech, but with the soul itself, extending ourselves in prayer to him, since we shall then be able to pray to him properly, when we approach by ourselves alone to the alone."
        Plotinus. Enn. V. I, 6. (P. 2, p. 171)

(g) " Now this Divine Abyss can be fathomed by no creatures ; it can be filled by none, and it satisfies none ; God only can fill it in His Infinity. For this abyss belongs only to the Divine Abyss, of which it is written : *Abyssus abyssum invocat.* He who is truly conscious of this ground, which shone into the powers of his soul, and lighted and inclined its lowest and highest powers to turn to their pure Source and Origin, must diligently examine himself, and remain alone, listening to the voice which cries in the wilderness of this ground. This ground is so desert and bare, that no thought has ever entered there. None of all the thoughts of man which, with the help of reason, have been devoted to meditation on the Holy Trinity (and some men have occupied themselves much with these thoughts) have ever entered this ground. For it is so close and yet so far off, and so far beyond all things, that it has neither time nor place. It is a simple and unchanged condition: A man who really and truly enters feels as though he had been here throughout eternity, and as though he were one

4

therewith ; whereas it is only for an instant, and the same glance is found and reveals itself in eternity.   It shines forth ; and God thus bears witness that man existed in God from all eternity, before his creation ; that is, he was in God, and thus man was God in God."

John Tauler.   (T. 2, p. 98.)

CYCLIC LAW

(a) " All things enter again into that whence they proceeded."   Jacob Böhme.   (B. 6, XV, 42.)

(b) " We are children of the eternity ; But this world is an outbirth out of the eternal ; and its palpability taketh its *original* in the *anger*, the eternal nature is its root.   But that which is an outbirth is corruptible, because it hath not been from eternity : and it must all return into the eternal essences (out of which it was born)."

Jacob Böhme.   (B. 3, VI, 40.)

(c) " Every thing entereth with its Ens into that whence it takes its original."   Jacob Böhme.   (B. 7, XXII, 7.)

(d) " The cosmogony of Origen was a theodicy.   . . . This visible world, which, as also Philo and the Platonists taught, is a copy of the ideal world, took its beginning in time : but it is not the first, nor will it be the last, of such worlds.   The matter of it as well as the form was created by God.   It was made by Him, and to Him it will return. The Stoical theory had conceived of the universe as analogous to a seed which expands to flower and fruit and withers away, but leaves behind it a similar seed which has a similar life and a similar succession : so did one universal order spring from its beginnings and pass through its appointed period to the end which was like the beginning in that after it all things began anew."

E. Hatch.   (H. 1, p. 204.)

(e) " God subsisted prior to creation ; there was a time when God did not create ; it was God's Sabbath of rest. Such Sabbaths recur,—when there is no material universe. This is when the Divine mind ceases from thinking. For God to think is to create."

Anna Kingsford. (K. 3, p. 88.)

(f) " THE DAYS AND NIGHTS OF BRAHMÂ :— This is the name given to the Periods called MANVAN-TARA (*Manu-antara*, or period between the Manus) and PRALAYA (Dissolution) ; one referring to the active periods of the Universe, the other to its times of relative and complete *rest*—according to whether they occur at the end of a ' Day,' or an ' Age ' (a life) of Brahmâ. These periods, which follow each other in regular succession, are also called *Kalpas*, small and great, the minor and the *Maha Kalpa* ; though, properly speaking, the *Maha Kalpa* is never a ' day,' but a whole life or age of Brahmâ, for it is said in the Brahmâ Vaivarta : ' Chronologers compute a Kalpa by the Life of Brahmâ ; minor Kalpas, as Samvarta and the rest, are numerous.' In sober truth they are infinite ; as they have never had a commencement, *i.e.*, there never was a *first* Kalpa, nor will there ever be a *last* one, in Eternity." H. P. Blavatsky. (B. 31, Vol. I, p. 368.)

(g) " Motion as well as matter being fixed in quantity, it would seem that the change in the distribution of matter which motion effects, coming to a limit in whichever direction it is carried, the indestructible motion thereupon necessitates a reverse distribution. Apparently, the universally co-existent forces of attraction and repulsion, which, as we have seen, necessitate rhythm in all minor changes throughout the Universe, also necessitate rhythm in the totality of its changes—produce now an immeasurable period during which the attracting forces predominating, cause universal concentration, and then an immeasurable period, during which the repulsive forces predominating, cause universal diffusion—alternate eras of evolution and dissolution."   Herbert Spencer.   (S. 10, p. 482.)

(*h*) " When we contemplate our Sidereal System as a whole, certain of the great facts which science has established imply potential renewals of life, now in one region now in another ; followed, possibly, at a period unimaginably remote, by a more general renewal."
                    Herbert Spencer.   (S. 10, p. 424.)

(*i*) " The principle of periodicity prevails in nature. The astronomical phenomena which are most familiar to us are all periodic.   . . .   There is a stupendous period in our system when the planets, having gone through all their mutual perturbations, commence a new cycle.   All periodic phenomena have one great feature in common ; at the close of a cycle the condition of the system is the same as it was at the commencement."
                    Sir Robert Ball.   (B. 34, p. 516.)

DURATION

(*a*) " PURE duration is the form which the succession of our conscious states assumes when our ego lets itself *live*, when it refrains from separating its present state from its former states. For this purpose it need not be entirely absorbed in the passing sensation or idea ; for then, on the contrary, it would no longer *endure*. Nor need it forget its former states ; it is enough that, in recalling these states, it does not set them alongside its actual state as one point alongside another, but forms both the past and the present states into an organic whole, as happens when we recall the notes of a tune, melting, so to speak, into one another."

Henri Bergson. (B. 26, p. 100.)

(*b*) " We can thus conceive of succession without distinction, and think of it as a mutual penetration, an interconnection and organization of elements, each one of which represents the whole, and cannot be distinguished or isolated from it except by abstract thought. Such is the account of duration which would be given by a being who was ever the same and ever changing, and who had no idea of space." (*Ibid.*, p. 101.)

(*c*) " In a word, pure duration might well be nothing but a succession of qualitative changes, which melt into and permeate one another, without precise outlines, without any tendency to externalize themselves in relation to one another, without any affiliation with number : it would be pure heterogeneity." (*Ibid.*, p. 104.)

(*d*) " Pure duration, that which consciousness perceives, must be reckoned among the so-called intensive magnitudes,

53

if intensities can be called magnitudes : strictly speaking, however, it is not quantity, and as soon as we try to measure it, we unwittingly replace it by space.

"But we find it extraordinarily difficult to think of duration in its original purity ; this is due, no doubt, to the fact that we do not *endure* alone, external objects, it seems, *endure* as we do, and time, regarded from this point of view, has every appearance of a homogeneous medium."

(*Ibid.*, p. 107.)

(*e*) "What is duration within us ? A qualitative multiplicity with no likeness to number ; an organic evolution which is yet not an increasing quantity ; a pure heterogeneity within which there are no distinct qualities. In a word, the moments of inner duration are not external to one another." (*Ibid.*, p. 226.)

DEATH, AFTER-DEATH STATES

NOTE ON DEATH AND AFTER-DEATH STATES

The mystical teaching with regard to Death and the after-death states has been in all ages that only the divine nature in man is immortal. All his lower nature —which includes much which survives bodily death—dies and fades out, or is disintegrated into its own proper cosmic elements.

Immortality is therefore conditional ; for if the individual has failed to realise his higher divine nature or *Self* whilst on earth ; if his *personality* consists merely of these lower elements : then he has nothing which can be carried forward, as it were, when these lower elements are dissolved away.

It is impossible to say what degree of wickedness or depravity will thus cause a man to " lose his own soul." Perhaps even the most depraved or worldly man may have in him some small smouldering spark of divinity ; and who knows when, or under what circumstances this may not be fanned into a flame ? Even so are " conversions " achieved. But certain it is that so long as any of this lower nature clings to us, we cannot enter into our divine heritage as " Sons of God "—either here or hereafter.

DEATH, AFTER-DEATH STATES

(a) " When thy material body is to be dissolved, first thou surrenderest the body by itself unto the work of change, and thus the form thou hadst doth vanish, and thou surrenderest thy way of life, void of its energy, unto the Daimon. The body's senses next pass back into their sources, becoming separate, and resurrect as energies ; and passion and desire withdraw into that nature which is void of reason.

" And thus it is that man doth speed his way thereafter upwards through the Harmony. To the first zone he gives the Energy of Growth and Waning ; unto the second [zone] Device of Evils [now] de-energized ; unto the third, the Guile of the Desires de-energized ; unto the fourth, his Domineering Arrogance, [also] de-energized ; unto the fifth, unholy Daring and the Rashness of Audacity, de-energized ; unto the sixth, Striving for Wealth by evil means, deprived of its aggrandisement ; and to the seventh zone, Ensnaring Falsehood, de-energized.

" And then, with all the energizings of the Harmony stript from him, clothed in his proper Power, he cometh to that Nature which belongs unto the Eighth, and there with those-that-are hymneth the Father.

" They who are there welcome his coming there with joy ; and he, made like to them that sojourn there, doth further hear the Powers who are above the Nature that belongs unto the Eighth, singing their songs of praise to God in language of their own.

" And then they, in a band, go to the Father home ; of their own selves they make surrender of themselves to Powers, and [thus] becoming Powers they are in God. This the good end for those who have gained Gnôsis—to be made one with God." Hermes. (M. 6, Vol. II, p. 15.)

(b) " For when the soul withdraws into itself, the spirit doth contract itself within the blood, and soul within the spirit. And then the mind, stript of its wrappings, and naturally divine, taking unto itself a fiery body, doth traverse every space, after abandoning the soul unto its judgment and whatever chastisement it hath deserved."
(Ibid., p. 151.)

(c) " Those who go hence without here having found the Soul (Ātman) and those real desires (free from illusion)— for them in all the worlds there is no freedom. But those who go hence having found here the Soul and those real desires—for them in all worlds there is freedom."
Chandogya Upanishad, VIII, 1, 6. (U. 1, p. 263.)

(d) " If, however, it is requisite that the soul of man being tripartite should be dissolved with the composite, we must say that pure souls which are liberated from the body, dismiss that which adhered to them in generation ; but that this is accomplished by others in long periods of time. That also which is dismissed, is the worst part, nor will this be destroyed, as long as that subsists from whence it originates. For nothing which is comprehended in being perishes. . . . Many souls also who once ranked among men, do not cease when liberated from bodies to benefit mankind. And these by employing divination benefit us in other respects, and demonstrate through themselves, that other souls also do not perish."
Plotinus. Enn. IV, 7, 14–15. (P. 1, p. 160.)

(e) " For what the soul doth here, in this life-time into

which it involveth itself, and taketh it into its will, that it taketh with it in its will, and after the ending of the body *cannot* be freed from it ; for afterwards it hath nothing else but *that*, and when it goeth into that and kindleth it, and seeketh with diligence, that is but an unfolding of the same thing, and the poor soul must *content itself with that* : Only in the time of the body can it break of that thing which it hath wrapped up in its will, and that standeth afterwards as *a broken wheel*, which is broken and useless, and no soul entereth into it any more, neither doth it seek any more therein." Jacob Böhme. (B. 3, XII, 27.)

(*f*) " In whatsoever essence and will the soul's fire liveth and burneth, according to that essence is also the *fiat* in the will-spirit, and it imageth such an image : so now when the outward body deceaseth then standeth that image thus in such a source and quality. In the time of the earthly life it may *alter its will* and then also its *fiat* altereth the figure ; but after the dying of the body it hath nothing more wherein it can alter its will."
Jacob Böhme. (B. 8, Part II, 266, 267.)

(*g*) " Like those globules of air and of fire which escape from corporeal substances in dissolution, and rise with more or less quickness according to the degree of their purity and the extent of their action, we cannot doubt that at their death men who have not permitted their proper essence to amalgamate with their earthly habitation will approach rapidly their natal region, there to shine, like stars, with dazzling splendour ; that those who have alloyed themselves partly with the illusions of this tene-brous abode will traverse with less speed the region which separates them from life ; and that those who have identified themselves with the impurities which surround us will remain buried in darkness and obscurity until the least of their corrupted substances be dissolved, and bear away with them an impurity which cannot cease till they themselves have finished." Saint-Martin.   (W. 2, p. 207.)

(*h*) " After death we are suspended, so to speak, from the Great Triad, or universal triangle, which extends from the First Being to Nature, and each of whose three actions draws to itself one of our constituent principles—divine, spiritual, and elementary—to reintegrate them if we are pure, and so set free our soul and enable it to reascend to its source.   But if we are not pure, the enemy, who does not oppose the separation of the corporeal parts which belong only to form, will combat the reintegration of the principles over which the soul has permitted his usurpation, and will retain the whole under his dominion, to the great detriment of the unfortunate soul who has become his victim."   Louis Claud de Saint-Martin.   (W. 2, p. 256.)

(*i*) " The general Egyptian belief was that a man's soul, after being ' purified ' in the after-death state, goes back to God, to live for the eternity as a god with the gods.   This does not mean, I hold, that there was no ' reincarnation,' that is, that the ' being ' of the man did not emanate other ' souls,' but that the ' soul ' of a particular life did not return—that all of it deserving of immortality became a god with the gods, or ' those-that-*are*,' and do not only *ex*-ist."   G. R. S. Mead.   (M. 6, Vol. I, p. 137.)

(*j*) " I do not doubt our permanent existence, for Nature cannot do without the *entelechie* (actual, distinctive being). But we are not all immortal in the same fashion, and in order to manifest one's self in the future life as a great entelechie, one must also become one."
                    Goethe.   (G. 1, Vol. II, p. 484.)

(*k*) " We are not temporally and spatially divided from the beyond, are not first transposed there by death, but are already rooted therein, and what divides us therefrom is merely the subjective barrier of the threshold of sensibility. This threshold thus limits consciousness and therewith self-consciousness."

Carl Du Prel. (D. 2, Vol. II, p. 3.)

(*l*) " Removal into the transcendental world can only be thought in a monistic sense as the displacement of the threshold of our consciousness and self-consciousness, whereby what was formerly unconscious rapport with nature becomes a conscious one. But if, when this happened, our normal rapport with nature was changed or suppressed, our normal consciousness and self-conscious-ness being diminished or even ceasing, that would in effect certainly resemble a spatial transfer to quite another world. Were our five senses to be suddenly taken away, and senses of an entirely different kind given to us, though standing on the same spot we should believe ourselves inhabitants of another star." *(Ibid.*, p. 4.)

(*m*) " When a man parts at death with his material body, that of him which survives is divisible into three parts, the *anima divina* or, as in the Hebrew, *Neshamah* ; the *anima bruta*, or *Ruach*, which is the *persona* of the man ; and the shade, or *Nephesh*, which is the lowest mode of soul-substance. In the great majority of persons the consciousness is gathered up and centred in the *anima bruta*, or *Ruach* ; in the few wise it is polarised in the *anima divina*." Anna Kingsford. (K. 2, p. 306.)

(*n*) " The Divine Breath, or Spirit, is the central life of the human soul, or true man ; and if the elements of this personality be no longer bound in obedience to the Divine Fire, they will become dissolved and dispersed in the void, and so the individual perish. ' Dying thou shalt die.' The rebellious Adam hath not eternal life. Death in the body is for him death in the soul. The soul is a purer and

finer essence than the mere matter of the body.   But-when
she is rebellious, and her elements are no longer bound to
their central fire, they continue, after the death of the
body, to disunite and disintegrate, until, at length, the
Holy Spirit being withdrawn, the soul dissolves into the
void and is no more.   This is eternal death.   On the other
hand, the soul redeemed by obedience to the Divine Will,
withdraws itself, and aspires ever more and more to its
centre, until—absorbed therein—it becomes like unto God,
wholly spiritual.   This is eternal life."

Anna Kingsford.   (K. 3, p. 27.)

(*o*) " Concerning the souls which have not yet attained
heaven, which stick in the source, quality or pain in the
principle in the birth, these have still human matters with
the works on them, and they search diligently after the
cause of their detention : and, therefore, many of them
come again with the starry spirit, and walk about in houses
and other places, and appear in human shape and form,
and desire this and that, and often take care about their
wills and testaments, supposing thereby to get the blessing
of holy people for their rest and quiet.   And if their earthly
business and employment stick in them and cleave to them
still, then, indeed, they take care about their children and
friends ; and this continueth so long, till they sink down
into their rest, so that their starry spirit be *consumed*, then
all is gone as to all care and perplexity, and they have no
more feeling knowledge thereof ; but merely that they see
it in the wonders of the Magia.   But they touch not the
Turba, nor seek what it is in this world, for they are once
sunk down from the Turba through death ; they desire
that no more, neither do they take any more care, for in
care the Turba is stirring ; for the soul's will must enter
with its spirit into earthly things, which it would fain
forsake, for it hardly got rid away from them before ;

it would not cumber itself to *let in* the earthly again. We speak freely and certainly that this sort do no more, *after they are come to grace*, purposely, take care about human earthly matters ; *but about heavenly* matters which come to them through man's spirit, that see them, and have their joy therein." Jacob Böhme. (B. 4, XXVI, 11–15.)

(*p*) "When the man dies, his lower three principles leave him for ever ; *i.e.*, body, life, and the vehicle of the latter, the astral body or the double of the *living* man. And then, his four principles—the central or middle principles, the animal soul or *Kama-rupa*, with what it has assimilated from the lower Manas, and the higher triad find themselves in *Kama-loka*. The latter is an astral locality, the *limbus* of scholastic theology, the *Hades* of the ancients, and, strictly speaking, a *locality* only in a relative sense. It has neither a definite area nor boundary, but exists *within* subjective space ; *i.e.*, is beyond our sensuous perceptions. Still it exists, and it is there that the astral *eidolons* of all the beings that have lived, animals included, await their *second death*. For the animals it comes with the disintegration and the entire fading out of their *astral* particles to the last. For the human *eidolon* it begins when the Atma-Buddhi-Manasic triad is said to ' separate ' itself from its lower principles, or the reflection of the *ex-personality*, by falling into the Devavhanic state." H. P. Blavatsky. (B. 33, p. 143.)

(*q*) " At the solemn moment of death every man, even when death is sudden, sees the whole of his past life mar-shalled before him, in its minutest details. For one short instant the *personal* becomes one with the *individual* and all-knowing *Ego*. But this instant is enough to show him the whole chain of causes which have been at work during his life. He sees and now understands himself as he is,

unadorned by flattery or self-deception. He reads his
life, remaining as a spectator looking down into the arena
he is quitting ; he feels and knows the justice of all the
suffering that has overtaken him. . . . As the man at
the moment of death has a retrospective insight into the
life he has led, so, at the moment he is reborn on to earth,
the *Ego*, awakening from the state of Devachan, has a
prospective vision of the life which awaits him, and realizes
all the causes that have led to it. He realizes them
and sees futurity, because it is between Devachan and
rebirth that the *Ego* regains his full *manasic* consciousness
and rebecomes for a short time the god he was, before, in
compliance with Karmic law, he first descended into matter
and incarnated in the first man of flesh. The ' golden
thread ' sees all its ' pearls ' and misses not one of them.''
                                              (*Ibid.*, p. 162.)

(*r*) '' Peace, peace ! he is not dead, he doth not sleep—
       He hath awaken'd from the dream of life—
       'Tis we, who, lost in stormy visions, keep
       With phantoms an unprofitable strife.
       He has outsoar'd the shadow of our night.''
                                   Shelley.   *Adonais.*

(*s*) '' WEEP not, beloved Friends ! nor let the air
        For me with sighs be troubled.   Not from life
        Have I been taken ; this is genuine life
        And this alone—the life which now I live
        In peace eternal ; where desire and joy
        Together move in fellowship without end.''
Wordsworth.—*Epitaphs*, I. (W. 1, Vol. V., p. 301.)

(*t*) '' The soul must raise the brute in man, with all its
appetites, to purity,—a mighty task, accomplished with
much pain, yet in infinitely shorter duration of pain than
if left in disembodied spirit-life ; and, indeed, we may

come to look upon pain in this world as one of our best privileges because of its powers of purification within the time-limit, and to know that by the mercy of the God of Love we may take our hell of cleansing in this world rather than in those worlds of disembodied spirits where progress is of infinite slowness—revolving upon itself, as a sand-spiral in a blast-furnace, without hope of death.

"Oh, how convey any warning of this terrible knowledge, which is not communicable by words! . . . But, O soul! repent and return while still in the body!"

The Golden Fountain. (G. 7, p. 143.)

DUALISTIC THEORIES OF THE COSMOS

(a) "For the sake of experiencing the true and the false,
The Great Ātman (Soul, Self) has a dual nature!
—Yea, the Great Ātman has a dual nature!"
Maitri Upanishad. (U. 1, p. 458.)

(b) "This world, O Kaccâna, generally proceeds on a duality; on the 'It is' and the 'It is not.' But, O Kaccâna, whoever perceives in truth and wisdom how things originate in the world, in his eyes there is no 'It is not' in this world. Whoever, Kaccâna, perceives in truth and wisdom how things pass away in this world, in his eyes there is no 'It is' in this world. . . . 'Everything is,' this is the one extreme, O Kaccâna; 'Everything is not,' this is the other extreme. The perfect one, O Kaccâna, remaining far from both these extremes proclaims the truth in the middle." Gautama Buddha. (O. 1, p. 249.)

(c) "For some think there are two craft-rival Gods, as it were,—one the artificer of good (things), the other of (things) worthless. Others call the better 'God' and the other 'Daimon,' as Zoroaster the Mage, who, they tell us, lived five thousand years before the Trojan War.

" Zoroaster, then, called the one Ōromazēs, and the other Areimanios, and further announced that the one resembled light especially of things sensible, and the other, contrariwise, darkness and ignorance, while that between the two was Mithrēs ; wherefore the Persians call Mithrēs the Mediator." Plutarch. (M. 6, Vol. I, p. 324.)

(d) " Nothing without contrariety or opposition can become manifest to itself ; for if it hath nothing that is contrary or opposite to it, then it continually goeth forward *out* and goeth not *in* again into itself, viz., into that out of which it is originally gone forth ; then it knoweth nothing of its original. If the natural life had no contrariety or opposition and were without a limit, then it would never ask or enquire after its ground out of which it proceeded, and so the hidden God would continue unknowable or unapprehended by the natural life."
Jacob Böhme. (B. 20, I, 14–15.)

(e) " The great struggle between Light and Darkness, of the God of Light and the God of Darkness, goes back to the earliest Egyptian tradition, and the fights of Rā and Āpep, Heru-Behutet and Set, and Horus, son of Isis, and Set, are ' in reality only different versions of one and the same story, though belonging to different periods.' The Horus and Set version is apparently the most recent. The names of the Light God and Dark God thus change, but what does not change is the name of the Arbiter, the Mediator, ' whose duty it was to prevent either God from gaining a decisive victory, and from destroying one another.' This Balancer was Thoth, who had to keep the opposites in equilibrium." G. R. S. Mead. (M. 6, Vol. I, p. 57.)

DIVINE DARK, THE

(a) " Supernal Triad, Deity above all Essence, Knowledge, and Goodness ; Guide of Christians to Divine Wisdom ; direct our path to the ultimate summit of Thy Mystical Lore, most incomprehensible, most luminous, and most exalted, where the pure, absolute, and immutable mysteries of theology, are veiled in the dazzling obscurity of the secret Silence, outshining all brilliance with the intensity of their Darkness, and surcharging our blinded intellects with the utterly impalpable and invisible fairness of glories surpassing all beauty."

Dionysius. (D. 1, p. 5.)

(b) " Do thou, in the diligent exercise of mystical contemplation, leave behind the senses, and the operations of the intellect, and all things sensible and intellectual, and all things in the world of being and non-being, that thou mayest arise, by Unknowing towards the union, as far as is attainable, with Him Who transcends all being and all knowledge. For by the unceasing and absolute renunciation of thyself and of all things, thou mayest be borne on high, through pure and entire self-abnegation, into the superessential Radiance of the Divine Darkness."

(Ibid., p. 5.)

(c) " He (the Beneficent Cause of all) is superessentially exalted above created things, and reveals Himself in His naked Truth to those alone who pass beyond all that is pure or impure, and ascend above the topmost altitudes of holy things, and, who leaving behind them all divine light and sound and heavenly utterances, plunge into the Darkness where truly dwells, as the Oracles declare, that ONE Who is beyond all."   (Ibid., p. 6.)

(d) " A darkness that shines brighter than light, that invisibly and intangibly illuminates with splendours of inconceivable beauty the soul that sees not."

Dionysius. (S. 15, p. 208.)

(e) " In this abyss of darkness where love lights the fire of death, I see the dawn of eternal life and the manifestation of God. Here is born and shines forth a certain inconceivable light illuminating the eternal life, and in it things grow visible to us. But the light shines in the pure essence of the spirit, above the gifts, in the void where bliss has delivered man out of himself, and where he receives it in the fullest measure of which the creature is capable. Yet is this dark light, in which the spirit contemplates all that desire can conceive, of such a nature that the contemplative dwelling in peace in the depths, sees and feels nothing beyond its ineffable radiance."

Ruysbroeck. (H. 5, p. 45.)

(f) " The immeasurable abyss of Divinity is a holy darkness which contains, enfolds, and transcends every attribute in the all-embracing circle of essential Unity, and the mystery of possession is consummated in these nameless depths."   (*Ibid.*, p. 51.)

(g) " Above knowledge I sense and discover an abyss of darkness, fathomless, limitless, and without qualities, above the names of created things, above the names of God. It is the end of transcending, the merging of the sublime in the nameless Eternal. It is the hope of peace felt to exist at the core of life, beyond the outer worlds, beyond the worlds of the soul ; it is the infinite Beatitude, nameless, yet the central point where all names are one. It is the mountain crest of human effort and the abyss of the transcendent Essence, wherein the happy spirits, distinct yet ever immersed, are visible to the inner eye of contemplation, which sees in the Divine darkness Father, Son, and Holy Ghost : a Trinity of Persons, a Unity of Essence, ocean of sure unending peace. And if we should be lifted to these heights we should, by the grace thereof, become the essential beatitude, the eternal activity and the immeasurable abundance of the three Persons, Who are Divinity and bliss in the simplicity of Their essence, ceaseless motion, and everlasting rest, love, and joy in the midst of activity and peace." *(Ibid.,* p. 85.)

EVOLUTION, BIOLOGICAL

(a) " EVOLUTION will thus prove to be something entirely different from a series of adaptations to circumstances, as mechanism claims; entirely different also from the realisation of a plan of the whole, as maintained by the doctrine of finality."

Henri Bergson. (B. 27, p. 106.)

(b) " It must not be forgotten that the force which is evolving throughout the organised world is a limited force, which is always seeking to transcend itself and always remains inadequate to the work it would fain produce."

(Ibid., p. 133.)

(c) " It may be said that the whole evolution of the animal kingdom, apart from retrogressions towards vegetative life, has taken place on two divergent paths, one of which led to instinct and the other to intelligence."

(Ibid., p. 141.)

(d) " A true evolutionism would propose to discover by what *modus vivendi*, gradually obtained, the intellect has adopted its plan of structure, and matter its mode of subdivision. This structure and this subdivision work into each other; they are mutually complementary; they must have progressed one with the other. And, whether we posit the present structure of mind or the present subdivision of matter, in either case we remain in the evolved: we are told nothing of what evolves, nothing of evolution." (Ibid., p. 389.)

(e) " It is very desirable to remember that evolution is

not an explanation of the cosmic process, but merely a generalized statement of the method and results of that process." T. H. Huxley. (H. 2, p. 6.)

(*f*) " Thus we have given to man a pedigree of prodigious length, but not, it may be said, of noble quality. The world, it has often been remarked, appears as if it had long been preparing for the advent of man ; and this, in one sense is strictly true, for he owes his birth to a long line of progenitors. If any single link in this chain had never existed, man would not have been exactly what he now is. Unless we wilfully close our eyes, we may, with our present knowledge, approximately recognise our parentage ; nor need we feel ashamed of it. The most humble organism is something much higher than the inorganic dust under our feet ; and no one with an unbiassed mind can study any living creature, however humble, without being struck with enthusiasm at its marvellous structure and properties."

Charles Darwin. (D. 6, Vol. I, p. 213.)

(*g*) " Our present normal physical senses were (from our present point of view) abnormal in those days of slow and progressive downward evolution and fall into matter. And there was a day when all that which in our modern times is regarded as phenomena, so puzzling to the physiologists now compelled to believe in them—such as thought transference, clairvoyance, clairaudience, etc. ; in short, all that which is called now " wonderful and abnormal "— all that and much more belonged to the senses and faculties common to all humanity. We are, however, cycling back and cycling forward ; *i.e.*, having lost in spirituality that which we acquired in physical development until almost the end of the Fourth Race, we (mankind) are as gradually and imperceptibly losing now in the physical all that we regain once more in the spiritual *re*-evolution. This process must go on until the period which will bring the Sixth Root-Race on a parallel line with the spirituality of the Second, long extinct mankind."

H. P. Blavatsky.   (B. 31, Vol. I, p. 536.)

ETERNITY

(a) " And eternity may be properly denominated a God unfolding himself into light, and shining forth, such as he essentially is, viz., as immutable and the same, and thus firmly established in life. . . .   Hence, if someone should thus denominate eternity, calling it life which is now infinite, because it is all, and nothing of which is consumed, because nothing pertaining to it is either past or future, since otherwise it would not be all things at once :— if someone should thus denominate it, he will be near to the true definition of it.   For what is afterwards added, viz., that it is all things at once, and that nothing of it is consumed, will be an exposition of the assertion, that it is now infinite life."

Plotinus.   Enn. III, 7, 4.   (P. 2, p. 122.)

(b) " What is eternity ?   Well, it is characteristic of eternity that in it youth and existence are the same, for eternity would not be eternal could it newly become and *were* not always."   Eckhart.   (E. 1, p. 49.)

(c) " He who sees what now is, hath seen all that ever hath been from times everlasting, and that shall be to eternity ; for all things are of one lineage and one likeness."

Marcus Aurelius.   (M. 1, VI, 37, p. 151.)

(d) " Do not think that mankind hath such a beginning, as we must say of ourselves, according to the *creation* : no, the image hath appeared in God *from eternity* in the virgin of wisdom ; but not *in substance* (or distinction) ; it was no woman, nor man, but it was both ; as *Adam* was both, before *Eve* was, which (divided distinction) signifieth the earthly, and also the beastial man ; for nothing sub-sisteth in eternity, unless it hath been from eternity."

> Jacob Böhme.   (B. 3, VI, 74.)

(*e*) " The Word, viz., the efflux from the willing of God, was the Eternal beginning, and continueth so eternally."

> Jacob Böhme.   (B. 20, III, 4.)

(*f*)
> " Eternity may be as time,
>   Time as eternity,
>   Unless an inward difference
>   Thou dost create in thee."

> Angelus Silesius.   (S. 4, p. 52.)

(*g*)   " Time surveyed in its wholeness is Eternity."

> Josiah Royce.   (R. 3, Vol. II, p. 337.)

(*h*) " The doctrine that eternity is timeless, that our ' immortality,' if we live in the eternal, is not so much future as already here and now, which we find so often expressed to-day in certain philosophical circles, finds its support in a ' hear, hear ! ' or an ' amen,' which floats up from that mysteriously deeper level. We recognize the pass-words to the mystical region as we hear them, but we cannot use them ourselves ; it alone has the keeping of ' the password primeval.' "

> William James.   (J. 5, p. 422.)

(*i*) " The One remains, the many change and pass ;
>   Heaven's light for ever shines, Earth's shadows fly.
>   Life, like a dome of many-coloured glass,
>   Stains the white radiance of Eternity,
>   Until Death tramples it to fragments.—Die,
>   If thou wouldst be with that which thou dost seek !
>   Follow where all is fled !—Rome's azure sky,

Flowers, ruins, statues, music, words, are weak
The glory they transfuse with fitting truth to speak."
                                Shelley. *Adonais.*

EMANATION

NOTE ON EMANATION

The concept of an extra-cosmic *personal* God, who has *created* Man and the external world of Nature, and who remains apart therefrom, is very far indeed from the mystical doctrine which has been taught in all ages. The theology of the Christian Church, which has always been based upon a personal Creator, looks askance at the mystical doctrine of *emanation*, and denounces it as *pantheism.* Nevertheless it is the teaching of the philosophical Christian Mystics, as well as that of the pre-Christian philosophers. It can perhaps be more clearly understood to-day in connection with the concept of a unitary Cosmic Substance, or Substance-Principle.

See SUBSTANCE, p. 248.

EMANATION

(*a*) " We acknowledge that the will of the Abyss hath brought itself into a longing and imagination of itself, whence Nature and creature have their original : whence also the natural life hath its original, which now also out of the partibleness of the exhaled will hath its own will and imagination to form and image itself according to its longing and desire. As we see such changing in Nature, how Nature imageth itself into so many kinds and properties, and how these properties do every one desire their like again."   Jacob Böhme. (B. 18, 1, 17.)

(*b*) " The centre of everything (being a particle or spark from the expressed Word) doth again express or speak itself forth, and bringeth itself into a various distinct particularity, in manner and form of the divine speaking (or operation of the eternal Word) in its generation, and manifestation.''   (*Ibid.*, B. 16, VI, 12.)

(c) " Every thing's centre as a piece of the outspoken Word re-outspeaketh itself, and compriseth or frameth itself into separability after the kind and manner of the Divine speaking.''   (*Ibid.*, B. 19, 12.)

(d) " For all beings are but one only Being, which hath breathed forth itself out of itself.''   (*Ibid.*, B. 16, VI, 65.)

(e) " Every centre maketh its own out-breathing Nature, and Substance, out of itself, and yet all originateth out of the eternal One.''   (*Ibid.*, B. 19, 19.)

(f) " In God all beings are but one being, viz., an eternal One or unity, the eternal only *good*, which eternal One without severality were not manifest to itself. Therefore the same hath breathed forth itself out of itself that a plurality and distinct variety might arise, which variety or severality hath induced itself into a peculiar *will* and properties, the properties into desires, and the desires into beings.   (*Ibid.*, B. 16, VI, 8, 9.)

(g) " As there is a nature and substance in the outward world, so also in the inward spiritual world there is a nature and substance which is spiritual, from which the outward world is breathed forth and produced out of light and darkness, and created to have a beginning and time.''
                    (*Ibid.*, B. 13, II, 31.)

(h) " From him, indeed (who is) in the soul (*âtman*) come forth all breathing creatures, all worlds, all the Vedas, all gods, all beings. The mystic meaning (*upanishad*) thereof is : The Real of the real.''
          Maitri Upanishad, VI, 32.   (U. 1, p. 445.)

ESTHETIC EMOTION

(a) " The deeper the mind penetrates into the facts of esthetics, the more they are perceived to be based upon an ideal identity between the mind itself and things. At a certain point the harmony becomes so complete and the finality so close that it gives us actual emotion. The Beautiful then becomes the sublime, and, for a passing flash, the soul rises into the true mystic state and touches the Absolute."   E. Récéjac   (R. 4, p. 72.)

(b) " To me the meanest flower that blows can give
        Thoughts that do often lie too deep for tears."
Wordsworth.—*Ode to Immortality.* (W. 1, Vol. V, p. 345.)

(c) " Ah !   Then, if mine had been the Painter's hand,
        To express what then I saw ; and add the gleam,
        The light that never was, on sea or land,
        The consecration, and the Poet's dream."
Wordsworth.—*Elegiac Stanzas.* (W. 1, Vol. V., p. 312.)

(d) " Your enjoyment of the World is never right, till you so esteem it, that everything in it, is more your treasure than a King's exchequer full of Gold and Silver.   And that exchequer yours also in its place and service.   Can you take too much joy in your Father's works ?   He is Himself in everything.   Some things are little on the outside, and rough and common, but I remember the time when the dust of the streets were as pleasing as Gold to my infant eyes, and now they are more precious to the eye of reason.

" Your enjoyment of the world is never right, till every morning you awake in Heaven ; see yourself in your Father's Palace ; and look upon the skies, the earth, and the air as Celestial Joys : having such a reverend esteem of all, as if you were among the Angels.   The bride of a monarch, in her husband's chamber, hath no such causes of delight as you.

" You never enjoy the world aright, till the Sea itself floweth in your veins, till you are clothed with the heavens, and crowned with the stars : and perceive yourself to be the sole heir of the whole world, and more than so, because men are in it who are everyone sole heirs as well as you. Till you can sing and rejoice and delight in God, as misers do in gold, and Kings in sceptres, you never enjoy the world.

" Till your spirit filleth the whole world, and the stars are your jewels : till you are as familiar with the ways of God in all Ages as with your walk and table : till you are intimately acquainted with that shady nothing out of which the world was made : till you love men so as to desire their happiness, with a thirst equal to the zeal of your own : till you delight in God for being good to all : you never enjoy the world."

Thomas Traherne.   (T. 3, pp. 18, 20.)

FREE WILL

(a) "Of all things that are, one part is in our control, the other out of it; in our control are opinion, impulse to do, effort to obtain, effort to avoid—in a word, our own proper activities; out of our control are our bodies, property, reputation, office—in a word, all things except our proper activities. Things in our control are in their nature free, not liable to hindrance in the doing or to frustration of the attainment; things out of our control are weak, dependent, liable to hindrance, belonging to others. Bear in mind, then, that if you mistake what is dependent for what is free, and what belongs to others for what is your own, you will meet with obstacles in your way, you will be regretful and disquieted, you will find fault with both gods and men."

Epictetus. (H. 1, p. 221.)

(b) "That which is free, none may call his own, and he who maketh it his own, committeth a wrong. Now, in the whole realm of freedom, nothing is so free as the will, and he who maketh it his own, and suffereth it not to remain in its excellent freedom, and free nobility, and in its free exercise, (that is to say as God wills) doeth a grievous wrong. This is what is done by the Devil and Adam and all their followers."

Theologia Germanica. (T. 1, p. 202.)

(c) "Seeing now we thus know what we are, and that God letteth us know it, we should now look to it and generate some good out of us, for we have the centre of Eternal Nature *in us.* If we make an angel out of us, then we are *that* ; if we make a devil out of us, then we are *that*."   Jacob Böhme.   (B. 5, Part II, IX, 12.)

(*d*) " For thou must know that in the government of thy mind thou art *thine own* lord and master, there will rise up *no* fire in thee in the circle or whole circumference of thy body and spirit, *unless* thou awakenest it *thyself*."

(*Ibid.*, B. 1, X, 81.)

(*e*) " Each Ens of the forth-breathed word hath a free will again to breathe forth out of its own Ens a likeness according to itself."   (*Ibid.*, B. 7, XXII, 24.)

(*f*) " Every man is *free*, and is as *a god* to himself ; in this life man may *change* and alter himself either into wrath or into light."   (*Ibid.*, B. 1, XVIII, 43.)

(*g*)   " For what is freedom, but the unfettered use
Of all the powers which God for use had given ?
But chiefly this, him first, him last to view
Through meaner powers and secondary things
Effulgent, as through clouds that veil his blaze.
For all that meets the bodily sense I deem
Symbolical, one mighty alphabet
For infant minds ; and we in this low world
Placed with our backs to bright reality,
That we may learn with young unwounded ken
The substance from its shadow."
Samuel T. Coleridge.   Poems.   *The Destiny of Nations.*

(*h*) " We can now formulate our conception of freedom. Freedom is the relation of the concrete self to the act which it performs.   This relation is indefinable, just because we *are* free.   For we can analyse a thing, but not a process ; we can break up extensity, but not duration.   Or, if we persist in analysing it, we unconsciously transform the process into a thing and duration into extensity.   By the very fact of breaking up concrete time we set out its

moments in homogeneous space ; in place of the doing we
put the already done ; and, as we have begun by, so to
speak, stereotyping the activity of the self, we see spon-
taneity settle down into inertia and freedom into necessity.
Thus, any positive definition of freedom will ensure the
victory of determinism." Henri Bergson. (B. 26, p. 219.)

(*i*) " To sum up ; every demand for explanation in
regard to freedom comes back, without our suspecting it,
to the following question : ' Can time be adequately
represented by space ? ' To which we answer : Yes, if
you are dealing with time flown ; No, if you speak of time
flowing. Now, the free act takes place in time which is
flowing and not in time which has already flown. Freedom
is therefore a fact, and among the facts which we observe
there is none clearer. All the difficulties of the problem,
and the problem itself, arise from the desire to endow
duration with the same attributes as extensity, to interpret
a succession by a simultaneity, and to express the idea of
freedom in a language into which it is obviously untrans-
latable." Henri Bergson. (B. 26, p. 221.)

(*j*) " The problem of freedom has thus sprung from a
misunderstanding : it has been to the moderns what the
paradoxes of the Eleatics were to the ancients, and, like
these paradoxes, it has its origin in the illusion through
which we confuse succession and simultaneity, duration
and extensity, quality and quantity."
Henri Bergson. (B. 26, p. 240.)

FATE

(*a*) " Love only what befalls thee and is spun for thee
by fate. For what can be more befitting for thee."
Marcus Aurelius. (M. 1, VII, 57, p. 189.)

(*b*) " Fate has carried me
'Mid the thick arrows : I will keep my stand—

Not shrink and let the shaft pass by my breast
To pierce another."
George Eliot.   (E. 2, p. 260.)

(c) " That which ye sow ye reap.   See yonder fields !
The sesamum was sesamum, the corn
Was corn.   The Silence and the Darkness knew !
So is a man's fate born."
The Light of Asia.   (A. 2, Book VIII.)

(d) " From the remotest antiquity mankind as a whole have always been convinced of the existence of a personal spiritual entity within the personal physical man.   This inner entity was more or less divine, according to its proximity to the *crown*.   The closer the union the more serene man's destiny, the less dangerous the external conditions.   This belief is neither bigotry nor superstition, only an ever-present, instinctive feeling of the proximity of another spiritual and invisible world, which, though it be subjective to the senses of the outward man, is perfectly objective to the inner ego.   Furthermore, they believed that there are external and internal conditions which affect the determination of our will upon our actions. They rejected fatalism, for fatalism implies a blind course of some still blinder power.   But they believed in *destiny* or *Karma*, which from birth to death every man is weaving thread by thread around himself, as a spider does his cobweb ;   and this destiny is guided by that presence termed by some the guardian angel, or our more intimate astral inner man, who is but too often the evil genius of the man of flesh or the *personality*.   Both these lead on MAN, but one of them must prevail ;   and from the very beginning of the invisible affray the stern and implacable *law of compensation and retribution* steps in and takes its course, following faithfully the fluctuating of the conflict. When the last strand is woven, and man is seemingly enwrapped in the net-work of his own doing, then he finds himself completely under the empire of this *self-made* destiny.   It then either fixes him like the inert shell against the immovable rock, or like a feather carries him away in a whirlwind raised by his own actions."

H. P. Blavatsky.   (B. 33, p. 182.)

FALL OF MAN

(*a*) " What is the reason that souls become oblivious of divinity, being ignorant both of themselves and him, though their allotment is from thence, and they in short partake of God ?   The principle therefore of evil to them is audacity, generation, the first difference, and the wish to exercise an unrestrained freedom of the will.   When, therefore, they began to be delighted with this unbounded liberty, abundantly employing the power of being moved from themselves, they ran in a direction contrary [to their first course], and thus becoming most distant from their source, they were at length ignorant that they were thence derived."   Plotinus.   Enn. V, 1. 1.   (P. 2, p. 162.)

(*b*) " God knew very well that man would not stand, but fall."   Jacob Böhme.   (B. 16, X, 29.)

(*c*) " But it being known to God that-man would not stand, and that he had already imagined and lusted after good and evil, God said, ' It is not good for man to be alone, we will make him an helpmeet for him.'

" For God saw that Adam could not then generate magically, having entered with his lust into vanity.   Now therefore Moses saith, ' God caused a deep sleep to fall upon him, and he slept ' ; that is, seeing man would not continue in the obedience of the divine harmony in the properties, submitting himself to stand still as an instrument of the Spirit of God ; therefore God suffered him to fall from the divine harmony into a harmony of his own, *viz.*, into the awakened properties of evil and good ; the spirit of his soul went into these.

" And there in this sleep he died from the angelical world, and fell under the power of the outward Fiat, and thus bade farewell to the eternal image which was of God's begetting. Here his angelical form and power fell into a swoon and lay on the ground. And then by the Fiat God made the woman out of him, out of the matrix of Venus, *viz.*, out of that property wherein Adam had the begettress in himself ; and so out of one body he made two, and divided the properties of the tinctures, *viz.*, the watery and fiery constellations in the element, yet not wholly in substance but in the spirit, *viz.*, the properties of the watery and fiery soul.

" And yet it is but one thing still, only the property of the tincture was divided ; the desire of self-love was taken out of Adam, and formed into a woman according to his likeness. And thence it is that man now so eagerly desireth the matrix of the woman, and the woman desireth the limbus of the man, *viz.*, the fire-element, the original of the true soul, by which is meant the tincture of fire ; for these two were one in Adam, and therein consisted the magical begetting."

Jacob Böhme. (B. 15, *Of Regeneration*, I, 51–55.)

(*d*) " The Fall is a present and not a past fact. Man's real fall is that he is content with the shadow of good. He still eats of the tree of good and evil, and until the Christ fills the whole consciousness, man will ever be at war with himself, his brother, and his God." *"Christ in You."* (C. 10, p. 104.)

See also ADAM, p. 16.

GOD AND GODHEAD

NOTE ON GOD AND GODHEAD

THE following quotations bring out very clearly the fact that although it has been recognised by thinkers in all ages that God as the Absolute—or, as Böhme would say, "God as He is in Himself"—is utterly unknowable in any terms of human knowledge or intellect, and that nothing whatever can be affirmed of Him—or of IT (the THAT of the *Upanishads*)—yet for the purposes of practical religion, and more particularly for theology, it is necessary to have the concept of God as an *active* Being having *relations* with the universe and with ourselves. A secondary *aspect* of the Absolute is therefore postulated and the distinction made between the absolute unknowable Godhead and the active knowable —through manifestation—God.

In the mystic faculty, however, we have a means of knowing God as the Godhead by a deeper method or faculty than that of intellect. The mystic achieves the knowledge of THAT which he *is* and *always has been* in the deep ground of his nature. He finds it by looking *within*. He finds it as his own *Self*. He whose apprehension of God does not extend beyond the concept of a *relation* can never enter into this mystical experience; can never achieve a true knowledge of his own Self in its inmost root and ground; or of his inherent divine nature.

GOD AND GODHEAD

(*a*) "The Tao which can be expressed in words is not the All-embracing and Immutable Tao; the Name which can be uttered is not the Ever-applicable Name.

" Without a name, It is the beginning of Heaven and Earth ; conceived as having a name, It is the Progenitrix of all things.

" He alone who is free from earthly passions can perceive the deep mystery of the Unmanifested One ; he who is possessed by desires can only behold the Manifest's outward form.

" These two, the Manifest and the Unmanifest, although differing in name, in essence are identical. This sameness is the mystery, the deep within the deep, the door of many mysteries." Lao Tsze. *The Tâo Teh King.* (L. 1, p. 10.)

" All things under Heaven derive their being from the manifestation of Tao ; and Tao the Manifest is born in Tao the Unmanifest." (*Ibid.*, p. 15.)

(*b*) " Wherefore, O Hermes, never think that aught of things above or things below is like to God, for thou wilt fall from truth. For naught is like to That which hath no like, and is Alone and One." Hermes. (M. 6, Vol. II, p. 178.)

(*c*) " The one God, the first and sole and universal Maker and Lord, had nothing coeval with him, not infinite chaos, not measureless water, or solid earth, or dense air, or warm fire, or subtle breath, nor the azure cope of the vast heaven : but He was one, alone by Himself, and by His will He made the things that are, that before were not, except so far as they existed in His foreknowledge."

Hippolytus. (H. 1, p. 203.)

(*d*) " The Lord of the universe being Himself the substance of the whole, not yet having brought any creature into being, was alone : and since all power over both visible and invisible things was with Him, He Himself by the power of His word gave substance to all things with Himself." Tatian. (H. 1, p. 196.)

(*e*) " What, then, is that which really exists ? It is the Eternal, the Uncreated, the Undying, to whom time brings

no change.   For time is always flowing and never stays :
it is a vessel charged with birth and death : it has a before
and after, a ' will be ' and a ' has been ' : it belongs to the
' is not ' rather than to the ' is.'   But God is : and that
not in time but in eternity, motionless, timeless, changeless
eternity, that has no before or after : and being One, He
fills eternity with one Now, and so really ' is,' not ' has
been,' or ' will be,' without beginning and without ceasing.''
Plutarch.   (H. 1, p. 242.)

(*f*) '' He (God) is incomprehensible : not even the whole
universe, much less the human mind, can contain the
conception of Him : we know *that* He is, we cannot know
what He is : we may see the manifestations of Him in His
works, but it were monstrous folly to go behind His works
and inquire into His essence.   He is hence unnamed : for
names are the symbols of created things, whereas His
only attribute is to *be*.''   Philo.   (H. 1, p. 245.)

(*g*) '' You are not to think that the unbegotted God
' came down ' from anywhere nor went up.   For the
unutterable Father and Lord of all things neither comes
to any place nor walks nor sleeps nor rises, but abides in
His own place wherever that place may be, seeing keenly
and hearing keenly, not with eyes or ears, but with His
unspeakable power; so that He sees all things, nor is any one
of us hid from Him : nor does He move, He who is uncontained by space and by the whole world, seeing that He
was before the world was born.''
Justin Martyr.   (H. 1, p. 253.)

(*h*) '' To God, as Godhead, appertain neither will, nor
knowledge, nor manifestation, nor anything that we can
name, or say, or conceive.   But to God as God, (that is
as a person) it belongeth to express Himself, and know
and love Himself, and to reveal Himself to Himself ; and

all this without any creature. And all this resteth in God as a substance but not as a working, so long as there is no creature. And out of this expressing and revealing of Himself unto Himself, ariseth the distinction of Persons. But when God as God is made man, or where God dwelleth in a godly man, or one who is " made a partaker of the divine nature," in such a man somewhat appertaineth unto God which is His own, and belongeth to Him only and not to the creature. And without the creature, this would lie in His own Self as a Substance or well-spring, but would not be manifested or wrought out into deeds. Now God will have it to be exercised and clothed in a form, for it is there only to be wrought out and executed. What else is it for ? Shall it lie idle ? What then would it profit ? As good were it that it had never been ; nay better, for what is of no use existeth in vain, and that is abhorred by God and Nature. However, God will have it wrought out, and this cannot come to pass (which it ought to do) without the creature. Nay, if there ought not to be, and were not this and that—works, and a world full of real things, and the like,—what were God Himself, and what had He to do, and whose God would He be ? Here we must turn and stop, or we might follow this matter and grope along until we knew not where we were, now how we should find our way out again."

Theologia Germanica.   (T. 1, p. 109.)

(*i*) " This is that ingenerable and Eternal One who has no name and who has all names ; who was the first to know those of the Universe, who has heard those of the Universe. He is mightier than all might, upon whose incomprehensible Face no one is able to gaze. Beyond all mind does He exist in His own Form, Solitary and Unknowable. The Universal Mystery is He, the Universal Wisdom, of all things the Beginning. In Him are all Lights, all

Life, and all Repose. He is the Beatitude of which all in the Universe are in need, for that they might receive Him, they are there. All beings of the Universe does He behold within Himself, that One Uncontainable, who parts those of the Universe and receives them all into Himself. Without Him is nothing, for all the worlds exist in Him, and He is the boundary of them all. All of them has He enclosed, for in Him is all. No Space is there without Him, nor any Intelligence ; for without that Only One there exists nothing. The Eternities (æons) contemplate His incomprehensibility which is within them all, but understand it not. They wonder at it because He limits them all. They strive towards the City which is their Image. In this City it is that they move and live [and have their true being] ; for it is the House of the Father, the Robe of the Son, and the Power of the Mother, the Image of the Plêrôma. He is the First Father of all things, the First Eternal, the King of those that None can Touch ; He in whom all things lose themselves, He who has given all things from within Himself ; the Space which has grown from itself, He who is born of Himself, the Abyss of all being, the Great and True One who is in the Deep ; He in whom the Fulnesses (Plêrômata) did come, and even they are silent before Him. They have not named Him, because Unnameable and beyond thought is He, that First Fount whose Eternity stretches through all Spaces, that First Tone whereby all things hearken and understand. He it is whose limbs make a myriad, myriad Powers, and every Power is a being in itself."

The Gnôsis of the Light. (G. 6, p. 21.)

(*j*) " Theologists teach that we must distinguish in the Godhead between essence and (real) being. Essence in the Godhead is the Godhead itself, and is the first thing we apprehend about God. The Godhead is the whole

basis of divine perfection.   The Godhead in itself is motionless unity and balanced stillness; and is the source of all
emanations.   Hence I assume a passive (motionless)
welling-up.   We call this first utterance *existence*, for the
most intrinsic utterance, the first formal determination, is
existence in the Godhead : *being* in its mode of reality.
God is existence, but existence is not God.

" Now the origin of the Father is necessarily involved
in this assumption of a passive welling-up.   In other words,
the Godhead being in itself intelligence, therefore the
divine nature steps forth into relation to otherness : other
but not another, for this distinction is rational not real.
Thus the first Person arises in the Godhead passively, not
from any active beginning.   Hence its beginning is without
property (personality).

" The question is, what is the Person of the Father ?   I
answer that it is *being* (or *nature*) in the Godhead, not
according to essence but according to paternity, which is
the formal notion specifically determining the Father.
The Father is the beginning of all (the Persons of) the
Godhead."   Eckhart. (E. 1, p. 54.)

" The soul's beatitude consists in comprehending all
together, in one property, these eternal eternities which are
the formal expression of the divine nature.   For here is no
division : God is the superessential *one*, his own beatitude
and that of all creatures in the actuality of his Godhead.
Be sure that in this unity God knows distinctions but as
one impartible property.

" In this unity God is idle.   The Godhead effects neither
this nor that ; it is God who effects all things.   God in
activity is manifold and knows multiplicity.   God as *one*
is absolutely free from activity.   In this unity God knows
nothing save that he superessentially *is* in his own self."
                                   (*Ibid.*, p. 58.)

" Now mark ! The Godhead, self-poised, is self-sufficient. God as Godhead transcends all that creature as creature ever comprehended or can comprehend." (*Ibid.*, p. 68.)

(*k*) " All that is in the Godhead is one. Therefore can we say nothing. It is above all names, above all nature. The essence of all creatures is eternally a divine life in Deity. God works. So doth not the Godhead. Therein are they distinguished,—in working and not working. The end of all things is the hidden darkness of the eternal Godhead, unknown, and never to be known."

Eckhart. (V. 1, Vol. I, p. 189.)

" God in himself was not God—in the creature only hath He become God. I ask to be rid of God—that is, that God, by his grace, would bring me into the Essence—that Essence which is above God and above distinction. I would enter into that eternal Unity which was mine before all time, when I was what I would, and would what I was : —into a state above all addition or diminution ;—into the Immobility whereby all is moved."   (*Ibid.*, p. 191.)

(*l*) " The things which are in part can be apprehended, known, and expressed ; but the perfect cannot be apprehended, known, or expressed by any creature as creature. Therefore we do not give a name to the Perfect, for it is none of these. The creature as creature cannot know nor apprehend it, name nor conceive it."

Theologia Germanica.   (T. 1, p. 2.)

(*m*) " God is in Himself the Abyss, viz., the first world, of which no creature knoweth anything at all, for it standeth solely and alone with spirit and body in the Byss or ground. Thus also God Himself in the Abyss would not be manifest in Himself, but His Wisdom is from eternity become his ground or Byss."   Jacob Böhme. (B. 5, III, 24–25.)

(*n*) " If I would say what God is in his depth, then I

must say, he is outside of all nature and properties, viz., an understanding and original of all essences. The essences are his manifestation, and thereof alone we have ability to write ; and not of the unmanifested God, who, without his manifestation, also were not known to himself."

Jacob Böhme. (B. 7, V, 10.)

(*o*) " Reason speaketh very much concerning God and of His omnipotency ; but it understandeth little of God and His substance, *what* and *how* it is ; it severeth the soul totally off from God, as if it were a *sundry* being or substance apart."

Jacob Böhme. (B. 22, Ques. IX, 10.)

(*p*) " There are, assuredly, two forms of Brahma ; the formed and the formless. Now, that which is the formed is unreal ; that which is the formless is real, is Brahma, is light." *Maitri Upanishad*, VI, 3. (U. 1, p. 425.)

(*q*) " Clement anticipated Plotinus in conceiving of God as being ' beyond the One and higher than the Monad itself,' which was the highest abstraction of current philosophy. There is no name that can properly be named of Him : ' neither the One, nor the Good, nor Mind, nor Absolute Being, nor Father, nor Creator, nor Lord.' No science can attain unto Him , ' for all science depends on antecedent principles ; but there is nothing antecedent to the Unbegotten.' " E. Hatch. (H. 1, p. 255.)

(*r*) " Eckhart distinguishes between ' the Godhead ' and ' God.' The Godhead is the abiding potentiality of Being, containing within Himself all distinctions, as yet undeveloped. He therefore cannot be the object of knowledge, nor of worship, being ' Darkness ' and ' Formlessness.' The Triune God is evolved from the Godhead. The Son is the Word of the Father, His uttered thought ; and the Holy Ghost is ' the Flower of the Divine Tree,' the mutual life which unites the Father and the Son. . . . He insists that the generation of the Son is a continual process."

W. R. Inge.   (I. 1, p. 150.)

(s) " The Scripture (Upanishads) distinguishes two forms of Brahman ; the higher, attributeless (*param, nirgunam*) and the lower attribute-possessing (*aparam, sagunam*) Brahman.   In the former case it is taught that Brahman is without any attributes (*guna*), differences (*vicesha*), forms (*âkâra*), and limitations (*upâdhi*)—in the latter, for the purpose of worship, many attributes, differences, forms, and limitations are ascribed to him. . . .

" That the attributeless Brahman cannot be perceived depends on the fact that he is the inner Self (*antar-âtman*) of all ; as such he is on the one hand the greatest certainty of all, and cannot be denied by anyone ; on the other hand He is not to be perceived because in all perception He is the subject (*sâkshin*), and can therefore never become the object.—He is however beheld by the sages in the state of *Samrâdhanam* (perfect satisfaction), which consists in a withdrawal of the organs from all external things, and a concentration on their own inner nature. On the consciousness of being this attributeless Brahman, and on the accompanying conviction of the unreality of all plurality of names and forms, depends salvation. . . .

" The higher Brahman becomes the lower Brahman by being connected with pure or perfect limitations. The lower Brahman is to be recognised wherever the Scripture ascribes limitations, attributes, forms or differences of any sort to Brahman. This happens when the aim is not knowledge but worship ; and the fruit of this worship is, like that of works, which are to be placed in the same category, not liberation but happiness. This is, as it seems, mainly heavenly. It is however limited to the *Samsâra* (cycle of migration) ; though the heavenly lordship attained after death by the path of the gods as the result of the worship of the lower Brahman leads by means of *Krananukti*, or gradual liberation, to perfect knowledge and therefore complete liberation (from *Samsâra*). . . . The nature of Brahman is as little changed by these limitations as the clearness of the crystal by the colour with which it is painted—as the sun by its images swaying in the water—as space by bodies moving or burning in it."

Paul Deussen. (D. 4, pp. 456-7-8.)

(*t*) "In all things there is mystery and the greatest mystery we can approach is the soul of man. For the mystery of God is beyond our conceiving and it is for this reason that, strive as we may, it is as impossible to define God as it is to see Him. To define is to limit, for definition is merely the indication of limitations. Limits relate only to the finite. We refer to that spirit which we name God (men have given it countless names) as infinite and by the use of this word we imply that God is outside definition. The Infinite manifests Itself in the finite and would we find the Creator, we must seek Him in the made; since only through realization shall we approach Him, and we can only realize that which lies within the scope of our experience. And thus it is that St. Augustine's definition of the nature of God is probably the best, for it defines the impossibility of definition—the nature of God is as a circle whose centre is everywhere, and its circumference nowhere." Claude Houghton. (H. 11, p. 125.)

GOD, ONENESS OF MAN AND

NOTE ON THE ONENESS OF MAN AND GOD

THE DIVINE NATURE OF MAN has been both a mystical and philosophical teaching in all ages of which we have any literary records, and is to be found concealed in allegory and fable in most of the Scriptures of the world, as well as being openly stated in some.

The doctrine was rejected, however, by the early Christian Church theologians who formulated the traditional theology of the Church which is so much in question to-day. In much of the modern revolt from that theology however, this mystical doctrine is again coming to its own. It is only by a realisation of his inherent divine nature that man can achieve the conquest of the sin, suffering, and death to which he is now subject in his lower nature ; and the realisation of this is the natural course of his evolution.

See also "CHRIST IN YOU," p. 42, and KNOWLEDGE OF GOD, p. 101.

ONENESS OF MAN AND GOD

(a) " Verily, in the beginning this world was Brahma. It knew only itself (*ātmānam*) : ' I am Brahma ! ' Therefore it became the All. Whoever of the gods became awakened to this, he indeed became it ; likewise in the case of seers, likewise in the case of men. . . . This is so now also. Whoever thus knows ' I am Brahma ! ' becomes this All ; even the gods have not power to prevent his becoming thus, for he becomes their self (*ātman*)."

Brihad-Aranyaka Upanishad, I, 4, 10. (U. 1, p. 83.)

(b) " ' We also are His offspring.' Every one of us may call himself a son of God. Just as our bodies are linked to the material universe, subject while we live to the same forces, resolved when we die into the same elements, so by virtue of reason our souls are linked to and continuous with Him, being in reality parts and offshoots of Him. There is no movement of which He is not conscious, because we and He are part of one birth and growth ; to Him ' all hearts are open, all desires known ' ; as we walk or talk or eat, He himself is within us, so that we are His shrines, living temples and incarnations of Him."

Epictetus.   (H. 1, p. 155.)

(c) " Gods are immortal men, and men are mortal Gods."

Heracleitus.   (M. 1, Vol. II, p. 213.)

(d) " For thou art I, and I am thou.   Whate'er I speak, may it for ever be ; for that I have thy Name to guard me in my heart."

Greek Invocation to Hermes.   (M. 6, Vol. I, p. 85.)

" I know thee, Hermes, and thou (knowest) me ; (and) I am thou, and thou art I."   (*Ibid.*, p. 87.)

" For thou art I, and I am thou ; thy Name is mine, and mine is thine ; for that I am thy likeness."   (*Ibid.*, p. 89.)

(e) " He who knows what God is, and who knows what Man is, has attained.   Knowing what God is, he knows that he himself proceeded therefrom."

Chuang Tzu.   (C. 1, p. 88.)

(f) " The wise man recognises the idea of God within him.   This he develops by withdrawal into the Holy Place of his own soul.   He who does not understand how the soul contains the Beautiful within itself, seeks to realise the beauty without, by laborious production.   His aim should rather be to concentrate and simplify, and so to expand his being ; instead of going out into the manifold, to forsake it for the One, and so to float upwards towards the divine fount of being whose stream flows within him."

Plotinus.   (M. 4, p. 432.)

(g) " For when the vain imagination and ignorance are turned into an understanding and knowledge of the truth, the claiming anything for our own will cease of itself. Then the man says : ' Behold ! I, poor fool that I was, imagined it was I, but behold ! it is, and was, of a truth, God ! ' "   *Theologia Germanica.* (T. 1, p. 16.)

(*h*) " Now God in Eternity is without contradiction, suffering and grief, and nothing can hurt or vex Him of all that is or befalleth.   But with God, when He is made Man, it is otherwise." *Theologia Germanica.* (T. 1, p. 145.)

(*i*) " God became my second self that I might become his second self.   And St. Augustine declares : ' God became man that man might become God."

Eckhart. (E. 1, p. 70.)

(*j*) " God and I are one in knowing.   God's Essence is His knowing, and God's knowing makes me to know Him. Therefore is His knowing my knowing.   The eye whereby I see God is the same eye whereby He seeth me.   Mine eye and the eye of God are one eye, one vision, one knowledge, and one love." Eckhart. (V. 1, Vol. I, p. 191.)

(*k*) " Now behold, when this Perfect Good, which is unnameable, floweth into a Person able to bring forth, and bringeth forth the Only-begotten Son in that Person, and itself in Him, we call it the Father."

Theologia Germanica.   (T. 1, p. 214.)

(*l*) " God in the depths of us receives God Who comes to us ; it is God contemplating God ; God in Whom dwell healing and peace."   Ruysbroeck. (H. 5, p. 48.)

(*m*) " St. John says : ' All things were made by Him,' that means *one* life in Him.   That which man was in himself when created, that he was eternally in God.   As long as a man does not attain to the purity with which he came forth, when first created out of nothing, he will never truly come to God."   John Tauler. (T. 2, p. 99.)

(*n*) " For God is himself the *Being of all Beings*, and we are as gods in him, through whom he revealeth himself."

Jacob Böhme. (B. 3, VI, 4.)

(*o*) " All whatsoever it is that liveth and moveth is in God, and *God himself is all*, and whatsoever is formed or framed, is formed *out of* Him, be it either out of love or out of wrath."   Jacob Böhme.   (B. 1, XIII, 145.)

(*p*) " And we declare unto you that the eternal Being, and also this world, is *like* man : The *eternity* generateth nothing but that which is like itself ; for there is nothing in it but is like it, and it is unchangeable, or else it would *pass away*, or it would come to be *some other* thing, and that cannot be.

" And as you find man to be, just so is the eternity : consider man in body and soul, in good and evil, in joy and sorrow, in light and darkness, in power and weakness, in life and death : *All is in man*, both heaven and earth, stars, and elements ; and also the Number Three of the Deity ; neither can there be anything named that is not in man , all creatures (both in this world, and in the angelical world) are in man. *All of us*, together with the whole essence of all essences, are but one body, having many members, each member whereof is a *total* : and each member hath but one several work.

" O Man ! seek thyself, and thou shalt find thyself. Behold ! thy whole man (consisteth of) Three Principles, one whereof is not without the other, one of them is not beside or above the other, but they are in one another as one, and they are but *one* thing ; but according to the creation they are three."

Jacob Böhme.   (B. 3, VI, 46, 47, 48.)

(*q*) " God bringeth not a new or strange spirit into us ; but He openeth with His spirit our spirit, namely, the mystery of God's wisdom, which lieth in every man."

Jacob Böhme.   (B. 16, II, 26.)

(*r*) " Man in respect of his external comprehensible or finite body standeth only in a flitting figurative shadow or resemblance, and with his spiritual body he is the true essential Word of the Divine property, in which God speaketh and begetteth his Word, and there the Divine Science doth distribute, impart, impress, form and beget itself to an image of God."

Jacob Böhme.   (B. 16, VI, 41.)

(s)   " I am as rich as God : there's nothing any-
            where
    That I with Him (believe it !) do not share."

Angelus Silesius.   (S. 4, p. 44.)

" Am I not with God's Godhead
        essentially one ?
    How else is He my Father ? how else am I
        His son ? "

(Ibid., p. 46.)

" Spark from the Fire ! Drop from the Sea !
        O man, what art thou then
    Unless to thine Eternal Source
        Thou dost return again ? "

" Ere I was anything, the life of God was I,
    For me, therefore, He gave Himself to die."

(Ibid., p. 47.)

" I am God's Other-Self : He finds in me
    What is akin to Him eternally."

(Ibid., p. 48.)

" Before I was ' I,' I was God in God, and when
    The ' I ' shall be dead, I shall be God again."

(Ibid., p. 49.)

(t) " If we ask what was the highest purpose of the teaching of the Upanishads we can state it in three words as it has been stated by the greatest Vedânta teachers themselves, namely T a t   t v a m   a s i.   This means, Thou art that.   *That* stands for what I called the last result of Physical Religion which is known to us under different names in different systems of ancient and modern philosophy.   It is Zeus or the Εἶς Θεὸς cr τὸ ὄν in Greece ; it is what Plato meant by the Eternal Idea, what Agnostics call the Unknowable, what I call the Infinite in Nature. This is what in India is called Brahman, as masculine or neuter, the being behind all beings, the power that emits the universe, sustains it and draws it back again to itself. The *Thou* is what I called the Infinite in Man, the last result of Anthropological Religion, the Soul, the Self, the being behind every human Ego, free from all bodily fetters, free from passions, free from all attachments. The expression Thou art that, means Thine Ātman, thy soul, thy self is the Brahman, or, as we can also express it, the last result, the highest object discovered by Physical Religion is the same as the last result, the highest subject discovered by Anthropological Religion ; or, in other words, the subject and the object of all being and all knowing are one and the same.   This is the gist of what I call *Psychological Religion*, or Theosophy, the highest summit of thought which the human mind has reached, which has found different expressions in different religions and philosophies, but nowhere such a clear and powerful realisation as in the ancient Upanishads of India."

F. Max Müller. (M. 4, p. 105.)

(*u*) " We must remember also that the fundamental principle of the Vedânta-philosophy, was not ' Thou art *He*,' but Thou are *That*, and that it was not Thou *wilt be*, but Thou *art*. This ' Thou art ' expresses something that is, that has been, and always will be, not something that has still to be achieved, or is to follow, for instance, after death. . . .   By true knowledge the individual soul does

7

not *become* Brahman, but *is* Brahman, as soon as it knows what it really is, and always has been."

F. Max Müller. (M. 4, p. 284.)

(*v*) " What can man accomplish that is worth speaking of, either in life or in art, that does not arise in his own self from the influence of this sense for the infinite ? Without it, how can anyone wish to comprehend the world scientifically, or if, in some distinct talent, the knowledge is thrust upon Him, how should he wish to exercise it ? What is all science, if not the existence of things in you, in your reason ? What is all art and culture if not your existence in the things to which you give measure, form, and order ? And how can both come to life in you except in so far as there lives immediately in you the eternal unity of Reason and Nature, the universal existence of all finite things in the Infinite ? " Schleiermacher. (C. 3, p. 265.)

(*w*) " Deep as the universe is my life—and I know it ; nothing can dislodge the knowledge of it ; nothing can destroy, nothing can harm me."

Ed. Carpenter. (C. 2, p. 4.)

(*x*) " God, then, is this Infinite Spirit which fills all the universe with Himself alone, so that all is from Him and in Him, and there is nothing that is outside. Indeed and in truth, then, in Him we live and move and have our being. He is the life of our life, our very life itself. We have received, we are continually receiving our life from Him. We are partakers of the life of God ; and though we differ from Him in that we are individualized spirits, while He is the Infinite Spirit including us as well as all else beside, yet *in essence the life of God and the life of man are identically the same, and so are one.* They differ not in essence, in quality ; they differ in degree."

Ralph Waldo Trine. (T. 6, p. 12.)

(*y*) " By the self of any man I should understand his total consciousness of being. If there be any other consciousness which knows more of the universe in relation to him than he does himself, that consciousness ought to be regarded as his own deeper self because it includes his self-consciousness. Now there can be nothing in the universe outside of God. God is the all-inclusive consciousness, and, therefore, the Self beneath all selves."

Rev. R. J. Campbell. (C. 8.)

(*z*) " How slowly we learn that God and man are one. Do away with your limitations. Stand out free in the strong life of God. You are like children with your walls and partitions, your churches and chapels. We, too, wonder why we were so long learning the things that have since become quite clear to us. God is all life, seen and unseen." *" Christ in You."* (C. 10, p. 6.)

" The knowledge of God's oneness with man, with yourself, is the open door to freedom." (*Ibid.*, p. 50.)

" When you have risen out of your false belief in separateness, and know in your heart that God is ALL and in ALL, then, and then only, will you glide out of the false consciousness of sin, suffering, and pain, leaving it like a worn-out garment, rising into purer life renewed and regenerated."

(*Ibid.*, p. 125.)

GOD, CEASELESS ACTIVITY OF

(*a*) " For that indeed He [God] hath no other one to share in what He works, for working by Himself, He ever is at work, Himself being what He doth. For did He separate Himself from it, all things would [then] collapse, and all must die, Life ceasing.

" But if all things are lives, and also Life is one ; then one is God. And, furthermore, if all are lives, both those in Heaven and those on Earth, and One Life in them all is made to be by God, and God is it—then, all are made by God."   Hermes.   (M. 6, Vol. II, p. 184.)

(b) " Thus, making all, He makes Himself ; nor ever can He cease [His making], for He Himself is ceaseless."
    Hermes.   (M. 6, Vol. II, p. 276.)

(c) " For Me [Krishna] nothing remains that should be done throughout the three worlds, nor aught to gain that I have not gained ; yet I engage in works.   For if I should not engage in works unceasingly, even for a moment,— since all beings put forth their energy in mine—These worlds would sink away, were I not to carry on works, and I should cause confusion among them, and bring destruction to these beings."
    Bhagavad Gita, III, 22.   (J. 7, p. 60.)

(d)   " Look on me,
Thou Son of Prithâ ! in the three wide worlds
I am not bound to any toil, no height
Awaits to scale, no gift remains to gain,
Yet I act here ! and, if I acted not—
Earnest and watchful—those that look to me
For guidance, sinking back to sloth again
Because I slumbered, would decline from good,
And I should break earth's order and commit
Her offspring unto ruin, Bharata ! "
    Bhagavad Gita, III, 22.   (A. 1, p. 29.)

(e) " According to the mystery of Divine activity He comes perpetually by a perpetual first coming.   For this advent, which is outside time. operates in an eternal *now*, and the sleepless longing for Him ceaselessly renews the joy of this encounter."   Ruysbroeck.   (R. 5, p. 47.)

(f) " If He (God) would but suspend His power, no

doubt but Heaven and Earth would straight be abolished, which He upholds in Himself as easily and as continually as we do the idea of them in our own mind. . . . Every moment throughout all generations He continueth without failing to uphold all things for us."

Thomas Traherne. (T. 3, p. 142.)

(g) " Were there any power in God unemployed He would be compounded of Power and Act. Being therefore God is all Act, He is a God in this, that Himself is Power exerted. An infinite Act because infinite power infinitely exerted. An Eternal Act because infinite power eternally exerted. Wherein consisteth the generation of His Son, the perfection of His Love, and the immutability of God. For God by exerting Himself begot His Son, and doing it wholly for the sake of His creatures, is perfect Love ; and doing it wholly from all Eternity, is an Eternal Act, and therefore unchangeable. Thomas Traherne. (T. 3, p. 208.)

(h) " At least five thousand years ago the fundamental principle of this philosophy was enunciated as clearly as it can be stated to-day. It is that this finite universe— finite to our consciousness, finite to a finite mind—is one means of the self-expression and self-realisation of God. To all eternity God is what He is, the unchanging reality which underlies all phenomena, but it will take Him all eternity to manifest what He is even to Himself."

Rev. R. J. Campbell. (C. 8.)

GOD, KNOWLEDGE OF

NOTE ON KNOWLEDGE OF GOD

The mystical teaching concerning knowledge of God is simply that God is unknown to or by any but Himself. It is linked up with the teachings of the

Divine Nature of Man. Man can only know God as he himself becomes God. The lower personality, governed only by the rational mind or intellect, can neither know or legitimately postulate anything about God. This knowledge of God in virtue of man's realisation of his essential oneness with God, is the deep secret of the mystical consciousness; and when it has been discovered, it is incommunicable.

See also, GOD, ONENESS OF MAN AND (p. 91).

KNOWLEDGE OF GOD

(a) " This is the truth :—As, from a well-lit fire, sparks, of like nature to it, arise thousandfold, so, dear one, from the Imperishable go forth manifold beings, and return into it again. For divine is the spirit (*purusha*), the formless, who is within and without, unborn, breathless, wishless, pure, yet higher than the highest Imperishable. From him arises breath, the understanding with all the senses, from him arise ether, wind, and fire, the water, and earth the support of all. His head is fire, his eyes the moon and sun, the cardinal points are his ears, his voice is the revelation of the Veda. Wind is his breath, his heart the world, from his feet the earth ;—he is the inner Self in all beings."

Mundaka Upanishad. (D. 4, p. 131.)

(b) " Thou canst not see the seer of seeing, nor canst thou hear the hearer of hearing, nor canst thou understand the understander of understanding, nor canst thou know the knower of knowing. He is thy soul, which is innermost of all."

Brihad-āranyaka Upanishad. (D. 4, p. 142.)

(c) " And if any one, seeing God, knows what he sees, it is by no means God that he so sees, but something created and knowable. For God abides above created intellect and existence, and is in such sense unknowable and non-existent -that He exists above all existence and is known above all power of knowledge. Thus the knowledge of Him who is above all that can be known is for the most part ignorance." Dionysius. (S. 15, p. 225.)

(*d*) " Then, in this way know God ; as having all things in Himself as thoughts, the whole Cosmos itself.

" If, then, thou dost not make thyself like unto God, thou canst not know Him. For like is knowable to like [alone].

" Make [then] thyself to grow to the same stature as the Greatness which transcends all measure ; leap forth from every body ; transcend all Time ; become Eternity ; and [thus] shalt thou know God."

Hermes. (M. 6, Vol. II, p. 187.)

(*e*) " Thou shalt love God not-spiritually, that is, thy soul shall be not-spiritual : stripped of spirituality. For the while thy soul is specifically spirit she has form ; the while she has form she has neither unity nor union ; the while she lacks union she has never really loved God, for real love lies in union. Wherefore let thy soul be de-spirited of any spirit, let it be spiritless ; an thou lovest God as God, as spirit, as Person or as image, that must all go.

" —Then how shall I love him ?

" Love him as he is ; a not-God, a not-spirit, a not-Person, a not-image ; as sheer, pure, limpid unity, alien from all duality. And in this *one* let us sink down eternally from nothingness to nothingness. So help us God ! Amen." Eckhart. (E. 1, p. 52.)

(*f*) " Nothing is known of God : He is pure Unity :
        And what we know of Him, that we ourselves must
        be." Angelus Silesius. (S. 4, p. 48.)

(*g*) " God is an eternal seeker and finder of himself in the great wonders ; and that which he findeth, he findeth in the power ; he is the opener of the power. Nothing is like him, neither doth anything find him, but that which yieldeth itself to be his own, that entereth into him. That which denieth itself to be, in that thing the spirit of God is all things ; for it is the only will in the eternal nothing ; and yet it is all things, as God's spirit itself is. Therefore if you would fain find it, seek it not in me, but in yourself, though not in your reason either, which must be as dead, and your desire and will must be in God. And so God becometh the will and the deed in you : also the spirit of God bringeth your will into himself, and then you may well see what God is." Jacob Böhme. (B. 4, I, 57, 58.)

(*h*) " Every one hath the key to God in himself, let him but seek it in the right place."

Jacob Böhme. (B. 9, II, 306.)

(*i*) " This divine knowledge concerning God never relates to particular things, because it is conversant with the Highest, and therefore cannot be explained unless when it is extended to some truth less than God, which is capable of being described ; but this general knowledge is ineffable. It is only a soul in union with God that is capable of this profound loving knowledge, for it is itself that union. This knowledge consists in certain contact of the soul with the Divinity, and it is God Himself who is then felt and tasted, though not manifestly and distinctly, as it will be in glory. But this touch of knowledge and sweetness is so strong and so profound that it penetrates into the inmost substance of the soul, and the devil cannot interfere with it, nor produce anything like it—because there is nothing else comparable with it—nor infuse any sweetness or delight which shall at all resemble it. This knowledge savours, in some measure, of the divine essence and of everlasting life, and the devil has no power to simulate anything so great. . . . Such is the sweetness of deep delight of these touches of God, that one of them is more than a recompense for all the sufferings of this life, however great their number."

St. John of the Cross. (S. 5, pp. 207, 208.)

(j) " 'Tis not the skill of human art
        Which gives me power my God to know :
     The sacred lessons of the heart
        Come not from instruments below.

" Love is my teacher.   He can tell
     The wonders that He learnt above ;
   No other master knows so well :—
     'Tis Love alone can tell of Love.

" Oh ! then, of God if thou wouldst learn,
     His wisdom, goodness, glory see ;
   All human arts and knowledge spurn,
     Let Love alone thy teacher be."

Mme. Guyon.   (G. 2, p. 382.)

(k) " Thus, as soon as a man of Speculation can demonstrate that, which he calls the *Being and Attributes of God*, he thinks, and others think, that he truly *knows* God.   But what Excuse can be made for such an Imagination, when plain Scripture has told him, that *to know God is Eternal Life*, that is to know God is to have the Power, the Life, and the Spirit of God *manifested* in him ; and therefore it is Eternal Life.   ' No man knoweth the *Father, but the Son, and he to whom the Son revealeth him ;* ' because the *Revelation* of the Son is the *Birth of* the Son in the Soul, and this new Creature in Christ has alone *Knowledge* of God, what He is, and does, and works, in the Creature."

Wm. Law.   (L. 6, p. 125.)

(l) " GOD . . . without all beginnings of any essence, a working in Himself, generating, finding, or perceiving

Himself ; without any kind of source from any thing, or by any thing : He hath no other beginning nor end, He is immeasurable, no number can express His largeness, and greatness, He is deeper than any thought can reach ; He is nowhere far from any thing, or nigh unto any thing ; He is through all, and in all ; His birth is everywhere, and without and besides Him there is nothing else : He is time and eternity, byss and abyss, and yet nothing comprehends him save the true understanding, which is God Himself."

Jacob Böhme.   (B. 77, I, 8.)

(*m*) " Knowledge is not understanding.   To know God we must be God-like."

" *Christ in You.*"   (C. 10, p. 169.)

(*n*) " I have gone the whole round of creation : I saw
    and I spoke ;
I, a work of God's hand for that purpose, received
    in my brain
And pronounced on the rest of his handwork—
    returned him again
His creation's approval or censure : I spoke as I
    saw :
I report, as a man may of God's work—all's love,
    yet all's law.
Now I lay down the judgeship he lent me.   Each
    faculty tasked
To perceive him, has gained an abyss, where a dew-
    drop was asked.
Have I knowledge ? confounded it shrivels at
    Wisdom laid bare.
Have I forethought ? how purblind, how blank, to
    the Infinite Care !
Do I task any faculty highest, to image success ?
I but open my eyes,—and perfection, no more and
    no less,

In the kind I imagined, full-fronts me, and God is
　　seen God
In the star, in the stone, in the flesh, in the soul
　　and the clod."
　　Robert Browning. *Saul.* (B. 39, Vol. I, p. 278.)

GOD, IMMANENCE OF

(*a*)　　　" Be the dust ne'er so vile, be the motes
　　　　　　ne'er so small,
　　　　　The wise man sees God, great and
　　　　　glorious, in them all."
　　　　　　　　　Angelus Silesius. (S. 4, p. 34.)

" As in the flint the fire, as in the seed the tree,
So is God's likeness hid in everything I see."
　　　　　　　　　　　(*Ibid.*, p. 36.)

b) " I hear and behold God in every object, yet under-
　　stand God not in the least,
　　Nor do I understand who there can be more wonder-
　　ful than myself.

　　Why should I wish to see God better than this
　　　day ?
　　I see something of God each hour of the twenty-
　　　four, and each moment then,
　　In the faces of men and women I see God, and in
　　　my own face in the glass,
　　I find letters from God dropt in the street, and every
　　　one is sign'd by God's name,
　　And I leave them where they are, for I know that
　　　wheresoe'er I go,
　　Others will punctually come for ever and ever."
　　　　　　　　Walt. Whitman. (W. 4, p. 54.)

(c) " In the calm light of His splendor who fills all the universe, the imperishable indestructible of ages.
Dwell thou—as thou canst dwell—contented."

Ed. Carpenter.   (C. 2, p. 346.)

(d) " It is not sufficient for us intellectually to affirm the immanence of God in a blade of grass, but it is for us to carry the thought higher, and not to rest until we have realized that Divine immanence is in a far more intense degree in ourselves."

Archdeacon Wilberforce.   (W. 7, p. 14.)

" The one everlasting impossibility to man is to sever himself from immanent spirit."   (Ibid., p. 32.)

(e) " I *acknowledge* ONE only God : which is the eternal beginningless one only Good Substance, which dwelleth everywhere without a beyond besides or distinct from all Nature and Creature *in itself*, and needeth no Space or Place ; and is subject to no Measurableness, much less to any Comprehension of Nature and Creature.

And I do acknowledge that this one only God is *Threefold in Persons* in equal Omnipotence and Power, viz. : Father, Sonne, and Holy Spirit : and acknowledge that this *Triune* Substance fills all things alike at once, and also hath been the Ground and Beginning of all Things, and still is, and will abide so, *Eternally*."

Jacob Böhme.   (B. 11, para. 38, 39.)

GOD, THEOLOGICAL

(a) " According to this scientific or theological sense. . . . God is an infinite and eternal *substance*, and at the same time a person, the great first cause, the moral and intelligent governor of the universe."

Matthew Arnold.   (A. 3, p. 12.)

(b) " The thought of a God who *externally* dominates

over the course of nature and history is a compromise which cannot permanently be maintained. In the long run a religion based on such a conception must advance to the idea of a spiritual principle which is immanent in the object as it is in the subject, or else it must carry the opposition of the subject to the object to the point at which the latter is contemplated as purely evil or negative. That which is outside of God is necessarily that which is opposed to Him, and that which is opposed to the divine must be evil, so far as it can be regarded as having any positive existence at all."

Edward Caird. (C. 4, Vol. II, p. 63.)

(c) " Whatever sort of a being God may be, we *know* to-day that he is nevermore that mere external inventor of ' contrivances ' intended to make manifest his ' glory ' in which our great-grandfathers took such satisfaction, though just how we know this we cannot possibly make clear by words either to others or to ourselves. I defy any of you here fully to account for your persuasion that if a God exists he must be a more cosmic and tragic personage than that Being." William James. (J. 5, p. 74.)

(d) " I believe, in fact, that the logical reason of man operates in this field of divinity exactly as it has always operated in love, or in patriotism, or in politics, or in any other of the wider affairs of life, in which our passions or our mystical intuitions fix our beliefs beforehand. It finds arguments for our convictions, for indeed it *has* to find them. It amplifies and defines our faith, and dignifies it and lends it words and plausibility. It hardly ever engenders it ; it cannot now secure it. . . . The arguments for God's existence have stood for hundreds of years with the waves of unbelieving criticism breaking against them, never totally discrediting them in the ears of the faithful, but on the whole slowly washing out the mortar from between their joints. If you have a God already whom you believe in, these arguments confirm you. If you are atheistic, they fail to set you right. . . . The fact is that these arguments do but follow the combined suggestions of the facts and of our feeling. They prove nothing rigorously. They only corroborate our pre-existent partialities."

William James. (J. 5, pp. 436, 437, 439.)

(*e*) " If dogmatic theology really does prove beyond dispute that a God with characters like these exists, she may well claim to give a solid basis to religious sentiment. But verily, how stands it with her arguments ? It stands with them as ill as with the arguments for his existence. Not only do post-Kantian idealists reject them root and branch, but it is a plain historic fact that they never have converted any one who has found in the moral complexion of the world, as he experienced it, reasons for doubting that a good God can have framed it. To prove God's goodness by the scholastic argument that there is no non-being in his essence would sound to such a witness simply silly. . . . We must therefore, I think, bid a definitive good-by to dogmatic theology. In all sincerity our faith must do without that warrant. Modern idealism, I repeat, has said good-by to this theology forever."

William James. (J. 5, pp. 447, 448.)

GOOD AND EVIL

NOTE ON GOOD AND EVIL

The problem of Good and Evil—or, as it is more generally termed, the problem of Evil, as if Good were not just as much of a problem—is only a special aspect of the more general problem of *duality*, of the " pairs of opposites " which the Mind constructs, and which the intellect obstinately refuses to overpass. It is part of the general problem of Reality and Appearance, or Being and Becoming, or Subject and Object, or Unity and Multiplicity, or Spirit and Matter which it is the very function of the Mind to create, and which is only transcended in the Mystical consciousness. In theology there is the added difficulty that personality and attributes of goodness only are postulated of God ; and consequently a Devil has also to be postulated to account for the evil in the world.

The following quotations show that both mystics and intuitive writers have recognised that where God is postulated or accepted as ALL, he must be the root and source of what we *call* evil as well as what we call good. In short, the distinction is only in our mind, and not in Reality.

GOOD AND EVIL

(*a*) " The solution of the difficulties which these facts of life (misery and moral evil) presented, was found in a belief which was correlative to the growing belief in the goodness of God, though logically inconsistent with the belief in the universality of His Providence. It was, that men were the authors of their own misery. Their sorrows, so far as they were not punitive or remedial, came from their own folly or perversity. They belonged to a margin of life which was outside the will of the gods or the ordinances of fate. The belief was repeatedly expressed by Homer, but does not appear in philosophy until the time of the Stoics : it is found in both Cleanthes and Chrysippus, and the latter also quotes it as a belief of the Pythagoreans."

E. Hatch. (H. i, p. 220.)

(*b*) " If ye lay bound upon the wheel of change,
    And no way were of breaking from the chain,
  The Heart of boundless Being is a curse,
  The Soul of Things fell Pain.

" Ye are not bound ! the Soul of Things is sweet,
The Heart of Being is celestial rest ;
Stronger than woe is will : that which was Good
Doth pass to Better—Best.

" I, Buddh, who wept with all my brother's tears,
Whose heart was broken by a whole world's woe,
Laugh and am glad, for there is Liberty !
Ho ! ye who suffer ! know

" Ye suffer of yourselves.   None else compels,
None other holds you that ye live and die,
And whirl upon the wheel, and hug and kiss
Its spokes of agony,

" Its tire of tears, its nave of nothingness.
Behold, I show you Truth !   Lower than hell,
Higher than heaven, outside the utmost stars,
Farther than Brahm doth dwell,

" Before beginning, and without an end,
As space eternal and as surety sure,
Is fixed a Power divine which moves to good,
Only its laws endure."
        The Light of Asia.   (A. 2, Book VIII.)

(c) " For evil here happens from indigence, privation,
and defect.   And evil is the passion of matter frustrated
of form, and of that which is assimilated to matter."
        Plotinus.   Enn. V, 11, 10.   (P. 2, p. 193.)

(d) " And so I saw, and saw clearly that all that Thou
hast made is good ; and there are no substances at all
which Thou didst not make.   And because Thou didst not
make all things equal, each by itself is good, and the sum
of all is very good ; for our God made all things very good.
(Chap. XII.)
" And to Thee there is no such thing as evil, and even to

Thy creation as a whole there is not, because there is
nothing beyond it that can burst in and destroy the law
which Thou hast imposed upon it. In the details there
are things which, because they suit not some parts, are
counted evil, yet these same things suit other parts, and
are good to them, and are good in themselves." (Chap.
XIII.)   St. Augustine. (S. 2, p. 239.)

(*e*) " All things come from one source, from that ruling
Reason of the Universe, either under a primary impulse
from it or by way of consequence. And therefore the gape
of the lion's jaws and poison and all noxious things, such
as thorns and mire, are but after results of the grand and
the beautiful. Look not then on these as alien to that
which thou doest reverence, but turn thy thoughts to the
one source of all things."
         Marcus Aurelius. (M. 1, VI, 36, 37, p. 151.)

(*f*) " For beautiful to God are even things which men
think mean, in that in truth they have been made to
serve the laws of God." Isis to Horus, in the Hermetic
Fragment *The Virgin of the World.* (M. 6, Vol. III, p. 117.)

(*g*)   " Communion giveth rest.
           It is from ownhood's state
           That pains and woes arise,
           War, persecution, hate."
           Angelus Silesius. (S. 3, p. 83.)

(*h*) " The centre out of which evil and good floweth is
in thee ; that which thou awakest in thee, be it fire or light,
that will be taken in again by its *like*, either by God's
anger fire, or by God's *light* fire ; each of them electeth or
chooseth to itself that which is like its property."
           Jacob Böhme. (B. 8, I, 99.)

(*i*) " The wicked should not dare to say God maketh me
evil ; but the God in him, in Whose ground he standeth,

8

maketh him what he can serve to be according to the utmost possibility." Jacob Böhme. (B. 14, IX, 26.)

(*j*) "God sitteth *not* over the will and maketh it as a potter does a pot, but He generateth it out of His own properties. . . . God worketh to the producing of life out of everything ; out of the evil Ens an evil life, out of the good Ens a good life."

Jacob Böhme. (B. 14, IX, 10, 11.)

(*k*) "Power in the light is God's love-fire ; and the power in the darkness is the fire of God's anger ; and yet it is but *one* only fire ; but divided into two principles, that the one might be manifest in the other, for the *flame* of anger is the manifestation of the great Love, and in the darkness the light is made known, else it were not manifest to itself." Jacob Böhme. (B. 7, VIII, 27.)

(*l*) "The living Word of God, which is God Himself . . . speaketh itself through nature forth into a Spirit of the world *in Spiritu Mundi*, as a Soul of the Creation. . . . *In Spiritu Mundi*, many evil workings spring forth which appear *contrary* to God ; also, that one creature hurteth worrieth, and slayeth another ; also that wars, pestilence, thunder, and hail happen. All this lieth in the Spirit of the World, and ariseth from the first three properties, wherein they break and frame themselves in their opposite will. For God can give or afford *nothing* but that which is good, for he is alone the only good, and never a whit changed into any evil at all, neither can he, for he would then cease to be God. But in the word of his revelation or manifestation, wherein the forms, qualities, or dispositions arise, viz., wherein nature and creature ariseth, there existeth the working or framing into evil and good."

Jacob Böhme. (B. 14, V, 47, and VI, 63, 65.)

(*m*) "All is through and from God himself, and it is his own substance, which is himself, and he hath created it

out of himself ; and the evil belongeth to the forming and
mobility ; and the good to the love."

Jacob Böhme. (B. 2, Preface 14.)

(n) " We have good and evil in us, into which we frame
our willing, the essence thereof becometh stirring in us, and
such a property we draw also from without into us. . . .
If we lead ourselves to the good, then God's Spirit helpeth
us, but if we lead ourselves to the evil, then God's fierce
wrath and anger helpeth us ; what we will, of that property
we get a leader, and thereunto we lead ourselves. And
yet it is not the Deity's will that we perish, but His *anger's*
and *our will*."

Jacob Böhme. (B. 23, Point V, ch. VIII, 52, 54.)

(o) " God giveth power to every life, be it good or bad,
unto each thing, according to its desire, for He Himself is
All ; and yet He is not called God according to every being,
but according to the light wherewith He dwelleth in Himself,
and shineth with His power through all His beings. He
giveth in His power to all His beings and works, and each
thing receiveth His power according to its property ; one
taketh darkness, the other light ; each hunger desireth its
property, and yet the whole essence or being is all God's,
be it evil or good, for from Him and through Him are all
things ; what is not of His love, that is of His anger."

Jacob Böhme. (B. 6, VIII, 42.)

(p) " All that doth vex, plague and annoy thee, is only
thy selfhood : thou makest thyself thy own enemy and
bringest thyself into self-destruction and death."

Jacob Böhme. (B. 6, XV, 5.)

(q) " The history of Mankind offers unceasingly the
striking proof of this truth : that a particular evil is often
necessary in order to bring forth a general good."

Fabre d'Olivet. (F. 1, p. 536.)

(r) " Good is for every being the fulfilment of His proper law, and evil is that which is opposed thereto."

Saint-Martin.   (W. 2, p. 127.)

(s)   " I make the poem of Evil also—
            I commemorate that part also ;
    I am myself just as much Evil as good, and my nation is
            —And I say there is in fact no Evil,
    Or if there is, I say it is just as important to you, to
            the land, or to me, as anything else."

Walt Whitman.   (W. 5, p. 59.)

" I do not see one imperfection in the universe ;
And I do not see one cause or result lamentable at
        last in the universe."

(*Ibid.*, p. 219.)

(t) " For (over and over again) there is nothing that is evil except because a man has not mastery over it ; and there is no good thing that is not evil if it have mastery over a man ;

" And there is no passion or power, or pleasure or pain, or created thing whatsoever, which is not ultimately for man and for his use—or which he need be afraid of, or ashamed at.

" The ascetics and the self-indulgent divide things into good and evil—as it were to throw away the evil ;

" But things cannot be divided into good and evil, but all are good so soon as they are brought into subjection.

" And seest thou not that except for Death thou couldst never overcome Death—

" For since by being a slave to things of sense thou hast clothed thyself with a body which thou art not master of, thou wert condemned to a living tomb were that body not to be destroyed.

" But now through pain and suffering out of this tomb

shalt thou come ; and through the experience thou hast acquired shalt build thyself a new and better body ;

" And so on many times, till thou spreadest wings and hast all powers diabolic and angelic concentrated in thy flesh." Ed. Carpenter. (C. 2, p. 362.)

" All is well : to-day and a million years hence, equally. To you the whole universe is given for a garden of delight, and to the soul that loves, in the great coherent Whole, the hardest and most despised lot is even with the best ; and there is nothing more certain or more solid than this." (*Ibid.*, p. 5.)

(*u*) " As an Infinite Motherliness is the sole producing agent of all that is, and as all that is must have been in the thought-womb of Infinite Motherliness before coming into existence, the whole mystery of the dark side of life must be within the purpose of the eternal order, and there can be no independent rival to the Author of the Universe."
Archdeacon Wilberforce. (W. 7, p. 54.)

" God is All, All is God ; God is the only *ousia* (substance) in the universe. This negation of good which we hate, this contrast, either is or is not part of universal order. If it is part of universal order, then, in spite of all seeming paradox, it is of the ' all things that work together for good.' If it is not part of His universal order, then the philosophy of Infinity is shattered, and we are confronted with another creative originator in the universe, in everlasting antagonism to the good God—a paralyzing Dualism, which is only another name for Atheism. God is All, God is Love, God is Omnipotent, and God is Immanent. Therefore it is certain that a hidden purpose of benevolence and love, incomparably higher than would be accomplished by the abolition of what we call evil, must have actuated the Infinite Mind when He ' thought-created ' phenomena."
(*Ibid.*, p. 79.)

(*v*) " All finite life is a struggle with evil. Yet from the final point of view the whole is good. The Temporal Order contains at no one moment anything that can satisfy. Yet the Eternal Order is perfect. We have all sinned, and come short of the glory of God. Yet in just our life, viewed in its entirety, the glory of God is completely manifest. These hard sayings are the deepest expressions of the essence of true religion. They are also the most inevitable outcome of philosophy. . . . In the bare assertion of just these truths, that appear to our ordinary consciousness a stumbling-block and foolishness, the wisest of humanity, in India, in Greece, and in the history of Christian thought, are agreed. But the philosophical problem has always been to reconcile these doctrines with reason. An idealistic philosophy, when once understood, gives to all of them its own peculiar interpretation, but then makes them seem almost commonplace."

Josiah Royce. (R. 3, Vol. II, p. 379.)

" All things always work together for good from the divine point of view ; and whoever can make this divine point of view in any sense his own, just in so far sees that they do so, despite the inevitable losses and sorrows of the temporal order."   (*Ibid.*, p. 425.)

(*w*) " For Spinoza, God is not the cause of evil, because, from the point of view of the whole, contemplating the system of being in the only aspect in which it has any real or affirmative existence, evil vanishes away into illusion and nonentity."   John Caird. (C. 5, p. 74.)

(*x*) " What we call evil, is the only and best shape, which, for the person and his conditions at the time, could be assumed by the best good."

George Macdonald. (M. 7, end of Chap. XXV, p. 323.)

(*y*) " The little brown seed sown in the earth is unaware of the sun. until it comes through the darkness of matter, by its own inherent activity, unfolding to receive consciously that which has always been influencing its growth in the darkness ; and yet I say that even the sun would have no power, were it not for the central attraction within the seed.   Now we understand something of the meaning of evil and its friendly uses, that the dark earth is the medium for growth ; and I can best liken it to the creation of God, which is called evil, always pressing into activity the hidden force within the seed covering."

"*Christ in You.*"   (C. 10, p. 54.)

"Why are people suffering and sinful ?   Because they willingly choose to dwell in a divided consciousness of good and evil.   Whoever for even a second has seen that there is no evil, has passed from death to life.   He has entered the Heaven of Heavens, he has seen God.   The Fall is a thing of the present.   It is a false understanding."   (*Ibid.*, p. 167.)

(z)   "Believe thou, O my soul,
Life is a vision shadowy of Truth ;
And vice, and anguish, and the wormy grave,
Shapes of a dream !   The veiling clouds retire,
And lo ! the Throne of the redeeming God
Forth flashing unimaginable day
Wraps in one blaze earth, heaven, and deepest hell."
Samuel T. Coleridge. Poems. *Religious Musings.*

GNÔSIS, THE ANCIENT

NOTE ON THE GNÔSIS

Not a few modern scholars, students, and thinkers, have come to realise that there has always existed in the world, from the remotest ages of which we have any historical or literary records, a real *Gnôsis*, a profound knowledge of the constitution of Man and of the Universe of which he is a part.   This knowledge was the possession and heritage of a Hierarchy of Initiates, and was never imparted openly to the multitude, for two reasons : in the first place, and mainly, because what little might have been understood by a few, would have been exceedingly dangerous if applied practically by any but the profoundly wise and virtuous. This restriction applies with even more force to-day. In the second place, for the multitude this knowledge was in the nature of the case incomprehensible—and is so to-day.

This Hierarchy of Initiates, the great Occult Lodge of the Masters of Wisdom who guide the evolution of the Race, exists to-day. Very much has been given out by them through various sources, and in more or less plain language, during the last 50 years, which was never permitted to be given out before. Very much more is still being imparted for those who have ears to hear. What has already been thus given out throws an enormous light on the allegories and myths of the Ancient Scriptures of the world, and on ancient religious rites and ceremonies, as well as on the discoveries of modern science, and the philosophical thought of the age.

So far as Christianity is concerned, there are many lines of evidence which go to show that the Christian Scriptures contain this Gnôsis from beginning to end. Further than this, there is evidence to show that what " began to be called Christianity when Christ came in the flesh "—as St. Augustine put it—was in its origin a restatement of the ancient Gnôsis, and should have been understood as such, and thus presented to the world by the Christian Church. The inner, mystical, spiritual teaching, however,—the key to which is the divine nature of Man, of which Jesus Christ is the type—became obscured, and was finally lost to the understanding of the Church theologians and dogma makers, who took the mere letter of the Scriptures for the inspired words of a personal God— as witness the Garden of Eden story on which all the traditional Christian theology is based—and finally condemned Gnôsticism as a heresy. That what was known outwardly as Gnôsticism had itself suffered decay, and that

much of it was justly condemned, can hardly be disputed ;
but for those who are able to receive it—and they are not
a few to-day—the true Ancient Gnôsis or Wisdom Religion
is not difficult of recognition. It is perhaps rather too
much to hope, however, that that recognition will come as
yet from official ecclesiastical Christianity.

See also INITIATION (p. 132).

GNÔSIS, THE ANCIENT

(a) " The path by which to Deity we climb,
    Is arduous, rough, ineffable, sublime ,
    And the strong massy gates thro' which we pass,
    In our first course, are bound with chains of brass ;
    Those men the first who of Egyptian birth,
    Drank the fair water of Nilotic earth,
    Disclosed by actions infinite this road.
    And many paths to God Phoenicians showed ;
    This road the Assyrians pointed out to view,
    And this the Lydians and Chaldeans knew."
        Oracle of Apollo, from Eusebius. (A. 4, p. 181.)

(b) " Most excellent contemplators of nature and all
things therein, they (the ancient sages) scrutinise earth and
sea, and air and heaven, and the natures therein, their
minds responding to the orderly motion of the moon and
sun, and the choir of all the other stars, both variable and
fixed. They have their bodies, indeed, planted on earth
below ; but for their souls, they have made them wings,
so that they speed through æther and gaze on every side
upon the powers above, as though they were the true world-
citizens, most excellent, who dwell in cosmos as their city ;
such citizens as Wisdom hath as her associates, inscribed
upon the roll of Virtue, who hath in charge the supervising
of the common weal. . . . Such men, though (in comparison) few in number, keep alive the covered spark of

Wisdom secretly, throughout the cities (of the world), in order that Virtue may not be absolutely quenched and vanish from our human kind." Philo. (M. 6, Vol. I, p. 206.)

(c) " The more philosophical Gnôstics passed one by one outside the Christian lines. Their ideas gradually lost their Christian colour. They lived in another, but non-Christian form. The true Gnôstic, though he repudiates the name, is Plotinus. The logical development of the thoughts of Basilides and Justin, of Valentinus and the Naassenes, is to be found in Neo-Platonism—that splendid vision of incomparable and irrecoverable cloudland in which the sun of Greek philosophy set." E. Hatch. (H. 1, p. 132.)

(d) " The Gnôstic movement began long before the Christian era (what its original historical impulse was we do not know), and only one aspect of it, and that from a strictly limited point of view, has been treated by ecclesiastical historians. Recent investigations have challenged the traditional outlook and the traditional conclusions and the traditional ' facts.' With some to-day, and with many more to-morrow, the burning question is, or will be—not how did a peculiarly silly and licentious heresy rise within the Church—but how did the Church rise out of the great Gnôstic movement, and how did the dynamic ideas of the Gnôsis become crystallised into Dogmas ? "
Rev. F. Lamplugh. (L. 2, p. 10.)

(e) " The seeds of the Gnôsis were originally of Indian growth, and carried westward by the influence of that vast Buddhist movement, which in the fifth century before our era had overspread all the East from Thibet to Ceylon."
C. W. King. (K. 4, p. VI.)

(f) " The general name Gnôstics is used to designate several sects that sprang up in the Eastern parts of the Roman empire almost simultaneously with the establish-

ment of Christianity ; that is to say, these sects then, for
the first time, assumed a definite form, and ranged themselves under different teachers, by whose names they became
known to the world, although in reality their chief doctrines
had been held for centuries before in many of the cities of
Asia Minor. There, it is probable, they first came into
existence as ' Mystæ,' upon the establishment of a direct
intercourse with India under the Seleucidæ and the Ptole-
mies. The Colleges of Essenes and Megabyzæ at Ephesus,
the Orphies of Thrace, the Curetes of Crete are all merely
branches of one antique and common religion, and that
originally Asiatic."   C. W. King.   (K. 4, p. 1.)

(g) " For such an enterprise as that which I have under-
taken more than common resources are necessary. Without
specifying those which I employ, it will be enough to say
that they connect with the essential nature of man, and
that they have always been known to some among mankind
from the prime beginning of things, and that they will
never be withdrawn wholly from the earth while thinking
beings exist thereon. Thence have I derived my evidence,
and thence my convictions upon truths the search after
which engrosses the entire universe. After this avowal, if
I am accused of disseminating an unknown doctrine, at
least I must not be suspected of being its inventor, for if it
connect with the nature of man, not only am I not its
inventor, but it would have been impossible for me to
establish any other on a solid basis. The principles here
expounded are the true key of all the allegories and all the
mysterious fables of every people, the primitive source of
every kind of institution, and actually the pattern of those
laws which direct and govern the universe, constituting
all beings. In other words, they serve as a foundation to
all that exists and to all that operates, whether in man
and by the hand of man, whether outside man and

independently of his will. Hence, in the absence of these principles there can be no real science, and it is by reason of having forgotten these principles that the earth has been given over to errors. But although the light is intended for all eyes, it is certain that all eyes are not so constituted as to be able to behold it in its splendour. It is for this reason that the small number of men who are depositaries of the truths which I proclaim are pledged to prudence and discretion by the most formal engagements.''

Saint-Martin.   (W. 2, p. 82.)

(*h*) '' Here we take up our clue to weave onward as we proceed, unravelling the Mysteries by their traditional light. The objects encountering this research may, as we before said, be appalling to some, nugatory to others, and, at first view, too opposed we fear to the opinions of all , but if, by chance, a less oblivious soul or intellect, more allied than ordinary to antecedent realities, should find familiar scenes recur, thrilling into reminiscence, as of some long past life forgotten ; let such a one believe, and his faith will not betray him ; the road we are journeying is towards his Native Land.'' Mrs. Atwood. (A. 4, p. 180.)

(*i*) '' When we, O Mejnor, in the far time, were ourselves the Neophytes and Aspirants . . . we commenced research where modern conjecture closes its faithless wings. And with us, those were the common elements of science which the sages of to-day disdain as wild chimeras, or despair of as unfathomable mysteries.''
Bulwer Lytton. *Zanoni*. Book IV, Chap. X. (L. 3, p. 178.)

(*j*) '' That which is called the Christian Religion existed among the ancients, and never did not exist, from the beginning of the human race until Christ came in the flesh, at which time the true religion which already existed began to be called Christianity.''
St. Augustine. (*Episcopi Retract*, Lib. I, caput XIII, 3.)

HEAVEN AND HELL

(a)   " HEAVEN is within thee, with its joys :
        Hell, with its vengeful fire :
        'Tis what thou choosest, what thou wilt :
        Thou hast thy heart's desire."
                          Angelus Silesius.   (S. 4, p. 65.)

" Unless the lost did evermore
     Themselves from God dissever,
   God would not, could not doom their souls
     To misery for ever."
                          (*Ibid.*, p. 66.)

" Eternity's with God :
     (Mark well my rhyme !)
   In Hell there's only everlasting Time."
                          (*Ibid.*, p. 67.)

(b) " Every man carrieth in this world heaven and hell
in himself, which property soever he awakeneth, that
burneth in him, and of that fire the soul is capable : and so
when the body dieth and departeth, the soul need not go any
whither, but it will be cast home to the hellish dominion ;
whatsoever property it is of, those very devils which are
of those properties wait upon it, and take it into their
dominion, even till the judgment of God.   Though indeed
they are bound to no place, yet they belong to the same
dominion, and that very source or quality they have
everywhere."
        Jacob Böhme.   (B. 23, Point VI, Ch. IX, 52.)

(c) " Now seeing the departure of souls is various, so

125

also is their condition after their departure various, so that many of the souls departed are indeed for a long time in purgatory, if the soul had been defiled with gross sins, and had not rightly stepped into the true earnest regeneration, and yet do hang a little to it."

Jacob Böhme.   (B. 2, XIX, 38.)

(d) " There is nothing that is nearer you than heaven, paradise, and hell, into which of them you are inclined, and to which of them you tend (or walk), to that in this (life) time you are most near : you are between both. . . .   You have both the births in you."

Jacob Böhme.   (B. 2, IX, 27.)

(e) " Heaven is not a place, but a consciousness of God."

" Christ in You."   (C. 10, p. 5.)

(f) " Each soul makes its own Heaven, and there is a sense in which each created being augments Heaven by its own created environment.   By your rebirth into the spiritual kingdom, Heaven itself becomes greater.   In this sense you can understand better what I mean when I tell you that all are benefited by one, because you are a part of all.   I use the language of earth, but you have spiritual discernment.   We can never find true language to express Heaven and God, since the first is a state of consciousness, and the second infinity."

" Christ in You."   (C. 10, p. 156.)

INTELLECT

AN understanding of the functions and limitations of the Intellect is emerging more and more clearly—since Kant—in our modern philosophy and psychology; and with this emergence the existence of the transcendental Ego or Self becomes all the more firmly established. At the same time it is recognised that there is a real and vital continuity between the one and the other, and that it is only in consciousness that there *appears* to be a separation. The normal individual consciousness abstracts itself from the sum-total of the content of the Self in order that it may fulfil a special function in life. We might say, in fact, that just as we abstract ourselves from a normally larger consciousness when we are concentrating on some particular matter, so the individual is an abstraction, on a much larger scale, of the whole content of the Subject or Ego. The individual is a " dissociated complex " of the larger Whole, which only finds its completion in the Absolute.

INTELLECT

(*a*) " There remains around our conceptual and logical thought, a vague nebulosity, made out of the very substance of which has been formed the luminous nucleus that we call intellect." Henri Bergson. (B. 27, p. XIII.)

" The intellectual tendencies innate to-day, which life must have created in the course of its evolution, are not at all meant to supply us with an explanation of life : they have something else to do." (*Ibid.*, p. 22.)

" Intellect, such at least as we find it in ourselves, has

been fashioned by evolution during the course of progress ;
it is cut out of something larger, or, rather, it is the pro-
jection, necessarily on a plane, of a reality that possesses
both relief and depth." *(Ibid.,* p. 55.)

" Intellectuality and materiality have been constituted,
in detail, by reciprocal adaptation. Both are derived from
a wider and higher form of existence. It is there that we
must replace them, in order to see them issue forth."
(Ibid., p. 197.)

" The same movement by which the mind is brought to
form itself into intellect, that is to say, into distinct concepts, brings matter to break itself up into objects excluding
one another. The more consciousness is intellectualized,
the more is matter spatialized." *(Ibid.,* p. 199.)

" Intellect has detached itself from a vastly wider
reality, but there has never been a clean cut between the
two ; all around conceptual thought there remains an
indistinct fringe which recalls its origin. We compare the
intellect to a solid nucleus formed by means of condensa-
tion. This nucleus does not differ radically from the fluid
surrounding it. It can only be reabsorbed in it because it
is made of the same substance." *(Ibid.,* p. 203.)

" Intellect and matter have progressively adapted themselves one to the other in order to attain at last a common
form. This adaptation has, moreover, been brought about
quite naturally, because it is the inversion of the same
movement which creates at once the intellectuality of the
mind and the materiality of things." *(Ibid.,* p. 217.)

(*b*) " The ultimate elements in a theory of the world
must be of a nature impossible to define in terms recognisable to the mind." Profess. A. S. Eddington. (E. 3, p. 185.)

(*c*) " For my own part, I have finally found myself compelled to *give up the logic,* fairly, squarely, and irrevocably.
It has an imperishable use in human life, but that use is

not to make us theoretically acquainted with the essential nature of reality. Reality, life, experience, concreteness, immediacy, use what word you will, exceeds our logic, overflows and surrounds it. If you like to employ words eulogistically . . . you may say that reality obeys a higher logic, or enjoys a higher rationality. But I think that even eulogistic words should be used rather to distinguish than to commingle meanings, so I prefer bluntly to call reality if not irrational then at least non-rational in its constitution—and by reality here I mean reality where things *happen*, all temporal reality without exception."

William James. (J. 6, p. 212.)

(*d*) " We state what to ourselves has long appeared the grand characteristic of Kant's philosophy, when we mention his distinction, seldom perhaps expressed so broadly, but uniformly implied, between Understanding and Reason (*Verstand* and *Vernuft*). . . . Reason, the Kantists say, is of a higher nature than understanding; it works by more subtle methods, on higher objects, and requires a far finer culture for its development, indeed in many men it is never developed at all : but its results are no less certain, nay, rather they are much more so ; for Reason discerns Truth itself, the absolutely and primitively *True* ; while Understanding discerns only *relations*, and cannot decide without *if*. . . . Not by logic and argument does it work ; yet surely and clearly may it be taught to work : and its domain lies in that higher region whither logic and argument cannot reach ; in that holier region, where Poetry and Virtue and Divinity abide, in whose presence Understanding wavers and recoils, dazzled into utter darkness by that ' sea of light ' at once the fountain and the termination of all true knowledge."

Thomas Carlyle. *Miscellanies*, Art.
" State of German Literature." (C. 6, Vol. I, p. 69.)

9

INTUITION

(a) " Those who trust to their senses become slaves to objective existences. Those alone who are guided by their intuitions find the true standard. So far are the senses less reliable than the intuitions. Yet fools trust to their senses to know what is good for mankind, with alas ! but external results."   Chuang Tzu. (C. 1, p. 41.)

(b) " These fleeting intuitions, which light up their object only at distant intervals, philosophy ought to seize, first to sustain them, then to expand them and so unite them together. The more it advances in this work, the more will it perceive that intuition is mind itself, and, in a certain sense, life itself : the intellect has been cut out of it by a process resembling that which has generated matter. Thus is revealed the unity of the spiritual life. We recognise it only when we place ourselves in intuition in order to go from intuition to the intellect, for from the intellect we shall never pass to intuition."
                Henri Bergson. (B. 27, p. 282.)
" A philosophy of intuition will be a negation of science, will be sooner or later swept away by science, if it does not resolve to see the life of the body just where it really is, on the road that leads to the life of the spirit."
                                (*Ibid.*, p. 283.)
" Let us then concentrate our attention on that which we have that is at the same time the most removed from externality and the least penetrated with intellectuality. Let us seek, in the depths of our experience, the point where we feel ourselves most intimately within our own life. It is into pure duration that we then plunge back, a duration in which the past, always moving on, is swelling unceasingly with a present that is absolutely new."
                                (*Ibid.*, p. 210.)

INDIVIDUAL, NATURE OF THE

(a) " Now if living beings are, within the universe, just
' centres of indetermination,' and if the degree of this
indetermination is measured by the number and rank of
their functions, we can conceive that their mere presence
is equivalent to the suppression of all those parts of objects
in which their functions find no interest. They allow to
pass through them, so to speak, those external influences
which are indifferent to them ; the others isolated, become
' perceptions ' by their very isolation."

Henri Bergson. (B. 28, p. 28.)

" Will all these perceptions of a body by my different
senses give me, when united, the complete image of that
body ? Certainly not, because they have been gathered
from a larger whole.   To perceive all the influences from all
the points of all bodies would be to descend to the condition of a material object. Conscious perception signifies
choice, and consciousness mainly consists in this practical
discernment."   (Ibid., p. 46.)

" One general conclusion follows from the first three
chapters of this book : it is that the body, always turned
towards action, has for its essential function to limit, with
a view to action, the life of the spirit."   (Ibid., p. 233)

(b) " Finally, as to the origin and as to the end of
human individuals, our theory suggests that we are differen-
tiations from a finite conscious experience of presumably a
much longer time-span than our present one. This finite
consciousness of longer time-span, indicated to us in the
phenomena of memory and of race-instinct, is individuated,
is rational, is a live being, and is continuous in some sense
with our own individuality."

Josiah Royce. (R. 3, Vol. II, p. 233.)

" Our idealistic theory teaches that all individual lives

and plans and experiences win their unity in God, in such wise that there is, indeed, but one absolutely fixed and integrated Self, that of the Absolute. But our idealism also recognises that in the one life of the divine there is, indeed, articulation, contrast, and variety. So that, while it is, indeed, true that for every one of us the Absolute Self is God, we still retain our individuality, and our distinction from one another, just in so far as our life-plans, by the very necessity of their social basis, are mutually contrasting life-plans, each one of which can reach its own fulfilment only by recognizing other life-plans as different from its own."   (*Ibid.*, p. 289.)

" The finite beings whom we acknowledge in the concrete, are always, at any temporal moment, such as they are by virtue of an *inattention* which at present blinds them to their actual relations to God and to one another."

(*Ibid.*, p. 307.)

INITIATION

(*a*) " It is not without reason that in the mysteries of the Greeks, lustrations hold the first place, analogous to ablutions among the Barbarians [that is, non-Greeks]. After these come the lesser mysteries, which have some foundation of instruction and of preliminary preparation for what is to follow ; and then the great mysteries, in which nothing remains to be learned of the universe, but only to contemplate and comprehend nature [herself] and the things [which are mystically shown to the initiated].
Clement of Alexandria.   (M. 6, Vol. III, p. 150.)

(*b*) " This, therefore, is manifested by the mandate of the mysteries, which orders that they shall not be divulged to those who are uninitiated. For as that which is divine cannot be unfolded to the multitude, this mandate forbid

the attempt to elucidate it to any one but him who is
fortunately able to perceive it."

Plotinus.   Enn. VI, 9, 11.   (P. 2, p. 320.)

(c) " The knowledge which might formerly be transmitted in writing depended on instructions which sometimes rested on certain mysterious practices and ceremonies,
the value of which was more a matter of opinion or habit
than of reality, and sometimes rested on occult practices
and spiritual operations, the details of which it would have
been dangerous to transmit to the vulgar, or to ignorant
and ill-intentioned men.   The subject which engages us,
not resting on such bases, is not exposed to similar dangers.
The only initiation which I preach and seek with all the
ardour of my soul is that by which we enter into the heart
of God and make God's heart enter into us, there to form
an indissoluble marriage, which will make us the friend,
brother, and spouse of our Divine Redeemer.   There is
no other mystery to arrive at this holy initiation than to
go more and more down into the depths of our being and
not let go till we can bring forth the living vivifying root,
because then all the fruit which we ought to bear, according
to our kind, will be produced within us and without us
naturally."   Saint-Martin.   (W. 2, p. 253.)

See also GNÔSIS (p. 119).

INFINITE, THE

(a) " The scientific Infinite has its own prestige of
superstition, and its own mysticism, just like any other
Infinite."   E. Récéjac.   (R. 4, p. 74.)

(b) " It is easy work for the understanding to show that
everything said of the Idea is self-contradictory.   But
that can quite as well be retaliated, or rather in the Idea
the retaliation is actually made.   And this work, which is
the work of reason, is certainly not so easy as that of the

understanding. Understanding may demonstrate that the Idea is self-contradictory : because the subjective is subjective only and is always confronted by the objective,—because being is different from notion, and therefore cannot be picked out of it,—because the finite is finite only, the exact antithesis of the infinite, and therefore not identical with it ; and so on with every term of the description. The reverse of this, however, is the doctrine of Logic. Logic shows that the subjective which is to be subjective only, the finite which would be finite only, the infinite which would be infinite only, and so on, have no truth, but contradict themselves, and pass over into their opposites. Hence this transition, and the unity in which the extremes are merged and become factors, each with a merely reflected existence, reveals itself in their truth."

G. W. F. Hegel. (H. 9, p. 355.)

INFINITE, PERCEPTION OF, IN THE FINITE

(a) " The eternal centre, and the birth of life, and the substantiality, are everywhere. If you make a small circle, as small as a little grain (or kernel of seed), there is the whole birth of the eternal nature, and also the Number Three *in Ternario sancto* (contained) therein ; but you include not, nor comprise, the eternal nature, much less the Number Three ; but you comprehend the out-birth of the *centre* : the eternal nature is *incomprehensible*, as God also is.

" When I take up anything and carry it away, I do *not* carry away the eternity, much less God : and yet the eternity is in that very thing, but the thing is *out-born*, and stirreth not the eternity ; and that which is out-born comprehendeth not the eternity, but the eternity comprehendeth that which is out-born, thoroughly, without stirring ; for the eternity, as also the Deity, is in one place

as well as another (every where) : for there is no place (in
the eternity), but the out-birth maketh a *place* and room."
Jacob Böhme.   (B. 3, VI, 43, 44.)

(*b*) " Suppose a river, or a drop of water, an apple or a
sand, an ear of corn, or an herb : God knoweth infinite
excellencies in it more then we : He seeth how it relateth to
angels and men ; how it proceedeth from the most perfect
Lover to the most perfectly Beloved ; how it representeth
all His attributes ; how it conduceth in its place, by the
best of means to the best of ends : and for this cause it
cannot be beloved too much.   God the Author and God the
End is to be beloved in it ; Angels and men are to be
beloved in it ; and it is highly to be esteemed for all their
sakes.   O what a treasure is every sand when truly understood ! Who can love anything that God made too much ?
What a world would this be, were everything beloved as it
ought to be ! "   Thomas Traherne.   (T. 3, p. 126.)

(*c*) " The smallest thing by the influence of eternity, is
made infinite and eternal." Thomas Traherne.   (T. 3, p. 325.)

(*d*) " Flower in the crannied wall,
      I pluck you out of the crannies ;—
      Hold you here, root and all, in my hand,
      Little flower—but if I could understand
      What you are, root and all, and all in all,
      I should know what God and man is."
Alfred Tennyson.   (T. 4.)

(*e*) " Every atom contains the whole.   The whole of God
is in the blade of grass." " *Christ in You.* "   (C. 10, p. 165.)

IMAGINATION

(*a*) " If to see God with one's eyes in [sensible nature] is
a felicitous experience, the comprehension [of Him] by

means of imagination (*phantasia*) pertains to a higher order
of intuition. For this [power of imagination] is the [one]
sense of [all differentiated] senses, seeing that the spirit
(*pneûma*), whereby the imagination is brought into play, is
the most general sensory and the first body of the soul.   It
has its seat in the innermost place, and dominates the living
creature, as it were from a citadel.   For round it nature has
built up the whole economy of the head."

Synesius. (M. 5, p. 92.)

(*b*) " All things are arisen through the divine imagination, and do yet stand in such a birth, station, or government."   Jacob Bohme.   (B. 16, VI, 78.)

(*c*) " The original of all things lieth in the Idea, in the
eternal imaging."   Jacob Böhme.   (B. 22, XII, 4.)

(*d*) " And thus also we apprehend whence all things,
evil and good, exist, viz., from the *imagination* in the Great
Mystery, where a wonderful essential life generateth itself."

Jacob Böhme.   (B. 25, Text V, 39.)

(*e*) " There is nothing in this world that can touch or kill
the soul, no fire nor sword, but only the *imagination* ; that
is its poison ; for it is originally proceeded out of the
imagination, and continueth eternally therein."

Jacob Böhme.   (B. 4, II, 10.)

(*f*)   " Our nimble souls
     Can spin an insubstantial universe
     Suiting our mood, and call it possible,
     Sooner than see one grain with eye exact
     And give strict record of it.   Yet by chance
     Our fancies may be true and make us seers.
     'Tis a rare teeming world, so harvest-full,
     Even guessing ignorance may pluck some fruit."

George Eliot. (E. 2, p. 119.)

KNOWLEDGE

(a) " THE gift of knowledge is a supernatural illumination infused into the rational soul, and guides men's steps into the way of the higher perfection. . . . This gift is a Divine resemblance, for God knows all in an eternal knowledge. He contemplates eternally all His creatures in their everlasting type, which is co-substantial with Him ; it was according to this knowledge that He gave to the heavens, the earth and all that it contained, power, kingdom, and glory. . . . Jesus Christ was full of this knowledge, and His every act was comformable to this glorious light. He who possesses this gift brings perfection into the domain of the intellect."

Ruysbroeck. (H. 5, pp. 115–6.)

(b) " It behoves us not to receive without a certain distrust the extension by certain philosophers to the whole Universe, of a property demonstrated for those restricted systems which observation can alone reach. We know nothing of the Universe as a whole, and every generalization of this kind outruns in a singular fashion the limit of experiment." Lucien Poincaré. (P. 2, p. 70.)

" We cannot in any certain way apply to the Universe, which is not a finite system, a proposition demonstrated, and that not unreservedly, in the sharply limited case of a finite system. Herbert Spencer, moreover, in his book on *First Principles*, brings out with much force the idea that, even if the Universe came to an end, nothing would allow us to conclude that, once at rest, it would remain so indefinitely." (*Ibid.*, p. 81.)

(*c*) " Knowledge and atheism are incompatible. To know nature is to know that there must be a God."

Bulwer Lytton.

Zanoni, Book IV, Chap. X.   (L. 3, p. 180.)

(*d*) " There is an inmost centre in us all,
  Where truth abides in fulness ; and around,
  Wall upon wall, the gross flesh hems it in,
  This perfect, clear perception—which is truth.
  A baffling and perverting carnal mesh
  Binds it, and makes all error : and to KNOW
  Rather consists in opening out a way
  Whence the imprisoned splendour may escape,
  Than in effecting entry for a light
  Supposed to be without."

Robert Browning.

Paracelsus.   Part I.   (B. 39, Vol. I, p. 26.)

LOVE

(*a*) " FOR since the soul is different from God, but is derived from him, she necessarily loves him, and when she is there she has a celestial love ; but the love which she here possesses is common and vulgar. . . . The soul, therefore, when in a condition conformable to nature, loves God, wishing to be united to him, being as it were the desire of a beautiful virgin to be conjoined with a beautiful Love. . . . In the intelligible world the true object of love is to be found, with which we may be conjoined, which we may participate, and truly possess, and which is not externally enveloped with flesh. *He however who knows this, will know what I say*, and will be convinced that the soul has then another life."

Plotinus.   Enn. VI, 9, 9.   (P. 2, pp. 317, 318.)

(*b*) " Love is a great thing, yea, a great and thorough good ; by itself it maketh everything that is heavy, light ; and it bears evenly all that is uneven. For it carries a burden which is no burden, and makes everything that is bitter, sweet and pleasant to the taste. . . . Nothing is sweeter than Love ; nothing more courageous ; nothing higher ; nothing wider ; nothing more pleasant ; nothing fuller or better in Heaven and Earth : because Love is born of God, and cannot rest but in God, above all created things."

Thomas à Kempis.   (K. 1, Book III, Chap. 5, p. 98.)

(*c*) " Every moment the voice of Love is coming from
left and right,
We are bound for heaven · who has a mind to sight-
seeing ?

We have been in heaven, we have been friends of
        the angels ;
Thither, Sire, let us return, for that is our country."
                            Jalálu'd-dín Rúmí.   (J. 2, p. 48.)

(d) " At times, however, in a fleeting vision, the invisible
breath that bears them (the individual forms) is material-
ised before our eyes. We have this sudden illumination
before certain forms of maternal love, so striking and in
most animals so touching, observable even in the solicitude
of the plant for its seed. This love, in which some have
seen the great mystery of life, may possibly deliver us life's
secret. It shows us each generation leaning over the
generation that shall follow. It allows us a glimpse of the
fact that the living being is above all a thoroughfare, and
that the essence of life is in the movement by which life is
transmitted."   Henri Bergson.   (B. 27, p. 135.)

(e) " Love, lift me up upon thy golden wings
        From this base world unto thy heavens hight,
        Where I may see those admirable things
        Which there thou workest by thy soveraine might,
        Farre above feeble reach of earthly sight,
        That I thereof an heavenly Hymne may sing
        Unto the god of Love, high heavens king."
                                Edmund Spenser.
        Poetical Works.   " An Hymne of Heavenly Love."

(f) " It is love which is the centripetal power of the
universe ; it is by love that all creation returns to the
bosom of God. The force which projected all things is
will, and will is the centrifugal power of the universe.
Will alone could not overcome the evil which results from
the limitations of matter ; but it shall be overcome in the
end by sympathy, which is the knowledge of God in others,
—the recognition of the omnipresent Self. This is Love.

And it is with the children of the spirit, the servants of love, that the dragon of matter makes war."

Anna Kingsford.   (K. 3, p. 11.)

(g) " Great Love has many attributes, and shrines
For varied worship, but his force divine
Shows most its many-named fulness in the man
Whose nature multitudinously mixed—
Each ardent impulse grappling with a thought—
Resists all easy gladness, all content
Save mystic rapture, where the questioning soul
Flooded with consciousness of good that is
Finds life one bounteous answer."

George Eliot.   (E. 2, p. 180.)

(h) " What though with will rebellious I thwart thy
    omnipotent will,
Through purgatorial æons thy spirit will draw me
    still ;—
Draw me through shame and sorrow and pain and
    death and decay ;
Draw me from Hell to Heaven, draw me from night
    to day ;
Draw me from self's abysses to the self-less azure
    above ;
Draw me to thee, Life's Fountain, with patient
    passionate love."

Edmond Holmes.   (H. 10, p. 8.)

(i) " Love to God and man fulfils every law. Love is the key of all knowledge, wisdom and power. Dwell deep in this love and you will see as God sees. Yet even this expression of God is imitated by the false or shadow self of the senses."   " Christ in You."   (C. 10, p. 82.)

LOVE, THE MYSTIC'S

(a) "Now they who betake themselves to this service [of God do so], not because of any custom, or on some one's advice and appeal, but carried away with heavenly love, like those initiated into the Bacchic or Corybantic Mysteries, they are a-fire with God until they see the object of their love."   Philo. (M. 6, Vol. I, p. 212.)

(b) "This call is an inconceivable joy, an ocean from whose depths arises an august, transcendent activity ; the man opens, expands, becomes a gulf. . . . This gulf which has opened in the depths of his soul will not close. It is the wound of love ; the most exquisite and the most terrible thing in the world ; for such is the nature of this Sun that its rays eternally pouring down upon him who has once been pierced, continually increases and deepens his wounds."   Ruysbroeck. (H. 5, p. 32.)

"Pure and measureless love awakens joy within us ; but love is a fathomless and soundless abyss ; abyss calls to abyss ; it is the Abyss of God calling the men of God. And this supreme invocation, this call out of the depths of the Abyss, which bids us come, appears to us as a shining dawn of essential light. It encompasses us and draws us and we pass into the darkness, into the infinite darkness of God."   (*Ibid.*, p. 34.)

"Then the man becomes aware of a central point within the depths of himself, the birthplace and haven of all goodness. Within this sanctuary dwells love, and within it the man offers up all his activities to God. And his hunger and thirst after God grow so immeasurably that he feels he must faint from the extremity of his longing. At each lightning flash from God that strikes into the depths of his soul he is enkindled and enflamed anew ; he dies in life and arises again in death ; for it is a loving ardour that possesses the likeness of that Unity which is the object of his search ; and the hunger and the thirst are perpetually renewed. . . . The intense burning activity of desire and of love is the source of supreme peace."

(*Ibid.*, p. 38.)

" He only is a contemplative who is the slave of nothing, not even of his virtues. Beyond all else it requires that he shall cleave to God by the operation of love, that ardent white flame, inextinguishable, that fervour which burns open the spirit. And lastly, he must lose himself, without confusion of substance, in the holy darkness, where joy delivers him out of himself, never again to find himself according to the human mode." (*Ibid.*, p. 45.)

" So vast, so penetrating and all embracing is this active and possessing love of the Trinity that in its presence the silence of the creature is absolute. The wonder of the Inconceivable, held within this love, transcends and surpasses the power of created intelligence. But if love is borne into this region where miracles are known and experienced without surprise, the spirit, transcending itself, consummates with God the mystery of the Divine marriage, and in this union of the living depths, possessing himself, and clothed anew in his eternal likeness, the man contemplates and enjoys, after the Divine mode, the treasures that are God Himself." (*Ibid.*, p. 50.)

" If we will walk with God the paths of the higher love, we shall find His ceaseless activity joined to His endless rest, and we shall draw near, and we shall enter in, and this will be eternal peace." (*Ibid.*, p. 59.)

" No words can tell the hunger of desire, nor paint the storm within the realm of love. Love burns at one moment, and the next freezes ; it fears and grows bold, rejoices and saddens, hopes, despairs, weeps, mourns, sings, and adores. It is an intoxication whirling the soul into incredible tumults; yet within its depths is the sanest of all lives." (*Ibid.*, p. 63.)

" When love has lifted us above objects, above light, into the holy darkness, we are transfigured by the eternal Word, like unto the Father ; and as the air is penetrated by the sun, so do we receive in that peace which passeth understanding inward piercing and outward shining light."   (*Ibid.*, p. 77.)

" Love cannot be inactive ; its life is a ceaseless effort to know, to feel, and to realise the boundless treasures hidden within its depths. This is its insatiable desire."
                                        (*Ibid.*, p. 78.)

" The eternal love fills all the capacities of the soul with grace and light, thus bringing to birth the virtues. . . . It is a marvellous activity, bringing to the contemplative as he stedfastly perseveres, the joy of realising the Divine unity without intermediary. He experiences in himself that ghostly quickening that is the renewal of grace and of the virtues ; for grace flows even into the inferior faculties. It reaches to the depths within man and awakens that profound and vital love that is the desire for God ; and this love penetrates even to the heart, to the senses, to the flesh and blood, to the whole physical nature of the man."   (*Ibid.*, p. 100.)

(c)   " Love is the sage's stone ;
              It takes gold from the clod ;
              It turns naught into aught,
              Transforms me into God."
              Angelus Silesius.   (S. 3, p. 141.)

(d) " When love has allowed itself to be rapt above its created substance by transcendent joy, it finds and tastes upon the mountain the splendour and delights which God causes to flow into the inner sanctuaries of life, impressing upon the ravished soul a certain image of His own Majesty."
              Ruysbroeck.   (B. 36, p. 38.)

(e) " Oh ! Supreme and Eternal Good, who has moved

Thee, Infinite God, to illuminate me, Thy finite creature
with the light of Thy Truth ?   Thou, the same Fire of
Love art the cause, because it is always love which constrained and constrains Thee to create us in Thine image
and similitude, and to do us mercy, giving immeasurable
and infinite graces to Thy rational creatures."
St. Catherine of Sienna.   (S. 7, Cap. CXXXIV, p. 311.)

(f)   " Where am I led, ah me !
              To depths so high ?
              Living I die
         So fierce the fire of Love.

      " Ineffable Love Divine !
              Sweetness unformed, yet bright,
              Measureless, endless Light,
         Flame in this heart of mine ! "

                                 Jacopone da Todi.
         Laude XC, XCI.   (U. 2, pp. 363 and 475.)

(g) " The intellectual love of the mind towards God is
that very love of God whereby God loves himself, not in
so far as he is infinite, but in so far as he can be explained
through the essence of the human mind regarded under
the form of eternity ; in other words, the intellectual love
of the mind towards God is part of the infinite love wherewith God loves himself."
                   Spinoza.   (S. 12, Vol. II, p. 264.)

(h) " And aye on Meditation's heaven-ward wing
         Soaring aloft I breathe the empyreal air
         Of Love, omnific, omnipresent Love,
         Whose day-spring rises glorious in my soul."
         Samuel T. Coleridge.   Poems, *Religious Musings.*

(i) " Purification removes the obstacles to our union

10

with God, but our guide on the upward path, *the true hierophany of the mysteries of God, is love.*"

W. R. Inge.   (I. 1, p. 8.)

(*j*) " In mysticism the will is united with the emotions in an impassioned desire to transcend the sense-world in order that the self may be joined by love to the one eternal and ultimate Object of love ; whose existence is intuitively perceived by that which we used to call the soul, but now find it easier to refer to as the ' Cosmic ' or ' transcendental ' sense."   Evelyn Underhill.   (U. 3, p. 84.)

" The mystic is ' in love with the Absolute ' not in any idle or sentimental manner but in that deep and vital sense which presses forward at all costs and through all dangers towards union with the object beloved."

(*Ibid.*, p. 85.)

" Page after page of the jewels of mystical literature glow with this intimate and impassioned love of the Absolute ; which transcends the dogmatic language in which it is clothed and becomes applicable to mystics of every race and creed."   (*Ibid.*, p. 103.)

" The language of human passion is tepid and insignificant beside the language in which the mystics try to tell the splendours of their love. They force upon the unprejudiced reader the conviction that they are dealing with an ardour far more burning for an Object far more real."   (*Ibid.*, p. 107.)

(*k*) " Love goes into God's presence unannounced,
          while at the gate
     Reason and Knowledge must remain,
          and for an audience wait."

Angelus Silesius.   (S. 4, p. 59.)

(*l*) " We know that these things are deep mysteries and largely hidden ; but this I know : as the heart feels love in itself for God, in that same instant comes God into the soul of the lover. Now, where God is we know that there is neither evil, nor sadness, nor unhappiness, nor any recollection of such things ; therefore, to be a great and constant lover to Him is to be automatically lifted from all unhappinesses." *The Golden Fountain.* (A. 8, p. 71.)

" God, once found, is so poignantly ever-present to the soul that we must sing and whisper to Him all the day.

" O marvellous and exquisite God ! I am so enraptured by Thy nearness, I am so filled with love and joy, that there is no one, nothing, in heaven or earth to me save Thine Own Self, and I could die for love of Thee ! Indeed I am in deep necessity to find Thee at each moment of the day, for so great is Thy glamour that without Thee my days are like bitter waters and a mouthful of gravel to a hungry man. How long wilt Thou leave me here—set down upon the earth in this martyrdom of languishing for love of Thee ? And suddenly, when the pain can be endured no more, He embraces the soul. Then where do sorrow and waiting fly ? and what is pain ? There never were such things." *(Ibid.,* p. 47.)

LOGOS OR WORD

NOTE ON THE LOGOS

The concept of the Logos as the outspoken *Word* of God whereby all things have come into manifestation, is of remote origin, and has undergone many permutations. It was absorbed by Christian doctrine in the early centuries, and presented in the restricted form in which we have it in the traditional theology, as applying exclusively to the person of Jesus Christ as being the incarnation of the second person of the Divine Trinity.

Its mystical signification is one of the deepest secrets

of initiation ; and it is occultly connected with the power of sound to produce forms in the *Akasa* or universal Substance.

Of all the mystical writers, Jacob Böhme appears to be the only one who has really penetrated to this secret, and there is much more to be found in his writings than can be given in this work.

See also my Note on the TRINITY (p. 260).

LOGOS OR WORD

(a) " The Word (*Logos*) of the Creator, O [my] son, transcends all sight ; He [is] self-moved ; He cannot be increased, nor [yet] diminished ; Alone is He, and like unto Himself [Alone], equal, identical, perfect in His stability, perfect in order ; for that He is the One, after the God alone beyond all knowing."

Hermes.   (M. 6, Vol. III, p. 256.)

" The nature of His Intellectual Word (*Logos*) is a productive and creative Nature. This is as though it were His Power-of-giving-birth, or [His] Nature, or [His] Mode of being, or call it what you will,—only remembering this : that He is Perfect, and from the Perfect makes, and creates and makes to live, perfect good things." (*Ibid.*, p. 255.)

(b) " I have sufficiently demonstrated that they are not atheists who believe in One who is unbegotten, eternal, unseen, impassible, incomprehensible and uncontained : comprehended by mind and reason only, invested with ineffable light and beauty and spirit and power, by whom the universe is brought into being and set in order and held firm, through the agency of his own *Logos*."

Athenagoras.   (H. 1, p. 253.)

" It was by a natural process of development that Christian philosophers, while acquiescing in the general proposition that Jesus Christ was the *Logos* in human form, should go on to frame large theories as to the nature

of the *Logos*.   It was an age of definition and dialectic.
It was no more possible for the mass of educated men to
leave a metaphysical problem untouched, than it is possible
in our own days for chemists to leave a natural product
unanalyzed.   Two main questions engaged attention :
(1) what was the genesis, (2) what was the nature, of the
Logos.   In the speculations which rose out of each of these
questions, the influence of Greek thought is even more
conspicuous than before.''

E. Hatch.   (H. 1, p. 263.)

(c) '' The Word, viz., the efflux from the willing
God, was the Eternal beginning, and continueth so
eternally.   . . .   This efflux floweth out from God, and
the outflown (Word) is His wisdom, the beginning and
cause of all powers, colours, virtues, and properties.''

Jacob Böhme.   (B. 20, III, 4, 6.)

(d) '' The *beginning* of all and every substance or thing
is the Word, viz., the outbreathing of God's substance ;
and God was the Eternal One from Eternity, and continueth the same also in Eternity ; but the Word is the
efflux or *outflowing* of the divine willing or of the divine
knowledge.''   Jacob Böhme.   (B. 20, III, 2.)

(e) '' Moses said God made man of the dust of the earth,
and breathed into him the living breath, and then man
became a living soul.   But we are here to understand that
God did *not* in a personal and creaturely manner stand by
like a man and take a lump or clod of earth and make a
body of it ; no, it was not so.   But the Word of God was
in all properties in *Spiritu Mundi* and in the *ens*, or being
of the earth, stirring up from the spirit of the world, and
spake or breathed forth a life into every essence.''

Jacob Böhme.   (B. 14, Ch. V, pars. 85, 86.)

(f) '' Of what the Word is in its power and sound, of

that the Mysterium Magnum is a substance ; it is the eternal substantial Word of God."

Jacob Böhme. (B. 14, Ch. VIII, 61.)

(*g*) " The form and feature of bodies arise from the experience of the will, where the centre of everything (being a particle or spark from the expressed Word) doth again express or speak itself forth, and bringeth itself into a distinct particularity, in manner and form of the divine speaking (or operation of the eternal Word in its generation,) and manifestation."

Jacob Böhme. (B. 16, VI, 12.)

" Man in respect of his external comprehensible or finite body standeth only in a flitting figurative shadow or resemblance : and with his spiritual body he is the true essential *word* of the divine property, in which God speaketh and begetteth His *word* ; and there the divine science doth distribute, impart, impress, form, and beget itself to an image of God."   Jacob Böhme. (B. 16, VI, 41.)

(*h*) " Eternal activity without beginning or end, Cause without Cause, the Father contemplates Himself in the Abyss of His fecundity, and the act of understanding Himself begets another Person, the Son, His Eternal Word. The types of all creatures, not yet drawn from nothingness, dwelt eternally in the Eternal Begotten. God sees and contemplates them there in their types, but in Himself ; for there is nothing in God which is not God. This eternal existence which our types possess in God, the eternal being, is God ; endures eternally."

Ruysbroeck. (B. 36, p. 35.)

(*i*) " For the *Word* of God which saveth and redeemeth, which giveth Life and Light to the Soul, is not the Word printed on Paper, but is that eternal, ever-speaking Word, which is the Son of God, who in the Beginning was with God, and was the God by whom all Things were made.

This is the universal Teacher and Enlightener of all that are in Heaven and on Earth ; who from the Beginning to the end of Time, without Respect of Persons, stands at the Door of every Heart of Man, speaking into it not human Words but *divine Goodness* ; calling and knocking, not with outward Sounds but by the *inward Stirring* of an awakened Divine Life. And therefore, as sure as that is true, which St. John saith, that this eternal Word *is the Life of Men, and the Light that lighteth every Man that cometh into the World*, so sure is it that our Saviour and Salvation, our Teacher and Enlightener, from whom we have every good Thought, is *Christ within us* , not within this or that Man, but in every Man, wherever born, and in whom the Light of Life ariseth. And indeed how can it be otherwise ? For if God is the God of all Men ; and the *Word* of God the Life and Light of all Men ; and all Men are capable of Goodness ; and all Goodness can only be from God ; and no Goodness can belong to Man but that which is *within* him ; then every Man must have the *Word*, or *Christ* of God, within him, and can have it no-where else." Wm. Law. (L. 4, p. 153.)

(*j*) " It is true that if the Word did not sustain the universe in its existence and direct it in all its movements, it would stop instantaneously in its course and go back into the unmanifest. It is true that if the Word did not sustain all animals and plants, they would return at once into their respective germs, and the germ into the temporal spirit of the universe. It is true that if the Word did not sustain the action and display of all phenomena, the phenomenal would come immediately to its end. It is equally true in the spiritual order that except the Word sustain the thought and soul of man, thought would relapse into darkness, and the soul into that abyss which we navigate only by the immeasurable and merciful power of the same Word." Saint-Martin. (W. 2, p. 231.)

(k) " In Stoicism there was the theory of the one Law or Logos expressing itself in an infinite variety of material forms ; in Platonism, there was the theory of the one God, shaping matter according to an infinite variety of patterns. In the one, the processes of nature were the operations of active forces, containing in themselves the law of the forms in which they exhibit themselves, self-developing seeds, each of them a portion of the one *Logos* which runs through the whole.   In the other, they were the operations of the infinitely various and eternally active energy of God, moving always in the direction of His thoughts, so that those thoughts might themselves be conceived as the causes of the operations.   In both the one theory and the other, the processes were sometimes regarded in their apparent multiplicity, and sometimes in their underlying unity ; and in both the unity was expressed sometimes by the impersonal term *Logos*, and sometimes by the personal term God."   E. Hatch. (H. 1, p. 180).

" The relation of the *Logos* to God, as distinguished from its functions, is expressed by several metaphors, all of which are important in view of later theology.   They may be gathered into two classes, corresponding to the two great conceptions of the relation of the universe to God which were held respectively by the two great sources of Philo's philosophy, the Stoics and the Platonists.   The one class of metaphors belongs to the monistic, the other to the dualistic, conception of the universe.   In the former, the *Logos* is evolved from God ; in the other, created by Him. The chief metaphors of the former class are those of a phantom, or image, or outflow : the *Logos* is projected by God as a man's shadow or phantom was sometimes conceived as thrown off by his body, expressing its every feature, and abiding as a separate existence after the body was dead ; it is a reflection cast by God upon the space which He contains, as a parhelion is cast by the sun ; it is an outflow as from a spring. The chief metaphor of the second class is that of a son ; the *Logos* is the first-begotten of God ; and by an elaboration of the metaphor which reappears in later theology, God is in one passage spoken of as its Father, Wisdom as its Mother. It hence tends sometimes to be viewed as separate from God, neither God nor man, but ' inferior to God though greater than man.' "

(Ibid., p. 248.)

(*l*) " Whoever uses such words as *Logos*, the Word, *Monogenês*, the Only-begotten, *Prototokos*, the First-born *Hyios tou theou*, the Son of God, has borrowed the very germs of his religious thoughts from Greek philosophy. To suppose that the Fathers of the Church took these words without borrowing the ideas, is like supposing that savages would carry away fire-arms without getting at the same time powder and shot for firing them. . . . I have tried to show that the doctrine of the Logos, the very life-blood of Christianity, is exclusively Aryan, and that it is one of the simplest and truest conclusions at which the human mind can arrive, if the presence of Reason or reasons in the world has once been recognised."

F. Max Müller. (M. 4, p. X.)

" The *Logos*, the Word, as the thought of God, as the whole body of divine or eternal ideas, which Plato had prophesied, which Aristotle had criticised in vain, which the Neo-Platonists re-established, is a truth which forms, or ought to form, the foundation of all philosophy. And unless we have fully grasped it, as it was grasped by some of the greatest Fathers of the Church, we shall never be able to understand the Fourth Gospel, we shall never be able to call ourselves true Christians. For it is, as built upon the Logos, that Christianity holds its own unique position among all the religions of the world."

(Ibid., p. 521.)

MIND

(a) "FOR man's intellect, however keen, face to face with the countless evolutions of things, their death and birth, their squareness and roundness—can never reach the roots. There creation is, and there it has ever been." Chuang Tzū. (C. 1, p. 61.)

(b) " Reason (*Logos*) indeed, O Tat, among all men hath He distributed, but Mind not yet ; not that He grudgeth any, for grudging cometh not from Him, but hath its place below, within the souls of men who have no Mind."
Hermes. (M. 6, Vol. II, p. 86.)

(c) " The centre of the mind is come out of Eternity, out of God's omnipotence ; it can bring itself into what it will and whither it will."
Jacob Böhme. (B. 12, III, 20.)

(d) " *Yoga* teaches that the mind itself has, a higher state of existence, beyond reason, a super-conscious state, and when the mind gets to that higher state, then this knowledge, beyond reasoning comes to a man, metaphysical knowledge, beyond all physical knowledge. Metaphysical and transcendental knowledge comes to that man, and this state of going beyond reason, transcending ordinary human nature, sometimes may come by chance to a man who does not understand its science ; he, as it were, stumbles into it. When he stumbles into it, he generally interprets it as from outside. So this explains why an inspiration, or this transcendental knowledge, may be the same in different countries, but in one country it will seem to come through an angel, in another through a Deva, and in another through God. What does it mean ? It means that the mind brought the knowledge by its own nature, and that the finding of the knowledge was interpreted according to the beliefs and education of the person through whom it came. The real fact is that these various men, as it were, stumbled into this super-conscious state."   Swâmi Vivekananda.   (V. 2, p. 78.)

(e) " Our thought, in its purely logical form, is incapable of presenting the true nature of life, the full meaning of the evolutionary movement."

Henri Bergson.   (B. 27, p. X.)

See also INTELLECT (p. 127).

MIND, COSMIC

(a) " It is not possible such mysteries [as these] should be declared to those who are without initiation in the sacred rites. But ye, lend me your ears, [ears] of your mind !

" There was One intellectual Light alone,—nay, Light transcending Intellectual Light. He is for ever Mind of mind who makes [that] Light to shine.

" There was no other ; [naught] save the Oneness of Himself [alone]. For ever in Himself [alone], for ever doth He compass all in His own Mind,—His Light and Spirit."   Hermes.   (M. 6, Vol. III, p. 257.)

(b) " For us, along the great highways of time, those monuments stand—those forms of majesty and beauty. For us those beacons burn through all the nights. Unknown Egyptians, graving hieroglyphs ; Hindus, with hymn and apothegm and endless epic ; Hebrew prophet, with spirituality, as in flashes of lightning, conscience like red-hot iron, plaintive songs and screams of vengeance for tyrannies and enslavement ; Christ, with bent head, brooding love and peace, like a dove ; Greek, creating eternal shapes of physical and esthetic proportion ! Roman, lord of satire, the sword, and the codex :—of the figures, some far off and veiled, others nearer and visible ; Dante stalking with lean form, nothing but fibre, not a grain of superfluous flesh ; Angelo, and the great painters, architects, musicians ; rich Shakespeare, luxuriant as the sun, artist and singer of feudalism in its sunset, with all the gorgeous colours, owner thereof, and using them at will ; and so to such as German Kant and Hegel, where they, though near us, leaping over the ages, sit again, impassive, imperturbable, like the Egyptian gods. Of these, and the like of these, is it too much, indeed, to return to our favourite figure, and view then as orbs and systems of orbs, moving in free paths in the spaces of that other heaven, the cosmic intellect, the soul ? ''

Walt Whitman. (W. 6, p. 340.)

MAN AND THE UNIVERSE

NOTE ON MAN AND THE UNIVERSE

The mystical doctrine—we might say, the mystical *fact*—of Man's divine nature, of the unity of God and Man, carries with it by implication the oneness of Man with the manifested universe in all its aspects and activities. The individual man derives all his bodies, physical and subtle, and all his powers, from Cosmic Substance considered as the first out-breathing or emanation from the One Causeless-Cause. The individual man is merely a special case of universal principles—matter or substance, force, life, mind, spirit, etc. But all these are expressions of that One ultimate PRINCIPLE which we call the Absolute, or God. To know God, and the Universe as a manifestation of God, therefore, Man must know himself ; and in no other way can either God or the Universe as the expression of God be known in any sense which may be called real knowledge. It is this self-realisation which lies at the root of Man's evolution ; and thus also we may postulate that Man and the Universe in their Unity are not merely the outspoken *Word* or *Logos* of the ever-concealed Godhead, but are also the self-realisation of that Supreme Unity, without which it might even be said that IT could not know ITSELF.

See further, SELF KNOWLEDGE (p. 212) ; SOUL, NATURE OF (p. 229) ; and SOUL AND COSMOS (p. 236).

MAN AND THE UNIVERSE

(*a*) " That which is the finest essence—this whole world has that as its soul. That is Reality. That is Ātman (Soul). That art thou, Svetaketu."

Chandogya Upanishad, VI, 9, 4. (U. 1, p. 246.)

(*b*) " Him 'neath whose feet the mighty tide of days and years rolls past,

In whom the five-fold host of things and space itself stands fast,

Whom gods as light of lights adore, as immortality,

The Brahman know I as my deathless Self, for I am he."

Brihad-āranyaka Upanishad, IV, 4, 15–16–17.

(D. 4, p. 195.)

(*c*) " But he whose mind the inner Self in Thought hath learned to grasp,

Why should he longer seek to bear the body's pain and woe ?

For when a man in spite of all the stains of mortal sin,

The great awakening to the Self hath won, and learned to see,

Him as creator of the worlds, almighty shalt thou know,

His is the universe, because the universe is he."

Brihad-āranyaka Upanishad, IV, 4, 12–13. (D. 4, p.194.)

(d) " There is nothing under the canopy of heaven greater than the tip of an autumn spikelet. A vast mountain is a small thing. Neither is there any age greater than that of a child cut off in infancy. P'êng Tsu himself died young. The universe and I came into being together ; and I, and everything therein, are One."
Chuang Tzū. (C. 1, p. 38.)

(e) " Whatsoever can be thought to have a being anywhere in the creature, the same is likewise without the creature everywhere, for the creature is nothing else but an image and figure of the separable and various power and virtue of the Universal Being."
Jacob Böhme. (B. 21, par. 96.)

(f) " For the book in which all mysteries lie is man himself ; he himself is the book of the Being of all beings ; seeing he is the likeness [or similitude] of God ; the great *Arcanum* lieth *in* him, the revealing of it belongeth only unto God's spirit." Jacob Böhme. (B. 16, IX, 3.)

(g) " I do not consider man as an individual, but as an universal species, which I have called the *Kingdom of Man.* This Kingdom always presents itself to me as a unique being, delighting in an intelligible existence, which becomes sentient by individualisation. When philosophers have said that Nature makes only individuls, they have said the truth when they apply this axiom to physical nature ; but they have uttered an absurdity when they extend it to intellectual nature ; this superior nature, on the contrary, creates only the Kingdom modified by inferior nature first into species, afterwards into races, and finally into individuals." Fabre d'Olivet. (F. 1, p. 287.)

(h) " We live in succession, in division, in parts, in particles. Meantime, within man is the soul of the whole ; the wise silence ; the universal beauty, to which every part and particle is equally related ; the eternal ONE. And this deep power in which we exist, and whose beatitude is all accessible to us, is not only self-sufficing and perfect in every hour, but the act of seeing and the spectacle, the subject and the object, are one. We see the world piece by piece, as the sun, the moon, the animal, the tree ; but the whole, of which these are the shining parts, is the soul." Ralph Waldo Emerson. (E. 4, Vol. I, p. 112.)

> (*i*)   " 'Tis the sublime of man,
> Our noontide majesty, to know ourselves
> Parts and proportions of one wondrous whole !
> This fraternises man, this constitutes
> Our charities and bearings. But 'tis God
> Diffused through all, that doth make all one whole."

Samuel T. Coleridge. Poems. *Religious Musings.*

MAN, POWERS AND DESTINY OF

(*a*) " The perfect man is a spiritual being. Were the ocean itself scorched up, he would not feel hot. Were the Milky Way frozen hard, he would not feel cold. Were the mountains to be riven with thunder, and the great deep to be thrown up by storm, he would not tremble."
Chuang Tzū. (C. 1, p. 86.)

(*b*) " Such a man, as Adam was before his Eve, shall arise and again enter into, and eternally possess Paradise : not a man, or a woman, but as the Scripture saith, *they are virgins, and follow God, and the Lamb, they are like to the angels of God,* yet not only pure spirit, as the angels, but in heavenly bodies, in which the spiritual angelical body inhabiteth."   Jacob Böhme. (B. 7, XVIII, 3.)

(*c*) " In what quality soever thou excitest or *awakenest* the spirit, and makest it operative or qualifying, according to that same quality the thoughts rise up, and *govern* the mind. . . . For when thou, in thy body, liftest thyself against anything whatsoever, be it in love or wrath, thou kindlest the quality of that against which thou liftest thyself; and that (kindled quality) burneth in the corporeal whole of thy spirit. . . . But thou must know, that thou, in the government of thy mind, are *thine own* lord and master, there will rise up *no* fire in thee in the circle or whole circumference of thy body and spirit, *unless* thou awakenest it *thyself.*"   Jacob Böhme. (B. 1, X, 69, 71, 81.)

(d)   " Man should not stay a man :
                His aim should higher be.
                For God will only gods
                Accept as company."
                        Angelus Silesius.   (S. 3, p. 132.)

(e) " But if Man is, as I have just said, only a power in germ which civilization must develop, whence will come to him the principles of this indispensible culture ?   I reply that it will be from the two powers to which he finds himself linked and of which he must form a third.   These two powers, between which he finds himself placed, are Destiny (the inferior and instinctive part of Universal Nature ; called *necessity*) and Providence (the superior and intellectual part of Universal Nature ; the living law emanating from the Divinity, by means of which all things are determined with power to be).   Beneath him is Destiny, *nature necessitee et naturee* ; above him is Providence, *nature libre et naturante.*   He is himself, as Kingdom of Man, the mediatory will, the efficient form, placed between these two natures to serve them as a link, a means of communication, and to unite two actions, two movements, which would be incompatable without him.

" The three Powers which I have just named—Providence, Man, considered as the Kingdom of Man, and

Destiny—constitute the universal ternary. Nothing escapes their action ; all is subject to them in the universe ; all except *God* Himself who, enveloping them in His unfathomable Unity, forms with it the Sacred Tetrad of the Ancients, that immense quaternary, which is All in All and outside of which there is nothing."

Fabre d'Olivet. (F. 1, XL.)

(*f*) " At the time when Man appears upon the Earth he belongs to Destiny. . . . But he carries in him a divine germ which never could entirely be confused with him. This germ, reacted upon by Destiny itself, develops to oppose it. It is a spark of the Divine Will which, participating in the universal life, comes into the elementary nature to restore harmony in it. . . . When this germ is entirely developed, it constitutes the Will of the Universal Man, one of the three great Powers of the Universe.

" This Power, equal to that of Destiny which is inferior to it, and even to that of Providence which is superior to it, is quickened only by God Himself to whom the others are equally subjected, each according to his rank. It is the Will of Man, which, as powerful medium, unites Destiny and Providence ; without it, these two extreme powers not only would never unite, but they would not even understand each other."

Fabre d'Olivet. (F. 1, XLII, XLIII.)

(*g*) " Man is a divine germ which is developed by the reaction of his senses. All is innate in him, all ; that which he receives from the exterior is only the occasion of his ideas ; not his ideas themselves." Fabre d'Olivet. (F. 1, 22.)

(*h*)   " God wants not man to humble himself ;
            That is the trick of the ancient elf.
            This is the race that Jesus ran :
            Humble to God, haughty to man ;

11

Cursing the rulers before the people,
Even to the temple's highest steeple.
Thou also dwellest in eternity.
Thou art a man.   God is no more ;
Thine own humanity learn to adore,
And thy revenge abroad display,
In terrors at the last judgment day."
William Blake.   *The Everlasting Gospel.*

(*i*) " I the imperfect adore my own Perfect.   I am some-
how receptive of the great soul, and thereby I do overlook
the sun and the stars, and feel them to be but the fair
accidents and effects which change and pass.   More and
more the surges of everlasting nature enter into me, and I
become public and human in my regards and actions.
So come I to live in thoughts, and act with energies which
are immortal.   Thus revering the soul, and learning, as
the ancient said, that ' its beauty is immense,' man will
come to see that the world is the perennial miracle which
the soul worketh, and be less astonished at particular
wonders ; he will learn that there is no profane history ;
that all history is sacred ; that the universe is represented
in an atom, in a moment of time.   He will weave no longer
a spotted life of shreds and patches, but he will live with a
divine unity."
Ralph Waldo Emerson.   *The Oversoul.*
(E. 4, Vol. I, p. 124.)

(*j*) " He who believes in other worlds can accustom himself to look on this as the naturalist on the revolutions of an
ant-hill, or of a leaf.   What is the Earth to Infinity—what
its duration to the Eternal !   Oh, how much greater is the
soul of one man than the vicissitudes of the whole globe !
Child of heaven, and heir of immortality, how from some
star hereafter wilt thou look back on the ant-hill and its
commotions, from Clovis to Robespierre, from Noah to the

Final Fire. The spirit that can contemplate, that lives only in the intellect, can ascend to its star, even in the midst of the Burial-ground called Earth, and while the Sarcophagus called Life immures in its clay the Everlasting!"

Bulwer Lytton. *Zanoni*, Book I, Chap. V. (L. 3, p. 20.)

(*k*) " When once you perceive that man in his inmost nature is the product of the Divine Mind, imaging forth an image of Itself, you are certain that no negation can finally frustrate the evolution of the Divine principle which is the inmost centre in us all. It must ultimately blend with the ocean of uncreated life whence it came, and whither from all Eternity it is predestined to return."

Archdeacon Wilberforce. (W. 7, p. 41.)

MATTER AND SUBSTANCE

(*a*) " Matter both has been born, O son, and it has been [before it came into existence] ; for Matter is the vase of genesis, and genesis, the mode of energy of God, who's free from all necessity of genesis, and pre-exists.

" [Matter], accordingly, by its reception of the seed of genesis, did come [herself] to birth, and [so] became subject to change, and, being shaped, took forms ; for she, contriving the forms of her [own] changing, presided over her own changing self.

" The unborn state of Matter, then, was formlessness ; its genesis is its being brought into activity."

Hermes. (M. 6, Vol. III, p. 26.)

(*b*) " But it is acknowledged universally that a principle is indivisible, incommensurable, absolutely different from matter as presented to our senses. It is, in a word, a simple being, while matter, which is divisible and measurable, is not simple. . . . Matter itself may perish, but its principle remains unalterable and indestructible. It existed before bodies, and can remain after them. The principle of bodies may therefore be conceived apart from every form of matter, no particle of which can at the same time be conceived or exist unsustained or unanimated by its principle." Saint-Martin. (W. 2, p. 194.)

(c) " Matter is a phenomenal isolation of one aspect of Reality." F. H. Bradley. (B. 30, p. 338.)

(d) " Mind filters out matter from the meaningless jumble of qualities, as the prism filters out the colours of the rainbow from the chaotic pulsations of white light."
A. S. Eddington. (E. 3, p. 197.)
See SUBSTANCE (p. 248).

MATERIALISM

(a) " I understand the main tenet of Materialism to be that there is nothing in the universe but matter and force ; and that all the phenomena of nature are explicable by deduction from the properties assignable to these two primitive factors. . . . This I heartily disbelieve."
T. H. Huxley. (H. 2, p. 129.)
" As I have said elsewhere, if I were forced to choose between Materialism and Idealism, I should elect for the latter ; and I certainly would have nothing to do with the effete mythology of Spiritualism." (*Ibid.*, p. 133.)
" I must make a confession, even if it be humiliating. I have never been able to form the slightest conception of those ' forces ' which the Materialists talk about, as if they had samples of them many years in bottle. They tell me that matter consists of atoms, which are separated by mere space devoid of contents ; and that, through this void, radiate the attractive and repulsive forces whereby the atoms affect one another. If anybody can clearly conceive the nature of these things which not only exist in nothing-ness, but pull and push there with great vigour, I envy him

the possession of an intellect of larger grasp, not only than mine, but than that of Leibnitz or of Newton. . . . Besides, by the hypothesis, the forces are not matter ; and thus all that is of any particular consequence in the world turns out to be not matter on the Materialist's own showing. Let it not be supposed that I am casting a doubt upon the propriety of the employment of the terms ' atom ' and ' force,' as they stand among the working hypotheses of physical science. As formulæ which can be applied, with perfect precision and great convenience, in the interpretation of nature, their value is incalculable ; but, as real entities, having an objective existence, an indivisible particle which nevertheless occupies space is surely inconceivable ; and with respect to the operation of that atom, where it is not, by the aid of a ' force ' resident in nothingness, I am as little able to imagine it as I fancy any one else is." *(Ibid.,* p. 131.)

(*b*) " It is worth any amount of trouble . . . to know by one's own knowledge the great truth . . . that the honest and rigorous following up of the arguments which lead us to ' materialism ' inevitably carries us beyond it."

T. H. Huxley. (H. 4, p. 251.)

" To sum up. If the materialist affirms that the universe and all its phenomena are resolvable into matter and motion, Berkeley replies, True ; but what you call matter and motion are known to us only as forms of consciousness ; their being is to be conceived or known ; and the existence of a state of consciousness, apart from a thinking mind, is a contradiction in terms.

" I conceive that this reasoning is irrefrangable. And, therefore, if I were obliged to choose between absolute materialism and absolute idealism, I should feel compelled to accept the latter alternative." *(Ibid.,* p. 279.)

(*c*) " If materialists like Vogt and Büchner so misunderstand the commonplace, that philosophy must rest upon experience, as to take the experience of five human senses for that experience on which exclusively true philosophy should stand, and then to set up the materialistic system as this true philosophy—a philosophy so unintellectual, that in it the feat seems to be performed of solving the maximum of problems with the minimum of intelligence —such teaching, indeed, may find followers in a time of intellectual mediocrity; but our posterity, studying this time with historical criticism, will set up a laugh over this materialism announcing itself as a philosophy—a laugh which will be Homeric."

Carl Du Prel. (D. 2, Vol. II, p. 280.)

MOTION

(a) " The motion of a thing is not the highest ground of the power, but that out of which the cause of motion cometh."   Jacob Böhme. (B. 20, III, 55.)

(b) " It is, therefore, incontestable that movement may be conceived without extension, since the principle of movement, whether sensible or intellectual, is actually outside extension."

Louis Claude de Saint-Martin.   (W. 2, p. 383.)

(c) " Real movement is rather the transference of a state than of a thing."   Henri Bergson. (B. 28, p. 266.)

MANIFESTATION, PRE-

(a) " Nor Aught nor Naught existed ; yon bright sky
    Was not, nor heaven's broad roof outstretched
        above.
    What covered all ? what sheltered ? what con-
        cealed ?
Was it the water's fathomless abyss ?

There was not death—yet there was nought
    immortal,
There was no confine betwixt day and night ;
The only One breathed breathless by Itself,
Other than It there nothing since has been.
Darkness there was, and all at first was veiled
In gloom profound—an ocean without light—
The germ that still lay covered in the husk
Burst forth, one nature, from the fervent heat.

.   .   .   .   .

Who knows the secret ? who proclaimed it here ?
Whence, whence this manifold creation sprang ?
The Gods themselves came later into being—
Who knows from whence this great creation
    sprang ?
That, whence all this great creation came,
Whether Its will created or was mute,
The Most High Seer that it in highest heaven,
He knows it—or perchance even He knows not."

    Rig Veda. (R. 6, X. 129. Colebrooke's trans.)

(*b*) "Before Heaven and Earth existed there was something undefined but already perfect.

"How calm it was and formless ! Self-sufficient and unchanging ; all forereaching without effort,—the Universal Mother.

"I do not know its name, but for title call it Tao."

    Lao Tsze. *The Tâo Teh King.* (L. 1, p. 12.)

(*c*) "Naught was,—neither matter, nor substance, nor voidness of substance, nor simplicity, nor impossibility of composition, nor inconceptibility, nor imperceptibility, neither man nor angel, nor God ; in fine, neither anything at all for which man has ever found a name, nor any operation which falls within the range either of his perception or conception.

"Such, or rather far more removed from the power of man's comprehension, was the state of Non-Being, when the Deity beyond Being, without thinking, or feeling, or determining, or choosing, or being compelled, or desiring, willed to create universality."

Basilides.   (M. 6, Vol. II, p. 160.)

(*d*) "Out of the substance the true intellective spirit primarily proceedeth, which before the substance was only a will, and not manifest to itself : for the will doth therefore introduce itself into substance and essence that it might be manifest to itself." Jacob Böhme. (B. 7, IV, 9.)

(*e*) "God's holy life would not be manifested without Nature, but be only in an eternal stillness."

Jacob Böhme.   (B. 14, IX, 46.)

(*f*) "The will is no substance, but the willing's imagination maketh substance."

Jacob Böhme.   (B. 5, Part II, ch. II, 23.)

(*g*) "The will maketh out of itself the form of a spirit, and the form maketh a substance according to the property of the spirit."

Jacob Böhme.   (B. 23, Point IV, ch. VI, 10.)

(*h*) "The Divine Ens which is spiritual, *cannot* be manifested but through the strife of Nature."

Jacob Böhme.   (B. 14, VIII, 226.)

(*i*) "If there were no anguish there would be no fire ; if there were no fire there would be no light ; if there were no light there would be neither Nature nor substance, and God would not be manifested."

Jacob Böhme.   (B. 9, Part I, 141.)

(*j*) " Before this worlds great frame, in which all things
Are now contain'd, found any being place,
Ere flitting Time could wag his eyas wings
About that mightie bound which doth embrace
The rolling Spheres, and parts their houres by space,
That high eternall powre, which now doth move
In all these things, mov'd in it selfe by love.''

Edmund Spenser. Poetical Works.
An Hymne of Heavenly Love.

STANZAS FROM THE BOOK OF DZYAN

(*k*) 1. The Eternal Parent [1] wrapped in her Ever-Invisible Robes had slumbered once again for seven Eternities.

2. Time was not, for it lay asleep in the Infinite Bosom of Duration.

3. Universal Mind was not, for there were no Ah-hi [2] to contain it.

4. The Seven Ways to Bliss were not. The Great Causes of Misery were not, for there was no one to produce and get ensnared by them.

5. Darkness alone filled the Boundless All, for Father, Mother and Son were once more one, and the Son had not yet awakened for the new Wheel [3] and his Pilgrimage thereon.

6. The Seven Sublime Lords and the Seven Truths had ceased to be, and the Universe, the Son of Necessity, was immersed in Paranishpanna, [4] to be outbreathed by that which is, and yet is not. Naught was.

[1] " The incomprehensible DEITY, whose ' invisible robes ' are the mystic root of all matter, and of the Universe "

[2] " The collective hosts of spiritual beings—the Angelic Hosts of Christianity, the Elohim and ' Messengers ' of the Jews—who are the vehicle for the manifestation of the divine or universal thought and wile.''

[3] Great cycle of Manifestation.

[4] " The absolute perfection to which all existences attain at the close of a great period (cycle) of activity (manifestation).''

7. The Causes of Existence had been done away with ; the Visible that was, and the Invisible that is, rested in Eternal Non-Being—the One Being.

8. Alone the One Form of Existence stretched boundless, infinite, causeless, in dreamless sleep ; and Life pulsated unconscious in Universal Space, throughout that All-Presence which is sensed by the opened eye of the Dangma.[1]

9. But where was the Dangma when the Ālaya [2] of the Universe was in Paramartha,[3] and the Great Wheel was Anupâdaka ? [4]

H. P. Blavatsky.   (B. 31, Vol. I, p. 27.)

MYSTICISM, DEFINITIONS AND GENERAL NATURE OF

(a) " These interior subjects are so difficult to understand, that whoever knows no more than I do is compelled to say many superfluous and foolish things, in order to mention a few things which may be useful."

St. Theresa.   (S. 6, p. 9.)

(b) " Man is a stream whose source is hidden.   Always our being is descending into us from we know not whence."

Ralph Waldo Emerson.   (E. 4, Vol. I, p. 113.)

(c) " The mystic fact is a *naïve* and non-methodical attempt to apprehend the Absolute ; it is a *symbolic* and not a dialectic mode of thought."   E. Récéjac.   (R. 4, p. 4.)

" All mysticism must seek in Freedom its determining principles and its inspiration.   Afterwards it rises by means of mental ' *symbolic* ' representations.   We can have no other experience of the Absolute in this life than through symbolic representations."   (*Ibid.*, p. 5.)

[1] " A purified soul, one who has become a Jivanmukta, the highest adept, or rather a Mahama "
[2] " The ' Soul of the World,' the ' Oversoul ' of Emerson "
[3] Absolute Reality.   [4] Parentless.

" Mysticism is a tendency to arrive at consciousness of
the Absolute by means of symbols under the influence of
love." *(Ibid.,* p. 62)

" Mysticism is the tendency to draw near to the Absolute
in moral union by symbolic means." *(Ibid.* p. 64.)

" All mystic efforts are merely meant to recall man more
within himself and to make plain to him principles deeper
and more profound than he had at first perceived, by
reason of his carelessness or egotism. Under the name of
' divine Will ' nothing different to this should be sought
for." *(Ibid.,* p. 196.)

" No one can ' know ' the Absolute, and for this reason
it might have been better to call mysticism an ' experience '
instead of a ' knowledge.' But what kind of experience is
it ? Not an experience through the senses, and not
through pure Reason. The truest expression we can use
seems to be Pascal's phrase, ' God known of the Heart.' "
(Ibid., p. 83.)

" The true field of Mysticism is the Infinite of Reason
and Freedom." *(Ibid.,* p. 178.)

" Has Mysticism no place in other consciences but those
which seem exclusively devoted to it ? Perhaps there is
no tendency which has so wide a psychological dominion
over the whole world. Mysticism has its adepts everywhere. Besides actual mystics, how many others are
there who carry into Art, Literature, and even into Science
itself that pursuit of the Infinite which constitutes a fact
as human, as universal, as Reason itself ? "
(Ibid., p. 89)

" Mysticism claims to be able to know the Unknowable
without help from dialectics, and is persuaded that, by
means of love and will, it reaches a point to which thought,
unaided, cannot attain." *(Ibid.,* p. 7.)

" We may legitimately expect a preponderance of Freedom over the understanding in Mysticism and the term

mystic should be applied only to minds that have sought the Absolute in other than dialectical ways."

(Ibid., p. 43.)

" What are the appreciable results of this symbolic presence of the Absolute in the consciousness ? What do we acquire from it ? . . . By the ordinary mental species logical scientific and esthetic communications are made between the world and ourselves, but the mystic symbols aid us to effect a synthesis in which the consciousness aspires to feel that unity which dominates all the others, that creative Love which absorbs in itself Science, Art, etc. After these efforts of the mystic consciousness, it cannot be said, the least in the world, that Reason has gained any more ground in the Unknowable ; but the conditions which are established in us during this moral and analogical research after the Absolute are very remarkable : they tend to impart the greatest inward vigour to the will, to the moral principles, to the character, and to inspire us with a realizing sense of the Infinite. The representative action of symbols, therefore, culminates in a moral presence of the Absolute : and it reinforces, in an incomparable manner, the natural powers and the qualities proper to the subject."

(Ibid., p. 139.)

" Mysticism consists simply in an alliance of Freedom and the Imagination, and unless Freedom keeps rigidly within the Kantian sense of ' practical Reason,' aberration would be the outcome. But when Desire has the safeguard of evident morals, it may soar without going astray."

(Ibid., p. 61.)

" Mystics aspire to a full and perfect life of the soul ; their desire is to be in harmony with the Absolute under as many relationships as the Absolute in itself has modes of Being. They love, then, Nature, Art, Duty ; but moral Good comes before everything else, and it is by embracing it that they enter and take possession of all the other modes of consciousness which seem exempt from relativity." *(Ibid.,* p. 25.)

(*d*) " Mysticism has been the ferment of the faiths, the forerunner of spiritual liberty, the inaccessible refuge of the nobler heretics, the inspirer, through poetry, of countless youth who know no metaphysics, the teacher, through the devotional books, of the despairing, the comforter of those who are weary of finitude. It has determined, directly or indirectly, more than half of the technical theology of the Church. The scholastic philosophy endeavoured in vain to give it a subordinate place."

Josiah Royce. (R. 3, Vol. I, p. 85.)

" By this term, Mysticism, I now mean . . . not a vaguely applied name for superstition in general, or for beliefs in spirits, in special revelations, and in magic, but a perfectly recognisable speculative tendency, observable in very various ages and nations, and essentially characterized by the meaning that it gives to the ontological predicate.

" For the mystic, according to the genuinely historical definition of what constitutes speculative Mysticism, to be real means to be in such wise Immediate that, in the presence of this immediacy, all thought and all ideas, absolutely satisfied, are quenched, so that the finite search ceases, and the Other is no longer another, but is absolutely found. The object which fulfils this definition, and which is therefore worthy to be called real, is of necessity in itself One and only One ; since variety, when consciously faced, calls forth thought, and arouses demands for characterization and explanation." *(Ibid.,* p. 144.)

" Mysticism is a practical doctrine. It observes at once that you merely express your own need as knower when you thus regard the object as existent. Mysticism asks you hereupon to define your needs in an absolutely general way. What do you want when you want Being ?

Mysticism replies to this question, as the sage Yâjnavalkya replies, in the Upanishads, to the question of his wife Maitreyî : *You want yourself*,—the Self in its completion, in its fulfilment, in its final expression. In brief, when you talk of reality, you talk of self-possession, of perfection, and of peace. And that is, therefore, all that you mean by the Being of the world or of any type of facts. Being therefore is nothing beyond yourself. You even now hold it within you, in your heart of hearts. Being therefore is just the purely immediate. *To be* means to quench thought in the presence of a final immediacy which completely satisfies all ideas. And by this simple reflection, the mystic undertakes to define the Absolute." *(Ibid.,* p. 185.)

(*e*) " Those who use the term ' Mysticism ' are bound in self-defence to explain what they mean by it. Broadly speaking, I understand it to be the expression of the innate tendency of the human spirit towards complete harmony with the transcendental order ; whatever be the theological formula under which that order is understood."

Evelyn Underhill. (U. 3, p. X.)

" Mysticism, then, is not an opinion : it is not a philosophy. It has nothing in common with the pursuit of occult knowledge. It is not merely the power of contemplating Eternity. It is the name of that organic process which involves the perfect consummation of the Love of God : the achievement here and now of the immortal heritage of man. Or, if you like it better—for this means exactly the same thing—it is the art of establishing his conscious relation with the Absolute." *(Ibid.,* p. 97.)

" To be a mystic is simply to participate here and now in that real and eternal life ; in the fullest, deepest sense which is possible to man." *(Ibid.,* p. 534.)

" Four rules or notes which may be applied as tests to any given case which claims to take rank amongst the mystics.

" 1. True mysticism is active and practical, not passive and theoretical. It is an organic life-process, a something which the whole self does ; not something as to which its intellect holds an opinion.

" 2. Its aims are wholly transcendental and spiritual. It is in no way concerned with adding to, exploring, re-arranging, or improving anything in the visible universe. The mystic brushes aside that universe even in its most supernormal manifestations. Though he does not, as his enemies declare, neglect his duty to the many, his heart is always set upon the changeless One.

" 3. This One is for the mystic, not merely the Reality of all that is, but also a living and personal object of Love ; never an object of exploration. It draws his whole being homeward, but always under the guidance of the heart.

" 4. Living union with this One—which is the term of his adventure—is a definite state or form of enhanced life. It is obtained neither from an intellectual realization of its delights, nor from the most acute emotional longings. Though these must be present, they are not enough. It is arrived at by a definite and arduous psychological pro-cess—the so-called Mystic Way—entailing the complete remaking of character and the liberation of a new, or rather latent, form of consciousness, which imposes on the self the condition which is sometimes inaccurately called ' ecstasy,' but is better named the Unitive State." (*Ibid.* p., 96.)

" Attempts to limit mystical truth—the direct appre-hension of the Divine Substance—to the formulæ of any one religion, are as futile as the attempt to identify a precious metal with the die which converts it into current coin." (*Ibid.*, p. 115.)

" A discussion of mysticism as a whole will include two

branches. First the life process of the mystic : the re-making of his personality ; the method by which his peculiar consciousness of the Absolute is attained, and faculties which have been evolved to meet the requirements of the phenomenal, are enabled to do work on the transcendental plane. This is the ' Mystic Way ' in which the self passes through the states or stages of development which were codified by the Neo-platonists, and after them by the mediaeval mystics, as Purgation, Illumination, and Ecstasy. Secondly, the content of the mystical field of perception ; the revelation under which the contemplative becomes aware of the Absolute. This will include a consideration of the so-called doctrines of mysticism : the attempts of the articulate mystic to sketch for us the world into which he has looked, in language which is only adequate to the world in which the rest of us dwell. Here the difficult question of symbolism, and of symbolic theology comes in : a point upon which many promising expositions of the mystics have been wrecked. It will be our business to strip off as far as may be the symbolic wrapping, and attempt a synthesis of these doctrines ; to resolve the apparent contradictions of objective and subjective revelations, of the ways of negation and affirmation, emanation and immanence, surrender and deification, the Divine Dark and the Inward Light ; and finally to exhibit, if we can, the essential unity of that experience in which the human soul enters consciously into the Presence of God." *(Ibid.*, p. 112.)

" To be a mystic is simply to participate here and now in that real and eternal life ; in the fullest, deepest sense which is possible to man. It is to share, as a free and conscious agent—not a servant, but as a son—in the joyous travail of the Universe : its mighty onward sweep through pain and glory towards its home in God. This gift of ' sonship,' this power to free co-operation in the

world-process, is man's greatest honour. The ordered
sequence of states, the organic development, whereby his
consciousness is detached from illusion and rises to the
mystic freedom which conditions, instead of being conditioned by, its normal world, is the way he must tread if
that sonship is to be attained. Only by this deliberate
fostering of his deeper self, this transmutation of the
elements of character, can he reach those levels of consciousness upon which he hears, and responds to, the measure
' whereto the worlds keep time ' on their great pilgrimage
towards the Father's heart. The mystic act of union, that
joyous loss of the transfigured self in God, which is the
crown of man's conscious ascent towards the Absolute,
is the contribution of the individual to this, the destiny
of the Cosmos."   (*Ibid.*, p. 534.)

(*f*) " Mysticism, whether in religion or philosophy, is
that form of error which mistakes for a divine manifestation
the operations of a merely human faculty."

R. A. Vaughan.   (V. 1, Vol. I, p. 26.)

(*g*) " So also no one can be united with God unless he
first be enlightened. Thus there are three stages : first,
the purification ; secondly, the enlightening ; thirdly, the
union. [The purification concerneth those who are beginning or repenting, and is brought to pass in a threefold
wise ; by contrition and sorrow for sin, by full confession,
by hearty amendment. The enlightening belongeth to
such as are growing, and also taketh place in three ways :
to wit, by the eschewal of sin, by the practice of virtue and
good works, and by the willing endurance of all manner of
temptation and trials. The union belongeth to such as
are perfect, and also is brought to pass in three ways : to
wit, by pureness and singleness of heart, by love, and by
the contemplation of God, the Creator of all things.]"

Theologia Germanica.   (T. 1, p. 46.)

12

(*h*) " The faculty and action of the soul by which we have an however dim yet direct and (in its general effects) immensely potent, sense and feeling, an immediate experience of Objective Reality, of the Infinite and Abiding, of a Spirit not unlike yet distinct from our own, which penetrates and works within these our finite spirits and in the world at large, especially in human history ; and by which we will, and give a definite result and expression to, our various memories, thinkings, feelings, and intuitions, as waked up by their various special stimulants and by the influence of each upon all the others ; is met by the Mystical and the directly Operative element of Religion." Baron F. von Hugel. (H. 13, Vol. II, p. 390.)

(*i*) " Mysticism consists in the spiritual realisation of a grander and a boundless unity, that humbles all self-assertion by dissolving it in a wider glory. It does not follow that the sense of individuality is necessarily weakened. But habitual contemplation of the Divine unity impresses men with the feeling that individuality is phenomenal only. Hence the paradox of Mysticism. For apart from this phenomenal individuality, we should not know our own nothingness, and personal life is good only through the bliss of being lost in God."

J. A. Picton. (P. 3, p. 356).

(*j*) " Mysticism is the filling of the consciousness with a content (feeling, thought, desire) through involuntary emergence of the same from the Unconscious."

E. von Hartmann.

(H. 12, Section B, IX, *The Unconscious in Mysticism*.)

MYSTICISM AND MIND

(*a*) " The mind must employ some device if its transcendental perceptions—wholly unrelated as they are to the phenomena with which intellect is able to deal—are ever to be grasped by the surface consciousness. Sometimes the symbol and the perception which it represents become fused in that consciousness; and the mystic's experience then presents itself to him as ' visions ' or ' voices ' which we must look upon as the garment he has himself provided to veil that Reality upon which no man may look and live. The nature of this garment will be largely conditioned by his temperament—as in Rolle's evident bias towards music, St. Catherine of Genoa's leaning towards the abstract conceptions of fire and light —and also by his theological education and environment; as in the highly dogmatic visions and auditions of St. Gertrude, Suso, St. Catherine of Siena, the Blessed Angela of Foligno; above all of St. Teresa, whose marvellous self-analyses provide the classic account of these attempts of the mind to translate transcendental intuitions into concepts with which it can deal."

Evelyn Underhill.   (U. 3, p. 93.)

" It seems, then, that this swift and dazzling vision of Divine Personality may represent the true contact of the soul with the Absolute Life—a contact immediately referred to the image under which the Self is accustomed to think of its God.   In the case of Christian contemplatives this image will obviously be most usually the historical Person of Christ, as He is represented in sacred literature and arts."   (*Ibid.*, p. 346.)

(b) " We may legitimately expect a preponderance of Freedom over the understanding in Mysticism, and the term *mystic* should be applied only to minds that have sought the Absolute in other than dialectical ways.   When, after long processes of reasoning, we seem to touch the confines of the purely intelligible in some culminating point of consciousness, we must be careful not to mistake such rational appearance for the *mystic fact*.   To give an example. No one ever tried more eagerly than Saint Augustine to obtain some intuition of God. At the term of all his efforts when he had reached by reflection the 'arbitral' act of Reason, he felt himself powerless to fix that which he believed to be focussed on his inner gaze, and in confusion fell back into the region of images. If mystics get beyond this point, it is by a very special use of the imagination, about which we must learn. Saint Augustine understood it perfectly well, but his purely metaphysical genius did not lend itself to this sort of experience. 'I got as far,' he says, ' as the thinking force which is myself. . . . I had a flashing gleam of you, O my God, and then immediately sinking backward I said, Who can go further? Shall I seek visions? Many have tried them and have found only illusions.' "

E. Récéjac. (R. 4, p. 43.)

(c) " The interpretation of this Vision, however, was conditioned by the ' matter ' of each seer ; he it was who had to clothe the naked beauty of the Truth—as the Gnostic Marcus would have phrased it—with the fairest garment he himself possessed, the highest thoughts, the best science, the fairest traditions, the most grandiose imagination known to him. Thus it is that we have so many modes of expression among the mystics of the time, so many varieties of spiritual experience—not because the experience itself was ' other,' the experience was the ' same ' for all, but the speaking of it forth was conditioned by the religious and philosophical heredity of the seer."

G. R. S. Mead. (M. 6, Vol. II, p. 21.)

MYSTICISM, RATIONAL

(a) " When the most excellent faculties of the soul are conjoined above the utmost heights of virtue in the unity of the spirit the creature feels the touch of God. Only in this region of the unity of the spirit is this contact felt, and this is above the realm of reason, but not alien from it. The illumined reason shares the contact ; in a lesser degree than love feels it, but it is shared, though without power to understand its mode." Ruysbroeck. (H. 5, p. 24.)

(b) " Mysticism is not to be considered in isolation, but must be conceived in its organic connection with the totality of things. Every philosophy, in which mysticism is not a necessary part, must be from the outset defective in its principles ; but conversely, mysticism can no more be arbitrarily extracted from the true view of the Kosmos, than can the focus from an ellipse.

" Mysticism does not stand beside the other phenomena of Nature unconnected with them, but forms the last communication between all phenomena. So far from it being an obsolete view, much rather obsolete are those, though modern, conceptions in which it has no place. So far is mysticism from belonging only to a surmounted past, that much rather will it first attain its full significance in the future. As well the Kantian ' Critique of Reason,' as the physiological theory of sense-perception, and Darwinism, point convergently to a view of the world into which mysticism will be organically fitted."
Carl Du Prel. (D. 2, Vol. I, p. XXVI.)

(c) " That the mystic is dealing with experience, and trying to get experience quite pure and then to make it the means of defining the real, is what we need to observe. That meanwhile the mystic is a very abstract sort of person, I well admit. But he is usually a keen thinker. Only he uses his thinking sceptically, to make naught of other thinkers. He gets his reality not by thinking, but by consulting the date of experience. He is not stupid. And he is trying, very skilfully, to be a pure empiricist. Indeed,

I should maintain that the mystics are the only thorough-going empiricists in the history of philosophy."

Josiah Royce. (R. 6, Vol. I, p. 80.)

" The philosophical mystic, whatever his personal type, and whatever his nation or tongue, always uses the same general metaphysical and dialectical devices. His theoretical weapon is some *reductio ad absurdum* of Realism." (*Ibid.*, p. 176.)

(*d*) " The mystic, then, is not, as such, a visionary; nor has he any interest in appealing to a faculty ' above reason,' if reason is used in its proper sense, as the logic of the whole personality. The desire to find for our highest intuitions an authority wholly external to reason and independent of it,—a ' purely supernatural ' revelation,—has, as Récéjac says, ' been the cause of the longest and the most dangerous of the aberrations from which Mysticism has suffered.' . . . A revelation absolutely transcending reason is an absurdity : no such revelation could ever be made. . . . What we can and must transcend, if we would make any progress in Divine knowledge, is not reason, but the shallow rationalism which regards the data on which we can reason as a fixed quantity, known to all, and which bases itself on a formal logic, utterly unsuited to a spiritual view of things." W. R. Inge. (I. 1, p. 19.)

" When, therefore, Harnack says that ' Mysticism is nothing else than rationalism applied to a sphere above reason,' he would have done better to say that it is ' reason applied to a sphere above rationalism.' " (*Ibid.*, p. 21.)

(*e*) " Perhaps the most exact definition of the Absolute or Perfect Experience would be that it is a sublime passion supremely rational. ' Passion is the highest *reason* in a soul sublime ' (Wordsworth). Now it is into direct experience of this supremely rational, creative passion of the Absolute that the mystic aspires to enter. And, therefore, the logic that is the test of the validity of his rapture is internal, genetic, concrete ; not the merely discursive, conceptual logic of the logician. Let us endeavour once for all to rid our minds of the fallacy that abstract or conceptual logic is the only sort of rationality there is. This is the fatal blunder of the current popular pragmatism."

J. H. Tuckwell. (T. 5, p. 309.)

" Mysticism, then, genuine mysticism, is no bare, ecstatic, religious emotion stript of rationality, if indeed there could be such a thing ; nor does it, strictly speaking, transcend reason. Rather it is, let us repeat once more, a sublime, rational immediacy in which the elements of thought and feeling, after having diverged and been distinguished in our reflective, self-conscious mind, meet and harmoniously blend once more. (*Ibid.*, p. 311.)

MYTHS, THEIR NATURE AND INTENTION

(*a*) " When, therefore, thou hearest the myth-sayings of the Egyptians concerning the Gods—wanderings and dismemberings, and many such passions—thou shouldst remember what has been said above, and think none of these things spoken as they [really] are in state and action."

Plutarch. (M. 6, Vol. I, p. 276.)

" But that these things are not at all like lean tales and quite empty figments, such as poets and prose-writers weave and expand as though they were spiders spinning them out of themselves from a source that has no basis in fact, but that they contain certain informations and statements,—thou knowest of thyself." (*Ibid.*, p. 292.)

" And there are consecrated symbols, some obscure ones and others more plain, guiding the intelligence towards the mysteries of the Gods, [though] not without risk. For some going entirely astray have stepped into superstitions, while others, shunning superstition as a quagmire, have unwittingly fallen into atheism as down a precipice." *(Ibid.*, p. 348.)

(*b*) " What man of sense will suppose that the first and the second and the third day, and the evening and the morning, existed without a sun and moon and stars ? Who is so foolish as to believe that God, like a husbandman, planted a garden in Eden, and placed in it a tree of life, that might be seen and touched, so that one who tasted of the fruit by his bodily lips obtained life ? Or, again, that one was partaker of good and evil by eating that which was taken from a tree ? And if God is said to have walked in a garden in the evening, and Adam to have hidden under a tree, I do not suppose that anyone doubts that these things figuratively indicate certain mysteries, the history being apparently but not literally true. . . . Nay, the Gospels themselves are filled with the same kind of narratives." Origen. (H. 1, p. 78.)

(*c*) " Do not suppose that when God made heaven and earth and all things, He made one thing to-day and another to-morrow. Moses says so, of course, but he knew better ; he only wrote for the sake of the populace, who could not have understood otherwise. God merely *willed*, and the world *was*." Eckhart. (E. 1, p. 162.)

NATURE

(*a*) " AND here lies the true, unchangeable Distinction between God and *Nature,* and the *Natural Creature.* Nature and Creature are only for the *outward Manifestation* of the inward, invisible, unapproachable Powers of God ; they can rise no higher, nor be anything else in themselves, but as Temples, habitations, or Instruments in which the *Supernatural* God, can, and does manifest himself in various Degrees."   Wm. Law.   (L. 6, p. 27.)

(*b*) " Lo ! *Nature* (the only complete, actual poem) existing calmly in the divine scheme, containing all, content, careless of the criticisms of a day, or these endless and wordy chatterers.   And lo ! to the consciousness of the soul, the permanent identity, the thought, the something, before which the magnitude even of Democracy, art, literature, etc., dwindles, becomes partial, measurable —something that fully satisfies (which those do not). That something is the *All* and the idea of *All,* with the accompanying idea of eternity, and of itself, the soul, buoyant, indestructible, sailing Space for ever, visiting every region, as a ship the sea.   And again lo ! the pulsations in all matter, all spirit, throbbing for ever—the eternal beats, eternal systole and diastole of life in things —wherefrom I feel and know that death is not the ending, as was thought, but rather the real beginning—and that nothing ever is or can be lost, nor ever die, nor soul nor matter."   Walt Whitman.   (W. 6, p. 68.)

(*c*) " The world is too much with us ; late and soon,
　　Getting and spending, we lay waste our powers:
　　Little we see in Nature that is ours ;

185

We have given our hearts away, a sordid boon !
This sea that bares her bosom to the moon ;
The winds that will be howling at all hours,
And are up-gathered now like sleeping flowers ;
For this, for every thing, we are out of tune ;
It moves us not.—Great God ! I'd rather be
A Pagan suckled in a creed outworn ;
So might I, standing on this pleasant lea,
Have glimpses that would make me less forlorn ;
Have sight of Proteus rising from the sea ;
Or hear old Triton blow his wreathèd horn."
Wordsworth.—Sonnet XXXIII.   (W. 1, Vol. III, p. 35.)

(d) " The law of continuity furnishes an *a priori* argument
for the position we are attempting to establish of the most
convincing kind—of such a kind, indeed, as to seem to our
mind final. Briefly indicated, the ground taken up is
this, that if Nature be a harmony, Man in all his relations
—physical, mental, moral, and spiritual—falls to be
included within its circle. It is altogether unlikely that
man spiritual should be violently separated in all the
conditions of growth, development, and life, from man
physical. It is, indeed, difficult to conceive that one set
of principles should guide the natural life, and these at a
certain period—the very point where they are needed—
suddenly give place to another set of principles altogether
new and unrelated. Nature has never taught us to expect
such a catastrophe. She has nowhere prepared us for it.
And Man cannot in the nature of things, in the nature of
thought, in the nature of language, be separated into such
incoherent halves." Henry Drummond.   (D. 3, p. 35.)

(e) " Ever more clearly must our age of science realise
that any relation between a material and a spiritual world
cannot be an ethical or emotional relation alone ; that it
must needs be a great structural fact of the Universe,

involving laws as persistent, as identical from age to age, as our known laws of Energy or of Motion."

F. W. H. Myers. (M. 3, Vol. II, p. 288.)

(*f*) "For myself, I am bound to say that the term 'Nature' covers the totality of that which is. The world of psychical phenomena appears to me to be as much part of 'Nature' as the world of physical phenomena; and I am unable to perceive any justification for cutting the Universe into two halves, one natural and the other supernatural." T. H. Huxley. (H. 3, p. 35.)

(*g*)   " Spirit of Nature ! thou
Life of interminable multitudes ,
    Soul of those mighty spheres
Whose changeless paths thro' Heaven's deep
        silence lie ;
    Soul of that smallest being,
    The dwellings of whose life
Is one faint April sun-gleam ;—
    Man, like these passive things,
    Thy will unconsciously fulfilleth."

Shelley. *Queen Mab.*

(*h*) "System of Nature ! To the wisest man, wide as is his vision, Nature remains of quite *infinite* depth, of quite infinite expansion; and all Experience thereof limits itself to some few computed centuries and measured square-miles. The course of Nature's phases, on this our little fraction of a Planet, is partially known to us : but who knows what deeper courses these depend on ; what infinitely larger Cycle (of causes) our little Epicycle revolves on ? To the Minnow every cranny and pebble, and quality and accident, of its little native Creek may have become familiar ; but does the Minnow understand the Ocean Tides and periodic Currents, the Trade-winds, and Monsoons, and Moon's Eclipses ; by all which the condition of its little Creek is regulated, and may, from time to time (*un*-miraculously enough), be quite overset and reversed ? Such a Minnow is Man ; his Creek this Planet Earth ; his Ocean the immeasurable All ; his Monsoons and periodic Currents the mysterious Course of Providence through Æons of Æons.

We speak of the Volume of Nature : and truly a Volume it is,—whose Author and Writer is God. To read it ! Dost thou, does man, so much as well know the Alphabet thereof ? With its Words, Sentences, and grand descriptive Pages, poetical and philosophical, spread out through Solar Systems, and Thousands of Years, we shall not try thee. It is a Volume written in celestial hieroglyphs, in the true Sacred-writing ; of which even Prophets are happy that they can read here a line and there a line. As for your Institutes, and Academies of Science, they strive bravely ; and, from amid the thick-crowded, inextricably intertwisted hieroglyphic writing, pick out, by dextrous combination, some Letters in the vulgar Character, and therefrom put together this and the other economic Recipe, of high avail in Practice. That Nature is more than some boundless Volume of such Recipes, or huge, well-nigh inexhaustible Domestic-Cookery Book, of which the whole secret will in this manner one day evolve itself, the fewest dream." Thomas Carlyle. (C. 7, *Sartor Resartus*, p. 178.)

(*i*) " All nature, as such, is an untrue appearance. It is the way in which a mere part of the Reality shows itself, a way essential and true when taken up into and transcended by a fuller totality, but considered by itself, inconsistent and lapsing beyond its own being."

F. H. Bradley. (B. 30, p. 291.)

" Nature by itself has no reality. It exists only as a form of appearance within the Absolute." (*Ibid.*, p. 293.)

(*j*) " The whole order of nature evinces a progressive march towards *a higher life*. There is design in the action of the seemingly blindest forces. The whole process of evolution, with its endless adaptations, is a proof of this. The immutable laws that weed out the weak and feeble species, to make room for the strong, and which ensure the ' survival of the fittest,' though so cruel in their immediate action—all are working towards the grand end. The very *fact* that adaptations *do* occur, that the fittest *do* survive in the struggle for existence, shows that what is called ' unconscious nature ' is in reality an aggregate of forces manipulated by semi-intelligent beings (Elementals) guided by High Planetary Spirits, (Dhyan Chohans), whose collective aggregate forms the mainfested *verbum* of the unmanifested LOGOS, and constitutes at one and the same time the MIND of the Universe and its immutable LAW."

H. P. Blavatsky. (B. 31, Vol. I, p. 277.)

(*k*) " Help Nature and work on with her ; and Nature will regard thee as one of her creators and make obeisance.

" And she will open wide before thee the portals of her secret chambers, lay bare before thy gaze the treasures hidden in the very depths of her pure virgin bosom. Unsullied by the hand of matter she shows her treasures only to the eye of Spirit—the eye which never closes, the eye for which there is no veil in all her kingdoms.

" Then will she show thee the means and way, the first gate and the second, the third, up to the very seventh. And then, the goal—beyond which lie, bathed in the sunlight of the Spirit, glories untold, unseen by any save the eye of Soul."

H. P. Blavatsky. *The Voice of the Silence.*

(B. 32, p. 14.)

PERCEPTION

(a) " To perceive is to immobilize."

Henri Bergson. (B. 28, p. 275.)

" Our perception outlines, so to speak, the form of their (the individual perceived objects) nucleus ; it terminates them at the point where our possible action upon them ceases, where, consequently, they cease to interest our needs. Such is the primary and most apparent operation of the perceiving mind ; it marks out the divisions in the continuity of the extended, simply following the suggestions of our requirements and the needs of practical life."

(*Ibid.*, p. 227)

" As we have shown, pure perception, which is the lowest degree of mind,—mind without memory—is really part of matter, as we understand matter." (*Ibid.*, p. 297.)

" When we pass from pure perception to memory, we definitely abandon matter for spirit." (*Ibid.*, p. 313.)

" Spirit borrows from matter the perceptions on which it feeds, and restores them to matter in the form of movements which it has stamped with its own freedom."

(*Ibid.*, p. 332.)

PERSONALITY

NOTE ON PERSONALITY

The term *person* in its ordinary acceptation means a distinct individual. You are one person and I am another ; we are two persons, not one person. The root of the word is the Latin *persona*, a mask used by the actors of that time, and is derived from *per*, through, and *sonus*, sound—that is to say, it is something which is sounded *through*.

From the point of view of Mysticism, or of any monistic philosophy which recognises only One Life in the Universe, that of the Absolute or God : this root meaning of the term *person* is perfectly congruous. As individual beings we *are* ' masks ' *through* which the One Life is manifested in an individual manner, while at the same time—as being the real actor or doer—that Life in its own fulness or proper nature is concealed. Even if we go no deeper than the subconscious self of modern psychology, the normal *person* is a ' mask '; and often exhibits but a distorted representation of the deeper Self.

It is evident that in this sense we cannot use the term *person* or *personality* for the Absolute itself. Nevertheless the utmost subtlety of metaphysical dialectic has been used to show that God is a person ; and the doctrine of the Trinity has not merely been the stumbling-block of the plain rational thinker, but also the cause—since the time of Arius—of the utmost bitterness and strife within the Christian Church itself. And yet it is all so unnecessary ! Give your definition of person, and God either is or is not a person in logical accord with that definition. It is thus with all concepts of the mind—they depend in the first instance on definitions ; you simply take out what you put in. The conflict between rationality and theology, however, in the matter of the doctrine of the Trinity lies in the claim of theology to a supernatural revelation. It is only on this basis that theology can claim to be anything different from metaphysical speculation. It is now widely known that the doctrine of the Trinity is one of the oldest concepts in the world, and that it cannot claim any special origin in Biblical revelation. The three persons of the Trinity are in fact a necessity of the mind—which cannot grasp pure unity—and being *aspects* of the one absolute God—or rather Godhead (see p. 82)—they are rightly distinguished as *persons*. They represent the first or initial step which it is necessary for the mind to take from the pure incomprehensible unity of the Godhead, to the more or less comprehensible multiplicity of the Cosmos as it appears in our normal consciousness. Theology, however, has involved the Trinity and the *personality* of God in such an amazing chaos of dogma and superstition, that many otherwise clear thinkers have been utterly misled in dealing with this subject.

The following quotations will, I think, bring out both the philosophical and the mystical aspects of the question.

PERSONALITY

(*a*) " God, according to the Persons, is Everlasting Activity, but according to the Essence and its perpetual stillness, He is Eternal Repose."

Jan van Ruysbroeck.   (R. 1, Vol. I, p. 260.)

(*b*) " Our Idealism especially undertakes to give a theory of the general place and of the significance of Personality in the Universe. Personality to our view, is an essentially ethical category. A Person is a conscious being, whose life, temporally viewed, seeks its completion through deeds, while this same life, eternally viewed, consciously attains its perfection by means of the present knowledge of the whole of its temporary strivings. Now from our point of view, God is a Person. Temporally viewed, his life is that of the entire realm of consciousness in so far as, in its temporal efforts towards perfection, this consciousness of the universe passes from instant to instant of the temporal order, from act to act, from experience to experience, from stage to stage. Eternally viewed, however, God's life is the infinite whole that includes the endless temporal process, and that consciously surveys it as one life, God's own life. God is thus a Person because, for our view, he is self-conscious, and because the Self of which he is conscious is a Self whose eternal perfection is attained through the totality of those ethically significant temporal strivings, these processes of evolution, these linked activities of finite Selves." Josiah Royce. (R. 3, Vol. II, p. 418.)

" Man, too, in our view, is a Person. He is not, indeed, an Absolute Person ; for he needs his conscious contrast with his fellows, and with the whole of the rest of the universe, to constitute him what he is. He is, however, a conscious being, whose life, temporally viewed, seeks its completion through deeds. From the eternal point of view this same life of the individual man, viewed as intentionally contrasted with the life of all the rest of the world, consciously attains its perfection by means of the knowledge of the whole of its temporal strivings." (*Ibid.*, p. 425.)

(c) " Of course the Absolute has personality, but it fortunately possesses so much more, that to call it personal would be as absurd as to ask if it is moral."

F. H. Bradley. (B. 30, p. 173.)

" The Absolute . . . is not personal, because it is personal and more. It is, in a word, super-personal."

(*Ibid.*, p. 531.)

(d) " What, then, is God ? Spirit ; essential substance. Is God, then, impersonal ? Impersonal if the word *persona* be taken in its radical meaning, but personal in the highest and truest sense of that word if the conception be of essential consciousness. God is a pure and naked fire burning in infinity, whereof a flame subsists in all creatures. The Kosmos is a tree having innumerable branches, each connected with and springing out of various boughs, and these again originating in one stem, and nourished by one root. And God is as a fire burning in this tree, and yet consuming it not. God is ' I AM.' Such is the nature of infinite and essential being. And such is God in the beginning before the worlds."

Anna Kingsford. (K. 3, p. 166.)

(e) " Besides, if we think of it, it would be monstrous

13

and inexplicable that we should be only what we appear to be, nothing but ourselves, whole and complete in ourselves, separated, isolated, circumscribed by our body, our mind, our consciousness, our birth and our death.   We become possible and probable only on the condition that we project beyond ourselves on every side, and that we stretch in every direction throughout time and space."

Maurice Maeterlinck.   (M. 9, p. 322.)

(*f*) " The falling apart of one Subject into two Persons, which is a fact in the empirical sense, is at least possible in the metaphysical sense.   It may seem a paradoxical suggestion that the man of manifest consciousness is only one person of a Subject, whose other persons belong at the same time to another order of things—to a metaphysical world ; but the fact of double consciousness within the empirical personality shows at least that there is no *psychological* difficulty in the conception."

Carl Du Prel.   (D. 2, Vol. II, p. 69.)

(*g*) " It is only on the analogy of human personality that we can conceive of the perfect personality of God ; and without personality the universe falls to pieces.   Personality is not only the strictest unity of which we have any experience ; it is the fact which creates the postulate of unity on which all philosophy is based.

" But it is possible to save personality without regarding the human spirit as a monad, independent and sharply separated from other spirits.   Distinction, not separation, is the mark of personality ; but it is separation, not distinction, that forbids union.   The error, according to the mystic's psychology, is in regarding consciousness of self as the measure of personality.   The depths of personality are unfathomable, as Heraclitus already knew ; the light of consciousness only plays on the surface of the waters. Jean Paul Richter is a true exponent of this characteristic doctrine when he says. ' We attribute far too small dimensions to the rich empire of ourself, if we omit from it the unconscious region which resembles a great dark continent. The world which our memory peoples only reveals, in its revolution, a few luminous points at a time, while its immense and teeming mass remains in the shade. . . . We daily see the conscious passing into unconsciousness ; and take no notice of the bass accompanyment which our fingers continue to play, while our attention is directed to fresh musical effects.' So far is it from being true that the self of our immediate consciousness is our true personality, that we can only attain personality, as spiritual and rational beings, by passing beyond the limits which mark us off as separate individuals. Separate individuality, we may say, is the bar which prevents us from realising our true privileges as persons.

"Lotze also says, ' Within us lurks a world whose form we imperfectly apprehend, and whose working, when in particular phases it comes under our notice, surprises us with fore-shadowings of unknown depths in our being.' "

W. R. Inge. (I. 1, p. 30.)

"Personality escapes from all attempts to limit and define it. It is a concept which stretches into the infinite, and therefore can only be represented to thought symbolically." (*Ibid.*, p. 366.)

"If it be further asked, Which is our personality, the shifting *moi* (as Fénelon calls it), or the ideal self, the end or the developing states ? we must answer that it is both and neither, and that the root of mystical religion is in the conviction that it is at once both and neither. The *moi* strives to realise its end, but the end being an infinite one, no process can reach it. Those who have "counted themselves to have apprehended" have thereby left the mystical faith ; and those who from the notion of a *progressus ad infinitum* come to the pessimistic conclusion, are

equally false to the mystical creed, which teaches us that
we are already potentially what God intends us to become."

(Ibid., p. 33.)*

(*h*) " The true understanding of personality becomes
clearer to you as you realise your relationship to the whole.
Your vision clears, you become filled with holy reverence
and mighty hope. Personality is greater than you know,
for the weakest person has the whole universe to draw
upon—is entirely unlimited."

" *Christ in You.*"   (C. 10, p. 35.)

PLANETARY SPHERES

(*a*) " The revolutions of the heavenly *Bodies*, therefore,
being from the first set in the celestial revolutions of the
æthereal *Soul*, for ever continue in this relationship ; while
the *Souls* of the [invisible] worlds, extending to their
[common] *Mind*, are completely surrounded by it, and from
the beginning have their birth *in* it. And *Mind* in like
manner, both partially and as a whole, is also contained in
superior states of existence."

Jamblichus.   (M. 6, Vol. III, p. 299.)

(*b*) " We say that [the Spiritual Sun and Moon, and the
rest] are so far from being contained within their Bodies,
that on the contrary, it is they who contain these Bodies
of theirs within the Spheres of their own vitality and
energy. And so far are they from tending towards their
Bodies, that the tendency of these very Bodies is towards
their Divine Cause. Moreover, their Bodies do not impede
the perfection of their Spiritual and Incorporeal Nature or
disturb it by being situated in it."

Jamblichus.   (M. 6, Vol. III, p. 300.)

(*c*) " Each of the [Seven] Planetary Spheres is a complete
World containing a number of divine offspring, which are

invisible to us, and over all of these Spheres the Star we
see is the Ruler.   Now Fixed Stars differ from those in the
Planetary Spheres in that the former have but one Monad,
namely, their system as a whole ; while the latter, namely,
the invisible globes in each of the Planetary Spheres, which
globes have an orbit of their own determined by the
revolution of their respective Spheres, have a double
Monad—namely, their system as a whole, and that domi-
nant characteristic which has been evolved by selection
in the several spheres of the system.   For since globes are
secondary to Fixed Stars they require a double order of
government, first subordination to their system as a
whole, and then subordination to their respective spheres.
And that in each of these spheres there is a host on the
same level with each, you may infer from the extremes.
For if the Fixed Sphere has a host on the same level as
itself, the Earth has a host of earthy animals, just as the
former a host of heavenly animals, it is necessary that
every whole should have a number of animals on the same
level with itself ; indeed it is because of the latter fact that
they are called wholes.   The intermediate levels, however,
are outside the range of our senses, the extremes only being
visible, the one through the transcendent brilliance of its
nature, the other through its kinship with ourselves."

Proclus.   (M. 6, Vol. III, p. 300.)

REASON

(*a*) " You ask, how can we know the Infinite ? I answer, not by reason. It is the office of reason to distinguish and define. The Infinite, therefore, cannot be ranked among its objects. You can only apprehend the Infinite by a faculty superior to reason, by entering into a state in which you are your finite self no longer, in which the Divine Essence is communicated to you. This is ecstasy. It is the liberation of your mind from its finite anxieties. Like only can apprehend like. When you thus cease to be finite, you become one with the Infinite. In the reduction of your soul to its simplest self (ἐπλωσις), its divine essence, you realise this Union, nay this Identity (ἔνωσις)."

Plotinus. (M. 4, p. 432.)

(*b*) " It is in vain that we pretend to arrive at the fulness of truth by reasoning. By this way we reach only rational truth ; still it is infinitely precious, and full of resources against the assaults of false philosophy. The natural lights of every man of aspiration have indeed no other font, and it is therefore of almost universal use ; but it cannot impart that sentiment and tact of active and radical truth from which our nature should derive its life and being. This kind of truth is given of itself alone. Let us make ourselves simple and childlike, and our faithful guide will cause us to feel its sweetness. If we profit by these first graces, we shall taste very soon those of the pure spirit, afterwards those of the Holy Spirit, then those of the Supreme Sanctity, and, lastly in the interior man we shall behold the all."

Louis Claud de Saint-Martin. (W. 2, p. 359.)

(c) " When each fact and end has foregone its claim, as such, to be ultimate or reasonable, then reason and harmony in the highest sense has begun to appear."

F. H. Bradley.   (B. 30, p. 429.)

See INTELLECT (p. 127.)

REALITY

(a) " The real whole might well be, we conceive, an indivisible continuity. The systems we cut out within it would, properly speaking, not then be *parts* at all ; they would be *partial views* of the whole. And with these partial views put end to end, you will not make even a beginning of the reconstruction of the whole, any more than, by multiplying photographs of an object in a thousand different aspects, you will reproduce the object itself."   Henri Bergson.   (B. 27, p. 32.)

" A philosophy which sees in *duration* the very stuff of reality."   (*Ibid.* p. 287.)

" He who installs himself in becoming sees in duration the very life of things, the fundamental reality."

(*Ibid.*, p. 334.)

" In the absolute we live and move and have our being. The knowledge we possess of it is incomplete, no doubt, but not external or relative. It is reality itself, in the profoundest meaning of the word, that we reach by the combined and progressive development of science and philosophy. . . . An identical process must have cut out matter and the intellect, at the same time, from a stuff that contained both. Into this reality we shall get back more and more completely, in proportion as we compel ourselves to transcend pure intelligence." (*Ibid.*, p. 210.)

(b) " Ultimate Reality is such that it does not contradict itself . . . and it is proved absolute by the fact that, either in endeavouring to deny it, or even in attempting to doubt it, we tacitly assume its validity."

F. H. Bradley.   (B. 30, p. 136.)

" Reality, set on one side and apart from appearance, would assuredly be nothing."   (*Ibid.*, p. 132.)

" The character of the real is to possess everything phenomenal in a harmonious form."   (*Ibid.*, p. 140.)

" The Reality, on the one hand, is no finite existence, and, on the other hand, every predicate—no matter what —must both fall within and must qualify Reality."

(*Ibid.*, p. 541.)

RELIGION

(*a*) " True religion is sense and taste for the infinite."

Schleiermacher.   (C. 3, p. 264.)

" The sum total of religion is to feel that, in its highest unity, all that moves us in feeling is one ; to feel that aught singular and particular is only possible by means of this unity ; to feel, that is to say, that our being and living is a being and living in and through God."

(*Ibid.*, p. 275.)

" The true nature of religion is neither this idea nor any other, but immediate consciousness of the Deity as He is found in ourselves and in the world."   (*Ibid.*, p. 303.)

(*b*) " We shall see how infinitely passionate a thing religion in its highest flights can be.   Like love, like wrath, like hope, ambition, jealousy, like every other instinctive eagerness and impulse, it adds to life an enchantment which is not rationally or logically deducible from anything else.   This enchantment, coming as a gift when it does come,—a gift of our organism, the physiologists will tell us, a gift of God's grace, the theologians say,—is either there or not there for us, and there are persons who can no more become possessed by it than they can fall in love with a

given woman by mere word of command. Religious
feeling is thus an absolute addition to the Subject's range
of life. It gives him a new sphere of power. When the
outward battle is lost, and the outer world disowns him, it
redeems and vivifies an interior world which otherwise
would be an empty waste." William James. (J. 5, p. 47.)

" Both thought and feeling are determinants of conduct,
and the same conduct may be determined either by feeling
or by thought. When we survey the whole field of religion,
we find a great variety in the thoughts that have prevailed
there ; but the feelings on the one hand and the conduct on
the other are almost always the same, for Stoic, Christian,
and Buddhist saints are practically indistinguishable in
their lives. The theories which Religion generates, being
thus variable, are secondary ; and if you wish to grasp
her essence, you must look to the feelings and the conduct
as being the more constant elements. It is between these
two elements that the short circuit exists on which she
carries on her principal business, while the ideas and
symbols and other institutions form loop-lines which may
be perfections and improvements, and may even some day
all be united into one harmonious system, but which are not
to be regarded as organs with an indispensible function,
necessary at all times for religious life to go on."

(*Ibid.*, p. 504.)

(c) " The ripeness of Religion is doubtless to be looked
for in this field of individuality, and is a result that no
organisation or church can ever achieve. As history is
poorly retained by what the technists call history, and is
not given out from their pages, except the learner has in
himself the sense of the well-wrapt, never yet written,
perhaps impossible to be written, history—so Religion,
although casually arrested, and, after a fashion preserved
in the churches and creeds, does not depend at all upon

them, but is a part of the identified soul, which, when greatest, knows not bibles in the old way, but in new ways —the identified soul, which can really confront Religion when it extricates itself entirely from the churches, and not before. Personalism fuses this, and favours it. I should say, indeed, that only in the perfect uncontamination and solitariness of individuality may the spirituality of Religion positively come forth at all. Only here, and on such terms, the meditation, the devout ecstasy, the soaring flight. Only here, communion with the mysteries, the eternal problems, whence ? whither ? Alone, and identity, and the mood—and the soul emerges, and all statements, churches, sermons, melt away like vapours. Alone, and silent thought and awe, and aspiration—and then the interior consciousness, like a hitherto unseen inscription, in magic ink, beams out its wondrous lines to the sense. Bibles may convey, and priests expound. but it is exclusively for the noiseless operation of one's isolated Self, to enter the pure ether of veneration, reach the divine levels, and commune with the unutterable."

Walt Whitman.   (W. 6, p. 333.)

(d) " What you call religion I call only a reasoning about religion. The dogmas and creeds are not religion. They are summaries of the reasons that men give to explain those facts of life which are religion, just as philosophies are summaries of the theories men make to explain other facts of life. Both creeds and philosophies come from the reason. They are speculations, not facts. They are pessimistic twins of the brain. Religion is a different matter. It is a series of facts."

H. Fielding.   (F. 2, p. 281.)

" Religion is not reason ; it is fact. It is beyond and before all reason. Religion is not what you say, but what you feel ; not what you think, but what you know.

Religions are the great optimisms. Each is to its believers
' the light of the world.' " *(Ibid.,* p. 284.)

" Religion is the recognition and cultivation of our
highest emotions, of our most beautiful instincts, of all
that we know is best in us." *(Ib:d,,* p. 298.)

" Religion is the music of the infinite echoed from the
hearts of men." *(Ibid.,* p. 312.)

(*e*) " True religious worship does not consist in the
acknowledgment of a greatness which is estimated by
comparison, but rather in the sense of a Being who surpasses
all comparison, because He gives to phenomenal existence
the only reality they can know. Hence the deepest
religious feeling necessarily shrinks from thinking of God
as a kind of gigantic Self amidst a host of minor selves.
The very thought of such a thing is a mockery of the
profoundest devotion." J. A. Picton. (P. 3, p. 356.)

(*f*) " For practical religion, the symbol which we shall
find most helpful is that of a progressive transformation of
our nature after the pattern of God revealed in Christ ; a
process which has as its end a real union with God, though
this end is, from the nature of things, unrealisable in time.
It is, as I have said in the body of the Lectures, a *progressus
ad infinitum*, the consummation of which we are nevertheless entitled to claim as already ours in a transcendental
sense, in virtue of the eternal purpose of God made known
to us in Christ." W. R. Inge. (I. 1, p. 367.)

REGENERATION

(*a*) " There is an eternal in the temporal body, which
verily disappeared in Adam as to the eternal light, which
must also be born again through Christ."
Jacob Böhme. (B. 7, VIII, 15.)

(b) " Such a man as Adam was before his Eve, shall arise again, enter into, and eternally possess, Paradise."

Jacob Böhme. (B. 7, XVIII, 3.)

(c) " The new man is not only a spirit ; he is even flesh and blood, as the gold in the stone is not only spirit ; it hath a body, but not such a one as the rude drossy stone is, but a body which subsisteth in the centre of nature, in the fire ; whose body the fire cannot consume."

Jacob Böhme. (B. 5, Part I, ch. XIV, 22, 23.)

(d) " The possibility of the new birth is in all men, else God were divided, and not in one place as He is in another."

Jacob Bohme. (B. 5, Part I, XIV, 59.)

(e) " Out of man's willing must God's spirit become generated ; it must itself become God in the willing spirit or else it attaineth not divine substantiality."

Jacob Böhme. (B. 5, Part II, X, 56.)

(f) " In that manner as precious pure gold lieth and groweth in a gross, drossy, dirty stone, wherein the drossiness helpeth to work, though it be not at all like the gold ; so also must the earthly body help to generate Christ in itself."   Jacob Böhme. (B. 14, III, 92.)

(g) " Most of the Gnostics held that in the spiritual rebirth something most real in all senses, some *substantial* as well as moral change, was wrought in them. If we read them aright, they believed that with truly spiritual ' repentance,' or the ' turning-back ' of the whole nature to God, that is with effective moral regeneration, the actual body or ground of resurrection was substantially brought to birth in them. Was this, then, simply some subtle body of identical or even somewhat changed physical form, capable of manifesting more extended powers than the ' flesh ' ? Yes and No. It was not *a* body in any order of subtle bodies in immediate sequence with the physical body, of which so much is heard among the psychics of all ages. It was rather the source of every possibility of embodiment,—the germ-ground, or *seminarium*, from which all such bodies could be produced."

G. R. S. Mead. (M. 5, p. 134.)

(*h*) " O Primal Origin of my origination ; Thou Primal Substance of my substance. First Breath of breath, the breath that is in me ; First Fire, God-given for the Blending of the blendings in me, First fire of fire in me ; First Water of my water, the water in me ; Primal Earth-essence of the earthy essence in me ; Thou Perfect Body of me ! . . . If, verily, it may seem good to you, translate me, now held in my lower nature, unto the Generation that is free from Death. In order that, beyond the insistent Need that presses on me, I may have Vision of the Deathless Source, by virtue of the Deathless Water, by virtue of the Deathless Solid, and by virtue of the Deathless Air. In order that I may become re-born in Mind ; in order that I may become initiate, and that the Holy Breath may breathe in me. In order that I may admire the Holy Fire ; that I may see the Deep of the [New] Dawn, the Water that doth cause the Soul to thrill ; and that the Life-bestowing Æther which surrounds all things may give me Hearing."

Mithriac Ritual. (M. 5, p. 137.)

REINCARNATION AND KARMA

NOTE ON REINCARNATION AND KARMA

To-day we have an extensive resuscitation and acceptance, mainly through the teachings of Theosophy, of the Eastern doctrine of Reincarnation, and its associated doctrine of Karma, or the law of inevitable cause and effect operating in the present *fate* of every individual as the result of actions in previous incarnations.

The doctrine, however, to be rightly understood, must

not be taken in its crudely exoteric form, as if it were the conventional ' I,' the lower personality which reincarnates. It may be as well therefore in this respect to consider the doctrine in the first instance in its cosmic aspect. In so far as the universe of matter and form is the expression of an indwelling universal LIFE, commonly called GOD ; and in so far as that LIFE is continuous, whilst matter and form are constantly being destroyed, so that Solar Systems, and even whole Universes come into and go out of existence periodically : we must consider in connection with the individual that we have the reflection in the microcosm of the macrocosmic *PRINCIPLE* of reincarnation , for so is the universe built up and constituted from centre to circumference : circle within circle, and cycle within cycle.

But the question as to *what* it is that reincarnates in the individual so as to enable him to say that ' he ' did so and so in his past incarnation to merit what is now happening to ' him,' is by no means an easy one to answer, for it involves some profound metaphysical questions as to the nature of the individual Ego, or Soul, and as to the relation which exists between the higher and the lower *self*.

What that relation is must be left, therefore, to the intuition of the reader of this work to apprehend as he may from what has herein been set forth of the mystical teaching concerning the nature of Man in his unity with the Universe, or with God who *is* the Universe—and which runs as a golden thread through the whole of this present work.

Special attention may be called to this subject under the headings of Death and after Death States (p. 54) ; Oneness of Man and God (p. 92) ; Man and the Universe (p. 156) ; Personality (p. 190) ; Self-knowledge (p. 212) ; Higher and Lower Self (p. 216) ; and Nature of the Soul (p. 229).

REINCARNATION AND KARMA

(a) " Such things, however, as happen to the good

without justice, as punishments, or poverty, or disease, may be said to take place through offences committed in a former life." Plotinus. Enn. IV, 3, 16. (P. 2, p. 229.)

(b) " There are, likewise, in the world, not only statues of the Gods, but the Gods themselves, beholding from on high, who easily, as it is said, escape the accusations of men, since they conduct all things in order from the beginning to the end, and distribute an appropriate allotment to every one, conformable to the mutations of lives, and to actions in a pre-existent state ; of which he who is ignorant, is of all men the most rash and rustic in divine concerns." Plotinus. Enn. II. 9, 9. (P. 2, p. 60.)

(c) " The present inequalities of circumstances and character are thus not wholly explicable within the sphere of the present life. But this world is not the only world. Every soul has existed from the beginning ; it has therefore passed through some worlds already, and will pass through others before it reaches the final consummation. It comes into this world strengthened by the victories or weakened by the defeats of its previous life. Its place in this world as a vessel appointed to honour or dishonour is determined by its previous merits or demerits. Its work in this world determines its place in the world which is to follow this."
Origen. (H. 1, p. 235.)

(d) " The Books say well, my Brothers ! each man's life
The outcome of his former living is ;
The bygone wrongs bring forth sorrows and woes,
The bygone right breeds bliss.

" That which ye sow ye reap. See yonder fields !
The sesamum was sesamum, the corn
Was corn. The Silence and the Darkness knew !
So is a man's fate born.

" He cometh, reaper of the things he sowed,
　　Sesamum, corn, so much cast in past birth ;
And so much weed and poison-stuff, which mar
　　Him and the aching earth."
　　　　　　The Light of Asia.   (A. 2, Book VIII.)

(*e*) " So if thou seekest fame or ease or pleasure or aught for thyself, the image of that thing which thou seekest will come and cling to thee—and thou wilt have to carry it about;

" And the images and powers which thou hast evoked will gather round and form for thee a new body—clamouring for sustenance and satisfaction ;

" And if thou are not able to discard this image now, thou wilt not be able to discard that body then ; but wilt have to carry it about.

" Beware then lest it become thy grave and thy prison —instead of thy winged abode, and palace of joy."
　　　　　　Ed. Carpenter.   (C. 2, p. 361.)

(*f*)　　　" Nay, but as when one layeth
　　　　　　His worn-out robes away,
　　　　And, taking new ones, sayeth,
　　　　　' These will I wear to-day ! '
　　　So putteth by the spirit
　　　　　Lightly its garb of flesh,
　　　And passeth to inherit
　　　　　A residence afresh."
　　　　　　The Song Celestial.   (A. 1, p. 13.)

(*g*) " I died from the mineral and became a plant ;
　　　I died from the plant and re-appeared in an animal ;
　　　I died from the animal and became a man ;
　　　Wherefore then should I fear ?   When did I grow
　　　　　less by dying ?
　　　Next time I shall die from the man
　　　That I may grow the wings of angels.

From the angel, too, must I seek advance ;
' *All things shall perish save His Face.*' [1]
Once more shall I wing my way above the angels ;
I shall become that which entereth not the
    imagination.
Then let me become naught, naught ; for the harp-string
Crieth unto me ' Verily unto Him do we return ! ' "

                      Jalālū'd-Din Rūmi.

(*h*) " The inability of the vast majority of persons to remember their previous existences is due to the fact that the return is that only of the permanent ego or soul, and not of the external personality ; and that they are very few in number who succeed during life in establishing with their soul relations so intimate as to gain cognisance of their soul's history.　But the fact that the outer personality is left thus uninformed on the subject, in no way invalidates either the truth or the value of reincarnation, since the function of the body is to serve as an instrument by and through which the soul obtains experiences, and the end of those experiences is attained when the soul applies them to its own advancement.　Nor is the fact—if it be a fact —that but comparatively few of the spirits with whom intercourse is held admit the doctrine, valid as an argument against it, since the agent of such communication is rarely the soul itself but only its astral envelope, and this is in no better position than the material body to pronounce upon the question."　Anna Kingsford.　(K. 3, p. XXXIII.)

(*i*) In the doctrine of transmigration, whatever its origin, Brahminical and Buddhist speculation found, ready to hand, the means of constructing a plausible vindication of the ways of the cosmos to man. . . .　Whether the cosmic process looks any more moral than at first, after such a vindication, may perhaps be questioned.　Yet this plea of justification is not less plausible than others ; and none but very hasty thinkers will reject it on the ground of inherent absurdity. Like the doctrine of evolution itself, that of transmigration has its roots in the world of reality ; and it may claim such support as the great argument from analogy is capable of supplying." T. H. Huxley. (H. 2, pp. 60, 61.)

(7) " It is only the knowledge of the constant rebirths of one and the same individuality throughout the life-cycle ; the assurance that the same MONADS—among whom are many Dhyan-Chohans, or the ' Gods ' themselves—have to pass through the ' Circle of Necessity,' rewarded or punished by such rebirth for the suffering endured or crimes committed in the former life ; that those very Monads, which entered the empty, senseless shells, or astral figures of the First Race emanated by the Pitris, are the same who are now amongst us—nay, we ourselves, perchance ; it is only this doctrine, we say, that can explain to us the mysterious problem of Good and Evil, and reconcile man to the terrible and *apparent* injustice of life. Nothing but such certainty can quiet our revolted sense of justice. For, when one unacquainted with the noble doctrine looks around him, and observes the inequalities of birth and fortune, of intellect and capacities ; when one sees honour paid to fools and profligates, on whom fortune has heaped her favours by mere privilege of birth, and their nearest neighbour, with all his intellect and noble virtues —far more deserving in every way—perishing for want or for lack of sympathy ; when one sees all this and has to turn away, helpless to relieve the undeserved suffering, one's ears ringing and heart aching with the cries of pain around him—that blessed knowledge of Karma alone prevents him from cursing life and men, as well as their supposed Creator."

(*k*) " Intimately, or rather indissolubly, connected with Karma, then, is the law of re-birth, or of the re-incarnation of the same spiritual individuality in a long, almost interminable, series of personalities. The latter are like the various costumes and characters played by the same actor, with each of which that actor identifies himself and is identified by the public, for the space of a few hours. The *inner*, or real man, who personates those characters, knows the whole time that he is Hamlet for the brief space of a few acts, which, represent, however, on the plane of human illusion the whole life of Hamlet. And he knows that he was, the night before, King Lear, the transformation in his turn of the Othello of a still earlier preceding night ; but the outer, visible character is supposed to be ignorant of the fact. In actual life that ignorance is, unfortunately, but too real. Nevertheless, the *permanent* individuality is fully aware of the fact, though, through the atrophy of the ' spiritual ' eye in the physical body, that knowledge is unable to impress itself on the consciousness of the false personality." H. P. Blavatsky. (B. 31, Vol. II, p. 306.)

(*l*) " You will see that for logic, consistency, profound philosophy, divine mercy and equity, this doctrine of Reincarnation has not its equal on earth. It is a belief in a perpetual progress for each incarnating Ego, or divine soul, in an evolution from the outward into the inward, from the material to the Spiritual, arriving at the end of each stage at absolute unity with the divine Principle. From strength to strength, from the beauty and perfection of one plane to the greater beauty and perfection of another, with accessions of new glory, of fresh knowledge and power in each cycle, such is the destiny of every Ego, which thus becomes its own Saviour in each world and incarnation."

H. P. Blavatsky. (B. 33, p. 154.)

SELF-KNOWLEDGE

(a) " He who knows himself, will also know from whence he is derived." Plotinus. Enn. VI. 9, 8. (P. 2, p. 314.)

(b) *Cogito, ergo sum.*

" For if the Self [that is Brahman] also [like ether, wind, fire, water, earth] were a modification, then, since the Scripture teaches nothing higher above it, every effect from ether downwards would be without Self (*nirâtmaka*, soulless, essenceless), since the Self [also] would be [only] an effect ; and thus we should arrive at Nihilism. Just because it is the Self, it is not possible to doubt the Self. For one cannot establish the Self [by proof] in the case of anyone, because in itself it is already known. For the Self is not demonstrated by proof of itself. For it is that which brings into use all means of proof, such as perception and the like, in order to prove a thing which is not known. For the objects of the expressions ether, etc., require a proof, because they are not assumed as known of themselves. But the Self is the basis of the action of proving, and consequently it is evident before the action of proving. And since it is of this character, it is therefore impossible to deny it. For we can call in question something, which comes to us [from outside], but not that which is our own being. For it is even the own being of him who calls it in question ; fire cannot call its own heat in question. And further, when it is said : ' It is I, who now know what at present exists, it is I, who knew the past, and what was before the past, it is I, who shall know the future and what is after the future,' it is implied in these words that even when the object of knowledge alters, the knower does not alter, because he is in the past, future, and present ; *for his essence is eternally present* ; therefore, even when the body turns to ashes, there is no passing away of the Self for its essence is the present, yea, it is not even for a moment thinkable, that this essence should be anything else than this." Sankara. (D. 4, p. 127.)

(c) " We have shown how the viewing of things from without, whether by the subjective method of Kant or the objective method of empirical science, leads finally to an inscrutable entity (the thing-in-itself, affection, force), which is for ever unattainable by way of external experience. For wherever we may turn to grasp the thing-in-itself— there stand ever between it and ourselves, as a darkening medium, the innate forms of our intellect, showing us how it appears in time, space and causality, but not what it is in itself.   All things in the world are accessible to me only from without—with one exception.   This exception is my own self (*Atman*), which I am able to comprehend *firstly*, like everything else, from without, and *secondly*, unlike anything else, from within. . . .   My ego, as object of inner experience, is free from space and causality, and there remains only the form of time in which expanded inner experience is reflected in the intellect.   Thus time is the only barrier which hinders me from knowing by the inner view, what I am as thing-in-itself."
Paul Deussen.   (D. 5, p. 103—pars. 146, 147.)

(d) " For, of a truth, thoroughly to know oneself, is above all art, for it is the highest art.   If thou knowest thyself well, thou art better and more praiseworthy before God, than if thou didst not know thyself, but didst understand the course of the heavens and of all the planets and stars. . . .   For it is said, there came a voice from heaven, saying, ' Man, know thyself.'   Thus that proverb is still true, 'Going out were never so good, but staying at home were much better.' "

Theologia Germanica.   (T. 1, p. 28.)

(*e*) " As the world is the object of consciousness, so is the Ego the object of self-consciousness.   As consciousness seeks logically to penetrate its object, the world, and to determine its content, so also self-consciousness the Ego. In the latter undertaking, almost everything has still to be done. . . .   The philosophy of the next century will undoubtedly include in its programme, as a pendant to the Kantian problem, the as yet scarcely propounded question, *whether self-consciousness exhausts its object.*   Such a question is just as warrantable in regard to subjective as to objective consciousness, and we have every reason to expect that in both cases the answer must be negative ; thus, that the like relation exists between consciousness and the world, and between self-consciousness and the Ego. Self-consciousness may be as inadequate to the Ego, as consciousness to the world ; or the Ego may as much exceed self-consciousness as the world exceeds consciousness. . . .   If the existence of a transcendental world follows from the theory of knowledge accepted in this century, the theory of self-knowledge which will belong to the next century will bring with it the recognition of a transcendental Ego. . . .   The question of the soul, which has been stationary for centuries, would be advanced to a wholly new stage if it could be shown that self-consciousness only partially comprehends its object, whereby, indeed, the stumbling-block, Dualism, would be removed, and the question solved in the sense of Monism."

Carl Du Prel.   (D. 2, Vol. I, pp. 11, 12, 13.)

(*f*) " Your true consciousness is the knowledge that One and One only fills all space.   When you silently think of this you will know that in this understanding, in this continual realisation, true freedom lies.   You will cast off everything alien to this ; nay, you will transmute the very sins and ignorances into the pure gold and wealth of life. These must be the healing of the self by the Self, the forgiveness, the whole redemption from your Christ, your indwelling Lord.   You are in all and through all, in every place, since hidden within yourself is the centre of all worlds."

" Christ in You."   (C. 10, p. 174.)

" It is the silent, creative great One, dwelling in the abyss of each, in whom we live and have our being."

(*Ibid.*, p. 185.)

SELF, HIGHER AND LOWER

NOTE ON THE HIGHER AND THE LOWER SELF

A clear realisation of the distinction between the higher and the lower self, and yet of their essential unity, is the golden key which unlocks every riddle of our existence. The higher Self is, yet is not, the lower self : in just the same sense that God is, yet is not, the manifested universe.

The lower self corresponds with, and is the product of the manifested universe.   As such it is subject to cyclic law : to birth and death, to appearance and disappearance, to good and evil, and to all the pairs of opposites which constitute the very essence of manifestation.   But the higher Self is subject to none of these, for in its essential oneness with God it is transcendent, yet it is also at the same time immanent in the lower self, the microcosm, even as God is immanent in the manifested universe, the macrocosm, yet remains eternally transcendental in His own BEING.

BEING and BECOMING, or manifestation, are the contrasted aspects—created by the inherent duality of the mind—of the One eternal, immutable, absolute BENESS ; and, in the words of the ancient *Upanishad* " THAT ART THOU."   (See p. 157.)

The following quotations will serve to show very clearly how this has been recognised by mystical and philosophical writers in all ages. It should be linked up with the teaching of the " Christ in You " ; and the " salvation " or " redemption " of the lower self by a transformation or transmutation of that self into the full consciousness of the eternal, immortal Higher Self. Only that is immortal which is inherently so, and so long as we cling to the lower self that immortality is never achieved, even though the lower self may survive physical death, and last for ages as we reckon time.

If the Church would teach this, and restore to man the glorious dignity of his higher divine nature—which is the whole object of the New Testament Scriptures—instead of accentuating his lower nature, " rubbing it into him," so to speak, and making his " salvation " depend upon a particular historical event, she would quickly regain her rightful functions, and regenerate the world.

See further THE ONE SELF (p. 226), and NATURE OF SOUL (p. 229).

SELF, HIGHER AND LOWER

(a) " Joined to the Gods by his cognate divinity, a man looks down upon the part of him by means of which he's common with the Earth." Hermes. (M. 1, Vol. II, p. 316.)

" For man is the sole animal that is twofold. One part of him is simple : the [man] ' essential,' as say the Greeks, but which we call the ' form of the Divine Similitude.' "

(*Ibid.*, p. 319.)

(b) " For the unreal there is no being, nor any end of being for the real ; the truth as to these two is seen by those who behold reality.

" But know THAT to be imperishable whereby all this is stretched forth ; and none can cause the destruction of the everlasting.

" These temporal bodies are declared to belong to the eternal lord of the body ; imperishable, immeasurable ; therefore fight, O son of Bharata !

" He who sees him as slayer, or who thinks of him as slain, both understand not ; he slays not nor is slain.

" He is never born nor dies, nor will he, having being, evermore cease to be ; unborn, eternal, immemorial, this Ancient is not slain when the body is slain.

" He who knows this imperishable, eternal, unborn, and passing not away : how can that man, O son of Pritha, slay any, or cause any to be slain ?

" As putting off worn garments, a man takes others new ; so putting off worn-out bodies, the lord of the body enters others new.

" Swords cut him not, nor may fire burn him, O son of Bharata, waters wet him not, nor dry winds parch.

" He may not be cut nor burned nor wet nor withered ; he is eternal, all-present, firm, unshaken, everlasting.

" He is called unmanifest, unimaginable, unchanging ; therefore, knowing him thus, deign not to grieve ! "

Bhagavad Gita.   II, 16–25.   (J. 7, p. 43.)

(c) " Now there are two modes of life, the first of the First and the second of the Second God.   For it is evident that the First God should be standing and the second, on the contrary, moved.   The First, then, is occupied about things intelligible, and the Second about things intelligible and sensible.

" Marvel not that I say this ; for thou shalt hear what is still more marvellous.   For I say that it is not the motion that appertains to the Second, but the rest that pertains to the First, which is the innate ' motion ' from which both their cosmic order and their eternal community and their preservation [or salvation] is poured forth on things universal."   Numenius.   (M. 6, Vol. II, p. 170.)

(d) " The inward man is eternity and the spiritual time and world, which also consisteth of light and darkness, viz., of the love of God, as to the eternal light, and of the anger of God as to the eternal darkness ; whichsoever of these is manifest in him, his spirit dwelleth in that, be it darkness or light."   Jacob Böhme. (B. 13, 21.)

(e)   " The more thou thine own self
                   Out of thyself dost throw,
                   The more will into thee
                   God with his Godhead flow."
                              Angelus Silesius.   (S. 3, p. 85.)

            " Beware man of thyself,
              Self's burden thou wilt rue.
              It will impare thee more
              Than thousand devils do."
                                        (*Ibid.*, p. 97.)

            " Two eyes our souls possess :
              While one is turned on time,
              The other seeth things
              Eternal and sublime."   (*Ibid.*, p. 38.)

" Of all the wonders of the world man is the greatest still,
    For God or Devil he may be, according as he will."
                                        (*Ibid.*, p. 38.)

(f) " One impulse art thou conscious of, at best ;
        O, never seek to know the other !
        Two souls, alas ! reside within my breast,
        And each withdraws from, and repels, its brother.
        One with tenacious organs holds in love
        And clinging lust the world in its embraces ;
        The other strongly sweeps this dust above,
        Into the high ancestral spaces."

            Goethe. *Faust.* Scene II. (G. 1, Vol. I, p. 54.)

(g) " So through our whole life is protracted the strife between our earthly phenomenal form and our true transcendental being. What is beautiful from the point of view of the Subject is not beautiful from that of the Person, and therefore remains caviare for the multitude ; and actions, ethically valuable from the standpoint of the Subject, are worthless and unintelligible from that of Phenomenal Egoism. Nay, life itself, from the standpoint of earthly consciousness a vale of tears, is from the standpoint of transcendental consciousness a valuable possession, not in spite of suffering, but on account of it."
Carl Du Prel. (D. 2, Vol. II, p. 165.)

(h) " Juliana's (of Norwich) view of human personality is remarkable, as it reminds us of the Neoplatonic doctrine that there is a higher and a lower self, of which the former is untainted by the sins of the latter. ' I saw and understood full surely,' she says, ' that in every soul that shall be saved there is a godly will that never assented to sin, nor ever shall ; which will is so good that it may never work evil, but evermore continually it willeth good, and worketh good in the sight of God. . . . We all have this blessed will whole and safe in our Lord Jesus Christ.' This ' godly will ' or ' substance ' corresponds to the *spark* of the German mystics."
W. R. Inge. (I. 1, p. 205.)

(i) " I believe in you my soul, the other I am must not
    abase itself to you,
And you must not be abased to the other.

" Loaf with me on the grass, loose the stop from your
    throat,
Not words, not music or rhyme I want, not custom
    or lecture, not even the best,
Only the lull I like, the hum of your valvèd voice.

" Swiftly rose and spread around me the peace and
    knowledge that pass all the argument of the earth,
And I know that the hand of God is the promise of
    my own,
And I know that the spirit of God is the brother of
    my own,
And that all men ever born are also my brothers,
    and the women my sisters and lovers,
And that a kelson of the creation is love."
Walt Whitman.   (W. 4, p. 15.)

(*j*) " Sin of self-love possesseth all mine eye
    And all my soul and all my every part ;
    And for this sin there is no remedy,
    It is so grounded inward in my heart.
    Methinks no face so gracious is as mine,
    No shape so true, no truth of such account ;
    And for myself mine own worth do define,
    As I all other in all worths surmount.
    But when my glass shows me myself indeed,
    Beated and chopp'd with tann's antiquity,
    Mine own self-love quite contrary I read ;
    Self so self-loving were iniquity.
      'Tis thee, myself, that for myself I praise,
      Painting my age with beauty of thy days."
Shakespeare.   Sonnet LXII.

" Reduced to last analysis the matter seems to stand
about as follows. The Cosmic Conscious self, from all
points of view, appears superb, divine. From the point of
view of the Cosmic Conscious self the body and the self-
conscious self appear equally divine. But from the point
of view of the ordinary self consciousness, and so compared
with the Cosmic Conscious self, the self conscious self and
the body seem insignificant and even, as well shown in
Paul's case, contemptible."   R. M. Bucke.   (B. 35, p. 145.)

(*k*) '' The individual, so far as he suffers from his wrong-ness and criticises it, is to that extent consciously beyond it, and in at least possible touch with something higher, if anything higher exists. Along with the wrong part there is thus a better part of him, even though it may be but a most helpless germ. With which part he should identify his real being is by no means obvious at this stage ; but when stage 2 (the stage of solution or salvation) arrives, the man identifies his real being with the germinal higher part of himself ; and does so in the following way. *He becomes conscious that this higher part is conterminous and continuous with a MORE of the same quality, which is operative in the universe outside of him, and which he can keep in working touch with, and in a fashion get on board of and save himself when all his lower being has gone to pieces in the wreck.* . . . The practical difficulties are : 1, to ' realize the reality ' of one's higher part , 2, to identify one's self with it exclusively ; and 3, to identify it with the rest of ideal being.''

William James. (J. 5, pp. 508, 509.)

(*l*) '' Let me propose, as an hypothesis, that whatever it may be on its *farther* side, the ' more ' with which in religious experience we feel ourselves connected is on its *hither* side the subconscious continuation of our conscious life. Starting thus with a recognized psychological fact as our basis, we seem to preserve a contact with ' science ' which the ordinary theologian lacks. At the same time the theologian's contention that the religious man is moved by an external power is vindicated, for it is one of the peculiarities of invasions from the subconscious region to take on objective appearances, and to suggest to the Subject an external control. In the religious life the con-trol is felt as ' higher ' ; but since on our hypothesis it is primarily the higher faculties of our own hidden mind which are controlling, the sense of union with the power beyond us is a sense of something, not merely apparently, but literally true."   William James.   (J. 5, p. 512.)

(m) " Disregarding the over-beliefs, and confining ourselves to what is common and generic, we have in *the fact that the conscious person is continuous with a wider self through which saving experience comes*, a positive content of religious experience which, it seems to me, *is literally and objectively true as far as it goes*. . . . The further limits of our being plunge, it seems to me, into an altogether other dimension of existence from the sensible and merely ' understandable ' world.   Name it the mystical region, or the supernatural region, whichever you choose.   So far as our ideal impulses originate in this region (and most of them do originate in it, for we find them possessing us in a way for which we cannot articulately account), we belong to it in a more intimate sense than that in which we belong to the visible world, for we belong in the most intimate sense wherever our ideals belong.   Yet the unseen region in question is not merely ideal, for it produces effects in this world.   When we commune with it, work is actually done upon our finite personality, for we are turned into new men, and consequences in the way of conduct follow in the natural world upon our regenerative change.   But that which produces effects within another reality must be termed a reality itself, so I feel as if we had no philosophic excuse for calling the unseen or mystical world unreal."

William James.   (J. 5, p. 515.)

(n) " *Es Leuchtet mir ein*, I see a glimpse of it !   There is in man a HIGHER than Love of Happiness : he can do without Happiness, and instead thereof find Blessedness ! Was it not to preach-forth this same HIGHER that sages and martyrs, the Poets and the Priests, in all times, have spoken and suffered ; bearing testimony, through life and through death, of the Godlike that is in Man, and how in the Godlike only has he Strength and Freedom ? Which God-inspired Doctrine art thou also honoured to be taught ; O Heavens ! and broken with manifold merciful Afflictions, even till thou become contrite, and learn it ! O, thank thy Destiny for these ; thankfully bear what yet remains, thou hast need of them ; the Self in thee needed to be annihilated. By benignant fever-paroxysms is Life rooting out the deep-seated chronic Disease, and triumphs over Death. On the roaring billows of Time, thou art not engulfed, but borne aloft into the azure of Eternity. Love not pleasure ; love God. This is the EVERLASTING YEA, wherein all contradiction is solved : wherein whoso walks and works, it is well with him."

Thomas Carlyle. (C. 7, *Sartor Resartus*, p. 132.)

(*o*) " After being awakened in her human house, the soul finds herself locked in with two most treacherous and soiled companions—the human heart and mind ; and so great is her loathing and her distress, that for shame's sake these two are constrained to improve themselves. But their progress is slow, and now comes a long and painful time of alternation between two states   At one time the soul will conquer the creature, imposing upon it a sovereign beauty of holiness ; and at another the creature will conquer the soul, imposing upon her its hideous designs and desires, and causing her many sicknesses. Hence we have the warring which we feel within ourselves, for the soul now desires her home, and the creature its appetites.

" Until this awakening of the soul takes place, we mistake in thinking that we either live with our soul, or know our soul, or feel with our soul. She does but stir within us from time to time, awaking strange echoes that we do not comprehend ; and we live with the mind and the heart and the body only—which is to say, we live as the creature ;

and this is why on the complete awakening of the soul we feel in the creature an immense and altogether indescribable enhancement of life and of all our faculties, so that in great amazement we say, ' I have never *lived* until this day.' When first the will of the creature is wholly submitted to the lovely guidance of the divine part of the soul, then first we know the ineffable joys of the world of free spirit. For to live with the mind and the body is to be in a state of existence in nature.   But to live with the soul is to live above nature, in the immeasurable freedom and intensity of the spirit.   And this is the tremendous task of the soul —that she help to redeem the heart and mind from their vileness of the creature, and so lift the human upwards with herself to the Divine from whence she came.   This, then, is the transmutation or evolution by divine means of the human into the divine ; and for this we need to seek repentance or change of heart and mind, which is the will of the creature turning itself towards the beauties of the spirit, that Christ may awaken in us the glories of that sleeping soul which is His bride."

The Golden Fountain.   (G. 7, pp. 80, 81.)

(*p*) " I recognise that I have a double consciousness, that two distinct planes of thought and initiative compose my life : the one is the natural or the animal man, the product of evolution through the operation of the Cosmic Mind ; the other is the spiritual man, the essential inner nature, equipped with all the potentialities and the qualities of the infinite Creative Mother-Soul.   In the recognition of this quality lies the wisdom of life ; in the reconciliation of these two planes of consciousness lies the battle of life ; in the supremacy of the higher plane of consciousness lies the victory of life.   . . .   Upon what does victory depend ? It depends upon our use of our will-power in constraining our mental faculty to rise above the mere sense-impressions

of our lower consciousness, and intensify upon the eternal fact of our oneness with the infinite Life from which we have come forth as a child comes from its mother's womb."
Archdeacon Wilberforce.   (W. 7, p. 55.)

(q) "Two birds (the Paramātman and Jivātman, or supreme and individual souls) always united, of the same name, occupy the same tree.   One of them (the Jivātman) enjoys the sweet fruit of the fig (or fruit of acts), the other looks on as a witness [1] Dwelling on the same tree (with the supreme Soul), the deluded (individual) soul, immersed (in worldly relations), is grieved by the want of power ; but when it perceives the Ruler, (separate from worldly relations) and his glory, then its grief ceases.   When the beholder sees the golden-coloured maker (of the world), the Lord, the Soul, the source of Brahma, then having become wise, shaking off virtue and vice, without taint of any kind, he obtains the highest identity "
Mundaka Upanishad, III, 1, 1–3.

" The Supreme Self (Paramātman) and the Incarnate Self (Jivātman) are one in essence and are both on the primal Ray from the Absolute (the Tree of Life).   The Incarnate Self evolving in the souls of humanity, struggles upward to enjoy in the buddhic consciousness the fruit of experience and aspiration, while the Supreme Self is a witness and inactive.   The Incarnate Self is immersed in illusion and ignorance, suffering and sorrow, but when having conquered the lower nature and risen above it, it perceives the Supreme Self, then its sorrow ceases ; ignorance and illusion are dispelled, and the Truth is made manifest.   The pairs of opposites are discarded, and perfection having been attained, the two Selves become one Self in complete identity."   G. A. Gaskell.   (G. 5, p. 103.)

(r) " There is a spiritual consciousness, the Manasic mind illumined by the light of Buddhi, that which subjectively perceives abstractions ; and (there is) the sentient

[1] Quoted from *Rig Veda*, I, 164, 20

consciousness (the lower *Manasic* light), inseparable from our physical brain and senses. This latter consciousness is held in subjection by the brain and physical senses and, being in its turn equally dependent on them, must of course fade out and finally die with the disappearance of the brain and physical senses. It is only the former kind of consciousness, whose root lies in eternity, which survives and lives for ever, and may, therefore be regarded as immortal. Everything else belongs to passing illusions."

H. P. Blavatsky.   (B. 33, p. 179.)

(s)   " Life itself
May not express us all, may leave the worst
And the best too, like tunes in mechanism
Never awaked."

George Eliot.   (E. 2, p. 74.)

SELF, THE ONE

(a) " Verily, in the beginning this world was Brahma. It knew only itself (*ātmānam*) : ' I am Brahma ! ' Therefore it became the All. Whoever of the gods became awakened to this, he indeed became it ; likewise in the case of seers, likewise in the case of men. This is so now also. Whoever thus knows ' I am Brahma ! ' becomes this All ; even the gods have not power to prevent his becoming thus, for he becomes their self (*ātman*)."
Brihad-āranyaka Upanishad, I, 4, 10.   (U. 1, p. 83.)

(b) " The Self, verily, O Maitreyî, must be seen, heard, thought on, and investigated ; he who sees, hears, thinks on, and investigates the Self, has understood all this world." *Brihad-āranyaka Upanishad*, II, 4, 5.   (D. 4, p. 52.)

(c) " Verily, this whole world is Brahma. Tranquil, let one worship It as that from which he came forth, as that into which he will be dissolved, as that in which he breathes.

"Now, verily, a person consists of purpose. According to the purpose which a person has in this world, thus does he become on departing hence. So let him form for himself a purpose.

"He who consists of mind, whose body is life (*prāna*), whose form is light, whose conception is truth, whose soul (*ātman*) is space, containing all works, containing all desires, containing all odors, containing all tastes, encompassing this whole world, the unspeaking, the unconcerned —this Soul of mine within the heart is smaller than a grain of rice, or a barley-corn, or a mustard-seed, or a grain of millet, or the kernal of a grain of millet ; this Soul of mine within the heart is greater than the earth, greater than the atmosphere, greater than the sky, greater than these worlds.

"Containing all works, containing all desires, containing all odors, containing all tastes, encompassing this whole world, the unspeaking, the unconcerned—this Soul of mine within the heart, this is Brahma. Into him I shall enter on departing hence.

"If one would believe this, he would have no more doubt." *Chāndogya Upanishad*, III 14. (U. 1, p. 209.)

(*d*) "That which is the finest essence—this whole world has that as its soul. That is Reality. That is Ātman (Soul). That art thou, Svetaketu."
        Chāndogya Upanishad, VI, 14, 3. (U. 1, p. 249.)

(*e*) "Who, seeking, finds all being in the Self
        For him all error fades, all sorrow ends."
                Isā Upanishad, I, 6. (D. 4, p. 52.)

(*f*) 4. "That one (the Self), though never stirring, is
        swifter than thought. The Devas (senses) never

reached it, it walked before them. Though standing still, it overtakes the others that are running. Mâtarisoan (the wind, the moving spirit) bestows powers on it.

5. It stirs and it stirs not ; it is far, and likewise near. It is inside of all this, and it is outside of all this.

6. And he who beholds all beings in the Self, and the Self in all beings, he never turns away from it.

7. When to a man who understands, the Self has become all things, what sorrows, what trouble can there be to him who once beheld that unity ? "

Vâjasaneya-Samhitâ Upanishad.
(S. 1, Vol. I, pp. 311–12.)

(g) " If, then, there be an incorporeal eye, let it go forth from body unto the Vision of the Beautiful ; let it fly up and soar aloft, seeking to see not form, nor body, nor [even] types [of things], but rather That which is the Maker of [all] these,—the Quiet and Serene, the Stable and the Changeless One, the Self, the All, the One, the Self of self, the Self in self, the Like to Self [alone], That which is neither like to other, nor [yet] unlike to self, and [yet] again Himself." Hermes. (M. 6, Vol. III, p. 253.)

(h) " When, through declarations of identity like ' tat tvam asi ' (that thou art), identity has become known, then the soul's existence as wanderer, and Brahman's existence as creator have vanished away."
Sankara. (D. 4, p. 106.)

SELF-WILL

(a) " Self-will is opposition attempted by a finite subject against its proper whole." F. H. Bradley. (B. 30, p. 229.)

(b) " The visible world with its hosts and creatures is

nothing but the *outflown word* which hath introduced itself into properties, where in the properties an own self-will is existed. And with the receptibility of the willing is the creaturely life existed."
Jacob Böhme.   (B. 20, Ch. III, 22, 23.)

(*c*) " The beginning of every being is nothing else but an imagination of the outflown will of God, which hath brought itself into separability, formedness, and image likeness wherein lieth the whole creation."
Jacob Böhme.   (B. 18, Ch. I, 4.)

(*d*) " But he that lieth still in *self-will*, and giveth way for his internal ground (out of which man is originally), to lead and guide him, *he is the noblest and richest upon the earth.*"   Jacob Böhme.   (B. 16, XX, 35.)

(*e*) " For the more a man followeth after his own self-will, and self-will groweth in him, the farther off is he from God, the true Good [for nothing burneth in hell but self-will. Therefore it hath been said, ' Put off thine own will, and there will be no hell ']."
Theologia Germanica.   (T. 1, p. 121.)
See also SIN (p. 245).

SOUL, NATURE OF THE

(*a*) " That the Jîva (individual soul) is different from the Highest is altogether contrary to the canonical words : ' *tat tvam asi* ' (That thou art).   The same error occurs, if we assume that it (the Jîva) is a modification or a part of it (the Brahman), If you assert, that the error does not occur, because a modification or a part is not separate from that of which they are [modification or part], we contest this, because the unity in the main point would be wanting. And in the case of all these assumptions, you cannot get over it that either no cessation of transmigration is possible, or that in case it ceases, the soul, unless its Brahman-selfhood be assumed, must perish."

Sankara.   (D. 4, p. 111.)

(b) " Lo, verily, in the Soul's being seen, hearkened to, thought on, understood, this world—all is known."

" That Soul (*Atman*) is not this, it is not that (*neti, neti*). It is unseizable, for it can not be seized ; indestructible, for it can not be destroyed ; unattached, for it does not attach itself ; is unbound, does not tremble, is not injured."

Brihad-āranyaka Upanishad, IV, 6, 5, 16.

(U. 1, pp. 146, 147.)

(c) " Every soul, therefore, ought to consider in the first place, that soul produced all animals, and inspired them with life : viz., those animals which the earth and sea nourish, those which live in the air, and the divine stars contained in the heavens. Soul also made the sun ; soul made and adorned this mighty heaven. Soul, too, circumvolves it in an orderly course, being of a nature different from the things which it adorns, which it moves, and causes to live, and is necessarily more honourable than these. For these are corrupted when soul deserts them, and generated when it supplies them with life. But soul always exists, because it never deserts itself."

Plotinus. Enn., V, 1, 2. (P. 2, p. 164.)

(d) " The power and nature of the soul will become still more apparent and manifest, if anyone directs his attention to the manner in which it comprehends and leads heaven by its will. For it gives itself to the whole of this vast magnitude ; and every interval, both great and small, is animated by it : one body indeed, being situated differently from another, and some bodies being opposite, but others being suspended from each other. This, however, is not the case with soul. For it does not give life to individuals, through a division of itself into minute parts, but it vivifies all things with the whole of itself ; and the whole of it is present every where, in a manner similar to its generator, both according to oneness and ubiquity. Heaven, also, though it is ample, and different parts of it have a different situation, yet is one through the power of soul. And through this the sensible world is a God. The sun, likewise, is a God, because it is animated. And this is also the case with the other stars. Whatever we too possess, we possess on account of this. Plotinus. Enn., V, 1, 2. (P. 2, p. 165.)

(e) " Souls, Horus, son, are of the self-same nature in themselves, in that they are from one and the same place, where the Creator modelled them ; nor male nor female are they. Sex is a thing of bodies, not of souls."
Isis to Horus, in the Hermetic Fragment, *The Virgin of the World.* (M. 6, Vol. III, p. 128.)

(f) " Each soul, accordingly, while it is in its body is weighted and constricted by these four [elements : fire, water, air, earth]. Moreover it is natural it also should be pleased with some of them and pained with others.

" For this cause, then, it doth not reach the height of its prosperity ; still, as it is divine by nature, e'en while [wrapped up] in them it struggles and it thinks, though not such thoughts as it would think were it set free from being bound in bodies."
Isis to Horus, in the Hermetic Fragment, *The Virgin of the World.* (M. 6, Vol. III, p. 134.)

(g) " We must explain to you how the question stands by some further conceptions drawn from the Hermaic writings. Man has two souls, as these writings say. The one is from the First Mind, and partakes also of the Power of the Creator, while the other, the soul under constraint, comes from the revolution of the celestial [Spheres] ; into the latter the former, the soul that is the Seer of God, insinuates itself at a later period. This then being so, the soul that descends into us from the worlds (The Seven Spheres of the Harmony) keeps time with the circuits of these worlds, while the soul from the Mind, existing in us in a spiritual fashion, is free from the whirl of Generation ; by this the bonds of Destiny are burst asunder ; by this the Path up to the spiritual Gods is brought to birth ; by such a life as this is thát Great Art Divine, which leads us up to That beyond the Spheres of Genesis, brought to its consummation." Jamblichus. (M. 6, Vol. III, p. 298.)

(*h*) " With regard to partial existences, then, I mean in the case of the soul in partial manifestation (individual soul), we must admit something of the kind we have above. For just such a life as the [human] soul emanated before it entered into a human body, and just such a type as it made ready for itself, just such a body. to use as an instrument, does it have attached to it, and just such a corresponding nature accompanies [this body] and receives the more perfect life the soul pours into it. But with regard to superior existences and those that surround the Source of All as perfect existences, the inferior are set within the superior, bodies in bodiless existences, things made in their makers ; and the former are kept in position by the latter enclosing them in a sphere."

Jamblichus. (M. 6, Vol. III, p. 299.)

(*i*) " By this kingdom of God we understand the soul, for the soul is of like nature with the Godhead. Hence all that has been said here about the kingdom of God, how God is himself the kingdom, may be said with equal truth about the soul. St. John says : ' All things were made by him.' This refers to the soul, for the soul is all things. The soul is all things in that she is an image of God, and as such she is also the kingdom of God, for as God really is in himself without beginning, so in the kingdom of the soul he really is without end. 'God', says one philosopher, 'is in the soul in such a fashion that his whole Godhead depends upon her.' It is far more perfect for God to be in the soul than for the soul to be in God. The soul is not happy because she is in God, she is happy because God is in her. Rely upon it, God himself is happy in the soul, for God, when he broke out and wrought the soul, so far maintained his ground in her as to conceal in her his divine treasure, his heavenly kingdom. Hence Christ says : 'The kingdom of heaven is like a treasure hid in a field.' This field is the soul wherein lies hidden the treasure of the divine kingdom. Accordingly God and all creatures are happy in the soul." Eckhart. (E. 1, p. 59.)

"In God, be sure, the soul in its highest prototype has never known creature as creature, nor has she ever therein possessed either time or space. For in this image (of God in the soul) everything is God : sour and sweet, good and bad, small and great, all are one in this image. This image is no more changed by anything in time than the divine nature is changed by anything that is creature : for it apprehends and uses all things according to the law of godhood." (*Ibid.*, p. 60.)

"Consider then thyself, O noble soul, and the nobility within thee, for thou art honoured above all creatures in that thou art an image of God ; and despise what is mean for thou art destined to greatness ! " (*Ibid.*, p. 61.)

"Likewise I say concerning the soul : when the soul breaks through and loses herself in her eternal prototype, that is the death the soul dies in God." (*Ibid.*, p. 67.)

"It must be clearly understood that the soul has got to die to all the activity connoted by the divine nature if she is to enter the divine essence where God is altogether idle ; for this highest prototype of the soul beholds without means the essence of the Godhead absolutely free from activity. This supernal image is the paradigm whereto the soul will be led by her dying." (*Ibid.*, p. 68.)

" Now when the soul has gone out of her created nature and out of her uncreated nature wherein she discovers herself in her eternal prototype, and, entering into the divine nature, still fails to grasp the kingdom of God, then, recognising that thereinto no creature can ever get, she forfeits her very self, and going her own way seeks God no more ; thus she dies her highest death. In this death the soul loses every desire and image and all understanding and form, and is bereft of any nature. . . . Now when the soul has lost herself in every way, as here set forth, she finds herself to be the very thing she vainly sought. *Herself* the soul finds in the supernal image wherein God really is in all his Godhead, where he is in himself the kingdom. There the soul recognises her own beauty. Thence she must go out to get into her very self and realise that she and God are one felicity : the kingdom which, without seeking, she has found." (*Ibid.*, p. 69.)

" Now mark this well ! I said of old, and say again, that I have now all that I shall possess eternally, for God in his felicity and in the fulness of his Godhead is enjoyed by my supernal prototype, though this is hidden from the soul. . . . The more the soul departs from all this manifoldness, the more God's kingdom is revealed in her." (*Ibid.*, p. 69.)

" For as the Godhead is apart from name and nameless, so also the soul, like God, is nameless, for she is the very same as he is." (*Ibid.*, p. 70.)

(*j*) " According to the esoteric Vedânta doctrine, which already finds expression in the Upanishads, the soul is identical with Brahman, and the entire existence of the manifold world is an illusion. For him who sees through this illusion, there is neither a migration of the soul nor an entering into Brahman, but ' Brahman is he, and into Brahman he is resolved.' "   Paul Deussen.   (D. 4, p. 358.)

(*k*) " For perfect knowledge, there is no world, and therefore also no transmigration of the Soul.   According to the highest truth the Soul cannot wander, because it is the omnipresent, that is, spaceless, Brahman itself.   But this the Soul does not know : what prevents its knowing is the *Upâdhis* (bodies, vehicles) which veil from the Soul its own proper nature.   These Upâdhis it regards as belonging naturally to its own Self, while in truth they are to be referred to the non-Ego, and therefore, like the whole world of plurality, are non-existent and without reality."
Paul Deussen.   (D. 4, p. 396.)

(*l*) " The old Eleatic argument carried out consistently is, that if there is but one Infinite or one God, the soul also can in its true essence be nothing but God.   Religions which are founded on a belief in a transcendent yet personal God, naturally shrink from this conclusion as irreverent and as almost impious.   Yet this is their own fault.   They have first created an unapproachable Deity, and they are afterwards afraid to approach it ; they have made an abyss between the human and the divine, and they dare not cross it.   This was not so in the early centuries of Christianity.   Remembering the words of Christ, ' I in them and thou in me, that they may be made perfect in one,' Athenasius declared, De Incarn. Verbi Dei, 54, ' He, the Logos or Word of God, became man that we might become God.' "   F. Max Müller.   (M. 4, p. 323.)

(*m*) " When the original oneness of earth and heaven, of the human and the divine natures has once been dis-covered, the question of the return of the soul to God assumes a new character.   It is no longer a question of an ascension to heaven ; an approach to the throne of God, an ecstatic vision of God and a life in a heavenly Paradise. The vision of God is rather the knowledge of the divine element in the soul, and of the consubstantiality of the divine and human natures. Immortality has no longer to be asserted, because there can be no death for what is divine and therefore immortal in man. There is life eternal and peace eternal for all who feel the divine Spirit as dwelling within them and have thus become the true children of God."   F. Max Müller. (M. 4, p. 424.)

(n) " The soul its origin from One discerns,
   And the soul's rest is when the soul returns.
   But up that steep incline which once we trod,
   When we came down—we know not why—from God,
   We also know that none to climb begin,
   Nor dare until they cast away their sin."
                       A. E. Waite.   (W. 3, p. 136.)

SOUL AND COSMOS

(a) " As far, verily, as this world-space extends, so far extends the space within the heart. Within it, indeed, are contained both heaven and earth, both fire and wind, both sun and moon, lightening and the stars, both what one possesses here and what one does not possess ; everything here is contained within it."
Chāndogya Upanishad, VIII, 1, 3.   (U. 1, p. 263.)

(b) " Now Genesis (or Becoming) and Time, in Heaven and on Earth, are of two natures.
   In Heaven they are unchangeable and indestructible, but on Earth they're subject unto change and to destruction.

Further, the Æon's soul is God ; the Cosmos' soul is Æon ; the Earth's soul, Heaven.

And God's in Mind ; and Mind, in Soul ; and Soul, in Matter ; and all of them through Æon.

But all this Body (Cosmos), in which are all the bodies, is full of Soul, and Soul is full of Mind, and [Mind] of God.

It (Soul) fills it (Cosmos) from within, and from without encircles it, making the All to live.

Without, this vast and perfect Life [encircles] Cosmos ; within, it fills [it with] all lives ; above, in Heaven, continuing in sameness ; below, on Earth, changing becoming.

And Æon doth preserve this [Cosmos], or by Necessity, or by Foreknowledge, or by Nature, or by whatever else a man supposes or shall suppose. And all this—God energizing." Hermes. (M. 6, Vol. II, p. 177.)

(c) " One Life through all the immense creation runs,
One Spirit is the moon's, the sea's, the sun's ;
All forms in the air that fly, on the earth that creep,
And the unknown nameless monsters of the deep,—
Each breathing thing obeys one Mind's control,
And in all substance is a single Soul."
Virgil. *Æneid*, VI. (M. 2, p. 173.)

(d) Socrates. " Shall we not affirm that this human body of ours possesses a soul ?

Prot. " We certainly shall.

So. " Then from what source, friend Prot- archus, did it get it, unless indeed the body of the universe had a soul also ? For the universe certainly has all the properties of our bodies, and those of a kind more beautiful in every respect.

Prot. " It is clear, Socrates, that our bodies have the animating principle from no other source." Plato. (P. 1, p. 40.)

(e) '' There is one common Substance, even though it be broken up into countless bodies individually characterized. There is one Soul, though it be broken up among countless natures and by individual limitations. There is one Intelligent Soul, though it seem to be divided.''
Marcus Aurelius. (M. 1, XII, 30, p. 339.)

(f) '' And out of the substance of the inward and outward world Man was created, out of and in the likeness of the birth of all substances.'' Jacob Böhme. (B. 13, 32.)

(g) '' The soul and spirit are not two distinct substances ; they live by one and the same life. But the soul dwells in grace, in measure, in the exercise of the virtues, while the spirit is united to God above reason and virtue, in the naked love which has lost all account of forms and images.''
Ruysbroeck. (B. 36, p. 31.)

(h)   '' A sense sublime
Of something far more deeply interfused,
Whose dwelling is the light of setting suns,
And the round ocean and the living air,
And the blue sky, and in the mind of man :
A motion and a spirit, that impels
All thinking things, all objects of all thought,
And rolls through all things.''
Wordsworth. *Tintern Abbey.* (W. 1, Vol. II, p. 165.)

(i) '' To every form of being is assigned,
An *active* principle :—howe'er removed
From sense and observation, it subsists
In all things, in all natures ; in the stars
Of azure heaven, the unenduring clouds,
In flower and tree, in every pebbly stone
That paves the brooks, the stationary rocks,
The moving waters, and the invisible air.

What'er exists hath properties that spread
Beyond itself, communicating good,
A simple blessing, or with evil mixed ;
Spirit that knows no insulated spot,
No chasm, no solitude ; from link to link
It circulates, the Soul of all the worlds.
This is the freedom of the universe ;
Unfolded still the more, more visible,
The more we know ; and yet is reverenced least,
And least respected in the human Mind,
Its most apparent home."

> Wordsworth. *The Excursion*, IX.
> (W. 1, Vol. VI, p. 315.)

(*j*) " Oh ! there is life that breathes not ; Powers there
        are
That touch each other to the quick in modes
Which the gross world no sense hath to perceive,
No soul to dream of."

> Wordsworth. *Kilchurn-Castle.*
> (W. 1, Vol. III, p. 125.)

(*k*) " Rise after rise bow the phantoms behind me,
      Afar down I see the hugh first Nothing, I know I
          was even there,
      I waited unseen and always, and slept through the
          lethargic mist,
      And took my time, and took no hurt from the fetid
          carbon.

" Long was I hugg'd close—long and long.

" Immense have been the preparations for me,
    Faithful and friendly arms that have help'd me.

" Cycles ferried my cradle, rowing and rowing like
    cheerful boatmen,

For room to me stars kept aside in their own rings,
They sent influences to look after what was to hold
  me.

" Before I was born out of my mother generations
    guided me,
My embryo has never been torpid, nothing could
    overlay it.

" For it the nebula cohered to an orb,
The long slow strata piled to rest it on,
Vast vegetables gave it sustenance.
Monstrous sauroids transported it in their mouths
    and deposited it with care.

" All forces have been steadily employ'd to complete
    and delight me,
Now on this spot I stand with my robust soul."

Walt Whitman.   (W. 4, p. 50.)

(*l*) " Throughout this varied and eternal world
Soul is the only element, the block
That for uncounted ages has remain'd.
The moveless pillar of a mountain's weight
Is active, living spirit.   Every grain
Is sentient both in unity and part,
And the minutest atom comprehends
A world of loves and hatreds ; these beget
Evil and good : hence truth and falsehood spring ;
Hence will and thought and action, all the germs
Of pain or pleasure, sympathy or hate,
That variegate the eternal universe.
Soul is not more polluted than the beams
Of heaven's pure orb, ere round their rapid lines
The taint of earth-born atmospheres arise."

Shelley. *Queen Mab.*

(*m*) " There is no great and no small
  To the Soul that maketh all ;
  And where it cometh all things are,
  And it cometh everywhere.

 " I am owner of the sphere,
  Of the seven stars and the solar year,
  Of Cæsar's hand, and Plato's brain,
  Of Lord Christ's heart, and Shakespeare's strain."
  Ralph Waldo Emerson. (E. 4, Vol. I, p. 1.)

SOUL, PRE-EXISTENCE OF THE

(*a*) " I have heard from men and women wise in divine matters a true tale as I think, and a noble one. My informants are those priests and priestesses whose aim is to be able to render an account of the subjects with which they deal. They are supported also by Pindar and many other poets—by all, I may say, who are *truly inspired*. Their teaching is that the soul of man is immortal ; that it comes to an end of one form of existence, which men call dying, and then is born again, but never perishes. Since then the soul is immortal, and has often been born, and has seen the things here on earth and the things in Hades ; all things, in short there is nothing which it has not learned, so that it is no marvel that it should be possible for it to recall what it certainly knew before, about virtue and other topics. For since all nature is akin, and the soul has learned all things, there is no reason why a man who has recalled one fact only, which men call learning, should not by his own power find out everything else, should he be courageous, and not lose heart in the search. For seeking and learning is an art of recollection."
       Plato. (M. 4, p. 210.)

(*b*) " Now, also, we shall summarily observe, that

16

besides bodies, souls differ, especially in their manners, in the operations of the reasoning power, and from a pre-existent life. For in the '.Republic' of Plato it is said, that the choice of souls is made conformably to their antecedent lives."

Plotinus. Enn. IV, 3, 8. (P. 2, p. 215.)

(c) " For if souls brought down to body memory of the divine things of which they were conscious in heaven, there would be no difference of opinion among men concerning the divine state. But all, indeed, in their descent drink forgetfulness—some more, some less. And for this cause on earth, though the truth is not clear to all, they nevertheless have all some opinion about it ; for opinion arises when memory sinks. Those, however, are greater discoverers of truth who have drunk less of forgetfulness, because they remember more easily what they have known before in that state." Macrobius. (M. 6, Vol. I, p. 415.)

(d) " The soul, however, is drawn down to these terrene bodies, and so it is thought to die when it is imprisoned in the region of things fallen and in the abode of death. Nor should it cause distress that we have so often spoken of death in connection with the soul, which we have declared to be superior to death. For the soul is not annihilated by (what is called) its death, but is (only) buried for a time ; nor is the blessing of its perpetuity taken from it by its submersion for a time, since when it shall have made it worthy to be cleansed clean utterly of all contagion of its vice, it shall once more return from body to the light of Everlasting Life *restored* and whole."

Macrobius. (M. 6, Vol. I, p. 417.)

(e) " Never the spirit was born ; the spirit shall cease to
be never ;
Never was time it was not ; End and Beginning
are dreams !

Birthless and deathless and changeless remaineth
    the spirit for ever ;
Death hath not touched it at all, dead though the
    house of it seems ! "

    Bhagavad-Gita. Sir Edwin Arnold. (A. 1, p. 13.)

(*f*)   " Perhaps I lived before
In some strange world where first my soul was shaped,
And all this passionate love, and joy, and pain,
That come, I know not whence, and sway my deeds,
Are old imperious memories, blind yet strong,
That this world stirs within me."

                George Eliot.   (E. 2, p. 115.)

(*g*) " In the history of philosophy it is an often-recurring opinion that man, as a pre-existing being, freely betakes himself to the earthly existence. According to Philo, souls, impelled by attraction to bodily materialization, are continually descending from heaven to earth, their connection with the body being thus their free act.   According to Plotinus, also, the soul is not united to the body by a foreign power, but every soul enters a body corresponding to its condition and its will : each determining its position in life by its own act and inclination.   At birth we lose recollection of the transcendental existence, as somnambulists lose recollection of their sleep life on waking ; but this loss of memory applies only to the earthly person ; only for this is it true that, as Plotinus says, one of our two existences is concealed from us. ' This activity, however, is not concealed from the whole self, but only from a part of it ; just as, when the vegetative function is active, the perception of this activity by the faculties of sense is not transmitted to the general consciousness of the man.' "

        Carl Du Prel. (D. 2, Vol. II, p. 203.

(*h*) " Our birth is but a sleep and a forgetting :
The Soul that rises with us, our life's Star,
    Hath had elsewhere its setting,
    And cometh from afar :
    Not in entire forgetfulness,
    And not in utter nakedness,
But trailing clouds of glory do we come
    From God, who is our home."

Wordsworth. Ode to Immortality.
(W. 1, Vol. V, p. 340.)

SEPTENARY CLASSIFICATIONS

(*a*) " We find seven especial properties in nature whereby this only Mother worketh all things, (to wit, *desire* which is astringent, *bitterness*, cause of all Motion, *anguish*, cause of all sensibility, *fire, light, sound*, and *substantiality*) ; whatsoever the six forms are spiritually that the seventh is essentially. . . . These are the seven forms of the Mother of all Beings, from whence all whatsoever is in this world is generated."

Jacob Böhme. (B. 6, XIV, 10, 14, 15.)

(*b*) " The Hebrew Scriptures describe the Lord Jehovah, or Logos, as operating as the Spirit of the fifth circle when they speak of God as a Man of War. And the Book of Wisdom (XVIII, 15) thus represents Him. For the Divine Word takes many forms, appearing sometimes as one, sometimes as another, of His Seven Angels, or Elohim. These are only Seven, because this number comprises all the Spirits of God. So that when the seventh is passed, the octave begins again, and the same series of processes is repeated without, as reflects—becoming by distance weaker and weaker—of the same Seven Lights."

Anna Kingsford. (K. 3, p. 81.)

(*c*) " Occult Science recognises *Seven* Cosmical Elements :

four entirely physical, and the fifth (Ether) semi-material, as it will become visible in the air towards the end of our Fourth Round, to reign supreme over the others during the whole of the Fifth. The remaining two are as yet absolutely beyond the range of human perception. These latter will, however, appear as presentments during the 6th and 7th Races of this Round, and will become known in the 6th and 7th Rounds respectively."

H. P. Blavatsky. (B. 31, Vol. I, p. 12.)

SIN

(a) " Sin is nought else, but that the creature turneth away from the unchangeable Good and betaketh itself to the changeable ; that is to say, that it turneth away from the Perfect to ' that which is in part ' and imperfect, and most often to itself." *Theologia Germanica.* (T. 1, p. 6.)

" Disobedience and sin are the same thing, for there is no sin but disobedience, and what is done of disobedience is all sin." (*Ibid.*, p. 59.)

" Mark this : Sin is nothing else than that the creature willeth otherwise than God willeth, and contrary to Him." (*Ibid.*, p. 182.)

" And what sin is, we have said already, namely, to desire or will anything otherwise than the One Perfect Good and the One Eternal Will, and apart from and contrary to them, or to wish to have a will of one's own." (*Ibid.*, p. 170.)

(b) " God dwelleth in All, and there is *nothing* that comprehendeth Him, unless it be one with Him ; and if it departeth out of that One, then doth it depart out from God into *itself*, and is *somewhat else besides* God ; and that divideth or separateth itself. And hence the law doth exist, that it must go again out of itself into that One, or else be separated from that One. Thus it may be known what sin is, viz., the human will which separateth itself

from God into its own selfness, and awakeneth its own self
and burneth in its own source."

Jacob Böhme.   (B. 24, III, 42–43.)

(c) " Consequent upon the conception of the moral law
as a positive enactment of God, the breach of moral law
was conceived as sin.   Into the early Christian conception
of sin several elements entered.   It was probably not in
the popular mind what it was in the mind of St. Paul, still
less what it became in the mind of St. Augustine.   But one
element was constant.   It was a trespass against God.
As such, it was on the one hand something for which God
must be appeased, and on the other hand something which
He could forgive.   To the Stoics it was shortcoming,
failure, and loss : the chief sufferer was the man himself :
amendment was possible for the future, but there was no
forgiveness for the past."   E. Hatch.   (H. 1, p. 159.)

(d) " Sin and evil must not be confused as they often
are.   Sin is that great falsity connected with our outer self
of the senses, it belongs to separateness and chaos.   It
would dare to set up its king and make its kingdom in our
midst ; but the Christ, now consciously real to us, as an
inward fact, is greater than we know, and shall put all
things under his feet.   His very life in us is re-creating,
making new, or filling with Himself, bringing the soul into
unity with God."   " Christ in You."   (C. 10, p. 45.)

(e) " The sense of separateness in every sense is your
great enemy.   We beg you to let the mind of the Christ
control.   IT is wisdom, IT is love, and IT is unity.   Let
this mind hold you, control you—sweeping through the
outer body of flesh as its lord and king ; so that
each breath shall rekindle and glow.   Ay, even the
very dry bones shall reunite and breathe.   So shall you

die to sin and the sense of separateness, but live unto Christ." *(Ibid.*, p. 51.)

SPARK, THE DIVINE

(*a*) " When somewhat of this Perfect Good is discovered and revealed within the soul of man, as it were in a glance or flash, the soul conceiveth a longing to approach unto the Perfect Goodness, and unite herself with the Father. And the stronger this yearning groweth, the more is revealed unto her ; and the more is revealed unto her, the more she is drawn towards the Father, and her desire quickened. Thus is the soul drawn and quickened into a union with the Eternal Goodness."

Theologia Germanica.   (T. 1, p. 214.)

(*b*) " There is in the soul something which is above the soul Divine, simple, a pure nothing ; rather nameless than named, rather unknown than known. Of this I am accustomed to speak in my discourses. Sometimes I have called it a power, sometimes an uncreated light, and sometimes a Divine spark. It is absolute and free from all names and all forms, just as God is free and absolute in Himself. It is higher than knowledge, higher than love, higher than grace. For in all these there is still *distinction.* In this power God doth blossom and flourish with all His Godhead, and the Spirit flourisheth in God. In this power the Father bringeth forth His only-begotten Son, as essentially in Himself. It rests satisfied neither with the Father, nor with the Son, nor with the Holy Ghost, nor with the three Persons, so far as each existeth in its particular attribute. It is satisfied only with the superessential essence. It is determined to enter into the simple Ground, the still Waste, the Unity where no man dwelleth. Then it is satisfied in the light ; then it is one : it is one in itself, as this Ground is the simple stillness, and in itself immovable ; and yet by this immobility are all things moved."   Eckhart. (E. 1, p. 157.)

SUBSTANCE

NOTE ON SUBSTANCE

The concept of a universal *Substance* is one which goes back to the remotest ages of which we have any literary records. The word itself, however, or its equivalent, is variously used according to whether it is taken in a physical, a metaphysical, or a theological sense. In its widest and most abstract connotation it is that which *sub-stands* the whole Universe ; that is to say, it is equivalent to the term Absolute or God, and includes life and consciousness as well as matter and force.

In any Monistic conception of the Universe, the One Substance must be both Subject and Object ; but in the natural dualism of the mind this becomes separated into two principles, the one being in a sense active, and the other passive ; hence Spirit and Matter. This duality leads quite naturally to a Trinity, for Spirit, or "Father," acting upon Substance, or "Mother," produces a third thing, a Form, or "Son," *i.e.*, the phenomenal universe as a manifestation of this activity. The doctrine of the Trinity is not a revelation, it is a necessity of thought. Christian theology derived it from earlier sources, and it is one of the oldest doctrines in the world. (See p. 260.)

When Substance is taken as the basis or matrix of the phenomenal world, the term is limited to the concept of an absolute space-filling *something*, the modern name for which is *Ether*. It was called Æther by the Greeks, and Âkâsa, or Mûlaprakriti, or Svabhâvat by the ancient Vedânta philosophers.

SUBSTANCE

(a) " But there is another essence opposed to this

[partible], which in no respect admits of a separation into parts, since it is without parts, and therefore impartible. It likewise admits of no interval, not even in conception, nor is indigent of place, nor is generated in a certain being, either according to parts, or according to wholes, because it is as it were at one and the same time carried in all beings as in a vehicle ; not in order that it may be established in them, but because other things are neither able nor willing to exist without it."

Plotinus. Enn. IV, 2, 1. (P. 2, p. 199.)

(b) " Now it is this Matter (*Hyle*) which, after being impressed by the [divine] ideas, fashioned every body in the cosmos which we see. Its highest and purest nature, by means of which the divinities are either sustained or consist, is called Nectar, and is believed to be the drink of the gods ; while its lower and more turbid nature is the drink of souls. The latter is what the Ancients called the River of Lethe [or Forgetfulness]."

Macrobius. (M. 6, Vol. I, p. 415.)

(c) " The unique Substance, viewed as absolute and void of all phenomena, all limitations, and all multiplicity, is the Real. On the other hand, viewed in His aspect of multiplicity and plurality, under which He displays Himself when clothed with phenomena, He is the whole created universe. Therefore the universe is the outward visible expression of the Real, and the Real is the inner unseen reality of the universe. The universe before it was evolved to outward view was identical with the Real ; and the Real after this evolution is identical with the universe."

Jāmi. (N. 1, p. 81.)

(d) " She (Wisdom, the Eternal Mother, the Eternal Commencing Ground) is the highest substantiality of the Deity : without her God would not be manifested or revealed, but would be *only* a *will* ; but through the Wisdom He bringeth Himself into substance."

Jacob Böhme. (B. 9, I, 69.)

(*e*) " Thus we understand the substance of all substances, that it is a magic substance, where a will can create itself into an essential life, and so pass into a birth, and in the great mystery awaken a source. . . . And thus also apprehend whence all things, evil and good, exist, viz., from the imagination in the great mystery, where a wonderful essential life generateth itself."

Jacob Böhme. (B. 25, V. 37, 38.)

(*f*) " For as there is a nature and substance in the outward world ; so also in the inward spiritual world there is a nature and a substance which is spiritual, from which the outward world is breathed forth, and produced out of light and darkness, and created to have a beginning and Time."   Jacob Bohme. (B. 13, II, 31.)

(*g*) " In this high consideration it is found that all is through and from God himself, and that it is his own substance, which is himself, and he hath created it out of himself ; and that the evil belongeth to the forming and mobility ; and the good to the love."

Jacob Böhme. (B. 2, Preface, 14.)

(*h*) " Now the clear Deity needs no coming, for it is in all places beforehand ; it needeth only to manifest itself to or in the place ; and all whatsoever cometh, that is Substance."

Jacob Böhme. (B. 10, Text IV, Point IV, 27, 28.)

(*i*) " By *Substance*, I understand that which exists in itself, and is conceived through itself ; that is, something of which the conception needs for its formation the conception of no other thing."   Spinoza. (C. 3, p. 78.)

(*j*) " The chief philosophical expression of Monism was

Stoicism. The Stoics followed the Ionians in believing that the world consists of a single substance. They followed Heraclitus in believing that the movements and modifications of that substance are due neither to a blind impulse from within nor to an arbitrary impact from without. It moved, he had thought, with a kind of rhythmic motion, a fire that was kindling and being quenched with regulated limits of degree and time. The substance is one, but immanent and inherent in it is a force that acts with intelligence. The antithesis between the two was expressed by the Stoics in various forms. It was sometimes the bare and neutral contrast of the Active and the Passive. For the Passive was sometimes substituted Matter . . . and for the Active was frequently substituted the term *Logos*, which, signifying as it does, on the one hand, partly thought and partly will, and, on the other hand, also the expression of thought in a sentence and the expression of will in a law, has no single equivalent in modern language. But the majority of Stoics used neither the colourless term the Active, nor the impersonal term the *Logos*. The *Logos* was vested with personality : the antithesis was between matter and God. This latter term was used to cover a wide range of conceptions. The two terms of the antithesis being regarded as modes of a single substance, separable in thought and name but not in reality."

E. Hatch. (H. 1, p. 175.)

(*k*) " The mere conception of self-cognition presupposes in the knowing substance a duality of attributes, one of which is directed upon the other. Self-cognition implies a substance going apart into subject and object. This substance is subject in so far as it knows, object in so far as it is known."   Carl Du Prel. (D. 2, Vol. II, p. 9.)

(*l*) " We hold with Goethe, that ' matter cannot exist and be operative without spirit, nor spirit without matter.'

We adhere firmly to the pure unequivocal Monism of Spinoza : matter, or infinitely extended substance, and Spirit (or Energy), or sensitive and thinking substance, are the two fundamental attributes of the all-embracing divine essence of the world, the universal substance."

Ernst Haeckel.   (H. 7, p. 8.)

(m) " The first thinker to introduce the purely monistic conception of substance into science and appreciate its profound importance was the great philosopher Baruch Spinoza (1632–1677). In his stately pantheistic system the notion of the *world* (the universe, or the cosmos) is identical with the all-pervading notion of God ; it is at one and the same time the purest and most rational *Monism* and the clearest and most abstract *Monotheism*. This universal substance, this ' divine nature of the world,' shows us two different aspects of its being, or two fundamental attributes—matter (infinitely *extended* substance) and spirit (the all-embracing energy of *thought*). All the changes which have since come over the idea of substance are reduced, on a logical analysis, to this supreme thought of Spinoza's ; with Goethe I take it to be the loftiest, profoundest, and truest thought of all ages. Every single object in the world which comes within the sphere of our cognisance, all individual forms of existence, are but special transitory forms—*accidents* or *modes*—of substance. These modes are material things when we regard them under the attribute of *extension* (or ' occupation of space '), but forces or ideas when we consider them under the attribute of thought (or ' energy '). To this profound thought of Spinoza our purified Monism returns after a lapse of two hundred years ; for us, too, matter (space-filling substance) and energy (moving force) are but two inseparable attributes of the one underlying substance."

Ernst Haeckel.   (H. 7, p. 76.)

SPACE

(*a*) "The whole deep between the stars and the earth is inhabited, and not void and empty. Each dominion hath its own Principle : which seems somewhat ridiculous to us men, because we see them not with our eyes ; not considering that our eyes are not of their essence and property, so that we are neither able to see nor perceive them ; for we live not in their Principle, therefore we cannot see them."   Jacob Böhme. (B. 7, VIII, 11.)

(*b*) "This moment exhibits infinite space, but there is a space also wherein all moments are infinitely exhibited, and the everlasting duration of infinite space is another region and room of joys. Wherein all ages appear together, all occurrences stand up at once, and the innumerable and endless myriads of years that were before the creation, and will be after the world is ended, are objected as a clear and stable object, whose several parts extended out at length, give an inward infinity to this moment, and compose an eternity that is seen by all comprehensors and enjoyers. Eternity is a mysterious absence of time and ages : an endless length of ages always present, and for ever perfect. For as there is an immovable space wherein all finite spaces are enclosed, and all motions carried on and performed ; so is there an immovable duration, that contains and measures all moving durations. Without which first the last could not be ; no more than finite places, and bodies moving without infinite space. All ages being but successions correspondent to those parts of the Eternity wherein they abide, and filling no more of it, than ages can do. Whether they are commensurate with it or no, is difficult to determine. But the infinite immovable duration is Eternity, the place and duration of all things, even of infinite space itself: the cause and end, the author and beautifier, the life and perfection of all."

Thomas Traherne. (T. 3, p. 323.)

(c) " *Akâca*, usually translated *ether*, is not so much this, as all-permeating, all-present space . . . as something corporeal, as an element;—a conception that is not far from the ideas of all those which take space to be something self-existent (that is, independent of our intellect) and therefore real." Paul Deussen. (D. 4, p. 231.)

(d) " There is really no such thing as space. For you, as for us, the spiritual law of attraction operates, but your consciousness of limitation, of distance, makes you blind and deaf to a great extent. At a later period of your unfoldment, to desire is to possess. Thus, if we wish to see you, our thought is a vital force, we are in your actual presence immediately, we are so close to you. Thought is so potent, so swift; every thought of ours becomes an outward expression. Although you may not see it, you cannot think without a result. Be very careful that you think from the spiritual plane. The phenomena of time and sense are like children's toys to us. They will be discarded as you dwell in the higher consciousness. What divides us now is simply and only that you are not dwelling in, not breathing, seeing, hearing from the spiritual plane. Every effort to rise helps another; but see to it that you are watchful, vigilant, purposeful, and loving."

" *Christ in You.*" (C. 10, p. 181.)

SUBJECT AND OBJECT

(a) " And inasmuch as the subjective is also objective, and the objective also subjective, and as the contraries under each are indistinguishably blended, does it not become impossible for us to say whether subjective an objective really exist at all ?   When subjective and objective are both without their correlates, that is the very axis of Tao.   And when that axis passes through the centre at which all Infinities converge, positive and negative alike blend into an infinite One."   Chuang Tzū.   (C. 1, p. 45.)

(*b*) " We are compelled to recognise that there must exist somewhere, in this world or in others, a spot in which everything is known, in which everything is possible, to which everything goes, from which everything comes, which belongs to all, to which all have access, but of which the long-forgotten roads must be learnt again by our stumbling feet."   Maurice Maeterlinck   (M. 9, p. 81.)

SYMBOLISM

(*a*) " Mysticism lives by symbols, the only mental representation by which the Absolute can enter into our relative experience."   E. Récéjac.   (R. 4, p. 3.)

(*b*) " Symbols are the most intimate of all signs, and are analogies created spontaneously by the consciousness to enable it to express to itself the things which have no empirical objectivity."   (*Ibid.*, p. 40.)

(*c*) " Symbolism is a *synthetic* expression, the inverse of verbal expression, which is always more or less *analytical*. The common function of both is to externalise the facts of consciousness, and for this reason both of them partake as much of us as of things, as much of our life itself as of objective verity. . . .   Symbolical signs have the same effect as direct perceptions : as soon as they have been ' seen ' within, their psychic action takes hold of the feeling and fills the consciousness with a crowd of images and emotions which are attracted by the force of Analogy. . . .   We revert to symbols to make up for the inadequacy of language and at moments when we feel that we would fain comprehend things with the whole soul ; by their aid only can we attain the state called ' mystic ' which is the synthesis of the heart, the Reason, and the Senses, around an object which is so perfect as to transport our whole being. . . . The symbol brings to the horizon of the consciousness an abundance of images which have a more or less strong bond of analogy, and which become for us (though not so really) an ' object.'   This remark is specially significant when mystic symbolism is in question."

(*Ibid.*, p. 134.)

(*d*) " It ought to be known, indeed, for the right Understanding of the Mystical Books, that in their esoteric Sense they deal, not with material Things, but with spiritual Realities ; and that as Adam is not a Man, nor Eve a Woman, nor the Tree a Plant in its true Signification, so also are not the Beasts named in the same Books real Beasts, but that the Mystic Intention of them is implied."

Anna Kingsford.   (K. 3, p. 18.)

(*e*) " In the Symbol proper, what we can call a Symbol, there is ever, more or less distinctly and directly, some embodiment and revelation of the Infinite ; the Infinite is made to blend itself with the Finite, to stand visible, and as it were, attainable there.   By Symbols, accordingly, is man guided and commanded, made happy, made wretched, He everywhere finds himself encompassed with Symbols, recognised as such or not recognised : the Universe is but one vast Symbol of God ; nay if thou wilt have it, what is man himself but a Symbol of God ; is not all that he does symbolical ; a revelation to Sense of the mystic god-given force that is in him ; a ' Gospel of Freedom,' which he, the ' Messias of Nature,' preaches, as he can, by act and word ? Not a hut he builds but it is the visible embodiment of a Thought ; but bears visible record of invisible things · but is, in the transcendental sense, symbolical as well as real."

Thomas Carlyle. (S. 7, *Sartor Resartus*, p. 152.)

(*f*) " On the question of symbolism, it is quite evident, from the structural resemblances we see in sacred Myths and Scriptures collected from all parts of the world, that the symbolism is one and universal, and therefore not of human origin. This unity, implying one Source for all sacred utterances, and the logical inference that the same symbols have the same meanings everywhere, has to be realised. When this highly important fact of symbolic unity is grasped, it completely sweeps away the possibility of the past existence of myth and scripture-making persons. No persons, however learned, could be credited with having knowledge of this obscure universal symbology so as to be able to compose true Myths or Scriptures."

G. A. Gaskell. (G. 5, p. 12.)

(*g*)   " Hieroglyphics old,
Which sages and keen-eyed astrologers
Then living on the earth, with labouring thought
Won from the gaze of many centuries :
Now lost, save what we find on remnants high
Of stone, or marble swart ; their import gone,
Their wisdom long since fled."

John Keats. Poetical Works. *Hyperion.*

TIME AND SPACE

(*a*) " WE may therefore surmise that time, conceived under the form of a homogeneous medium, is some spurious concept, due to the trespassing of the idea of space upon the field of pure consciousness. At any rate we cannot finally admit two forms of the homogeneous, time and space, without first seeking whether one of them cannot be reduced to the other." Henri Bergson. (B. 26, p. 98.)

(*b*) " Time is only an illusion produced by the succession of our states of consciousness as we travel through eternal duration, and it does not exist where no consciousness exists in which the illusion can be produced ; but ' lies asleep.' The present is only a mathematical line which divides that part of eternal duration which we call the future, from that part which we call the past. Nothing on earth has real duration, for nothing remains without change—or the same—for the billionth part of a second ; and the sensation we have of the actuality of the division of ' time ' known as the present, comes from the blurring of that momentary glimpse, or succession of glimpses, of things that our senses give us, as those things pass from the region of ideals which we call the future, to the region of memories that we name the past. In the same way we experience a sensation of duration in the case of the instantaneous electric spark, by reason of the blurred and continuing impression of the retina. The real person or thing does not consist solely of what is seen at any particular moment, but is composed of the sum of all its various and changing conditions from its appearance in the material form to its disappearance from the earth. It is these ' sum-totals ' that exist from eternity in the ' future,' and pass by degrees through matter, to exist for eternity in the 'past.' No one could say that a bar of metal dropped into the sea came into existence as it left the air, and ceased to exist as it entered the water, and that the bar itself consisted only of that cross-section thereof which at any given moment coincided with the mathematical plane that separates, and, at the same time, joins, the atmosphere and the ocean. Even so of persons and things, which, dropping out of the to-be into the has-been, out of the future into the past—present momentarily to our senses a cross-section, as it were, of their total selves, as they pass through time and space (as matter) on their way from one eternity to another: and these two constitute that ' duration ' in which alone anything has true existence, were our senses but able to cognize it there."

H. P. Blavatsky. (B. 31, Vol. I, p. 37.)

(c) " To sum up, if it is difficult for us to conceive that the future pre-exists, perhaps it is even more difficult for us to understand that it does not exist ; moreover, a certain number of facts tend to prove that it is as real and definite and has, both in time and in eternity, the same permanence and the same vividness as the past."

Maurice Maeterlinck. (M. 9, p. 176.)

(d) " Or thinkest thou it were impossible, unimaginable ? Is the Past annihilated, then, or only the past ; is the Future non-extant, or only the future ? Those mystic faculties of thine, Memory and Hope, already answer : already through those mystic avenues, thou the Earth-blinded summonest both Past and Future, and communest with them, though as yet darkly, and with mute beckonings. The curtains of Yesterday drop down, the curtains of To-morrow roll up ; but Yesterday and To-morrow both *are*, Pierce through the Time-element, glance into the Eternal. Believe what thou findest written in the sanctuaries of Man's Soul, even as all Thinkers, in all ages, have devoutly read it there : that Time and Space are not God, but creations of God ; that with God as it is a universal HERE, so it is an everlasting Now."

Thomas Carlyle. (C. 7, p. 181.)

(*e*) '' Time neither adds to, nor steals from, an atom in the Infinite.''

Bulwer Lytton.
Zanoni, Book II, Chap. IV. (L. 3, p. 57.)

TRINITY, DOCTRINE OF THE

NOTE ON THE DOCTRINE OF THE TRINITY

There is no obscurity or mystery about the doctrine of the Trinity in its philosophical and pre-Christian aspects. It arises in the necessity of the mind to *hypostasise*, to bring into its own region of *personality*, the otherwise incomprehensible unity of the Absolute. The moment the Absolute, or God, is conceived of as *acting*—and how can we otherwise conceive, seeing that the manifested universe exists ?—we have three factors : (*a*) the Actor or active Principle, (*b*) that which is acted upon, passive Substance, and (*c*) the result of the action, *i.e.*, the manifested universe itself.

When, as Hatch says (p. 263 *infra*) this concept is presented in terms of human parentage, we have a Trinity of Father, Mother, Son ; and this was more particularly the symbolism employed in the Gnostic and Mystical schools. The Son (or Logos) was the whole manifested universe ; not the universe of physical *matter*—or rather not that only— but the inner spiritual world as well as the outer material world of our present perceptions : this latter being only a very secondary and limited aspect or reflection of the real substantial world.

It was only when the Christian dogma makers came to materialise this symbolism, and to connect it up with, and confine it to, one particular historical character, that its simple philosophical form was corrupted and perverted, and the subsequent confusion, irrationality and strife was introduced. In the grossly material and literalising conceptions of these original obscurantists, the *Mother* principle was dropped out of the Trinity altogether, and she became the actual physical mother, by virgin birth, of a human being, the Jesus of the Gospels, to whom the term Son, or Logos, was now restricted. In place of the Mother the Holy Ghost was substituted; but when or how is lost in the obscurity of Christian origins. I give a quote below (*m*) from Max Muller to illustrate this obscurity and confusion. Belief in the Virgin Birth is now very widely rejected in the Protestant Church; though the mystical and symbolical meaning can hardly be said to have been recognised. But the Holy Ghost still keeps its place in the theological Trinity, which in this form remains as a stumbling-block to rational thought, and a source of contention and division in the Christian Church itself.

Of all the mystical writers on this subject, Jacob Böhme is the most philosophical and at the same time the most profoundly mystical. It is impossible, however, in a few words, or in a few quotations, to state his doctrine with any clearness, for he uses terms which have their own special meaning in his vocabulary, and which require many collated passages for their elucidation. Very briefly we may say, however, that he recognises and states quite clearly that the Eternal Unborn, Divine Nature, or Principle, requires for its manifestation a *Mother* principle, which he calls "the Virgin or Wisdom of God" (*Sophia*) (*g* and *k infra*), and which is a *Substantiality* (*h* and *k infra*), and the "heavenly corporeity" (*i infra*). This corresponds to some of the Gnostic systems; and we might also say that this substantiality corresponds to the Eastern concept of Mûlaprakriti, Âkâsa, or Svabhâvat. When we penetrate beneath the *form* of a doctrine we shall find the same fundamental concepts or truths ; and these have been presented in one form or another in all ages. The *inspired* writings of Jacob Böhme throw a flood of light on the inner meaning and symbolism of the Christian Scriptures when we are thus able to penetrate beneath the mere verbal form.

In connection with this subject of the Trinity, the quotations given from Böhme under the headings of Logos, Substance, and Virgin should also be consulted.

TRINITY, DOCTRINE OF THE

(a) " All are One, inasmuch as all are of One ; by unity, that is, of substance ; and yet notwithstanding there is guarded the mystery of the divine appointment, which distributes the Unity into a Trinity, ranging in their order the Three, Father, Son, and Holy Ghost ; three, that is, not in essence but in degree, not in substance but in form, not in power but in manifestation, but of one substance and of one essence and of one power, forasmuch as there is one God, from whom these degrees and forms and manifestations are set down under the name of Father, Son, and Holy Ghost." Tertullian, *Adv. Prax.* (S. 16, p. 25.)

(b) " Now from One Source all things depend ; while Source [dependeth] from the One and Only [One]. Source is, moreover, moved to become Source again ; whereas the One standeth perpetually and is not moved. Three then are they : " God, the Father and the Good," Cosmos and Man. God doth contain Cosmos ; Cosmos [containeth] Man. Cosmos is e'er God's Son, Man as it were Cosmos's child." Hermes. (M. 6, Vol. II, p. 150.)

(c) " We shall, however, be quite correct in saying that the Demiurge who made all this universe, is also at the same time Father of what has been brought into existence ;

while its Mother is the Wisdom of Him who hath made it
—with whom God united, though not as man (with woman),
and implanted the power of genesis. And she, receiving
the Seed of God, brought forth with perfect labour His only
beloved Son, whom all may perceive—this Cosmos."

Philo. (M. 6, Vol. I, p. 224.)

(*d*) " By a different conception of the genesis of the
world, and one that is of singular interest in view of the
similar conceptions which we shall find in some Gnostic
schools, God is the Father of the world : and the metaphor
of Fatherhood is expanded into that of a marriage : God is
conceived as the Father, His Wisdom as the Mother : ' and
she, receiving the seed of God, with fruitful birth-pangs
brought forth this world, His visible son, only and well-
beloved.' "

E. Hatch. (H. 1, p. 188.)

(*e*) " In the eternal generation of the Son all things are
actually present to the Father ; in the eternal proceeding
of the Holy Ghost from the Father and the Son all things
are immediate objects of love. For the union of the Father
and the Son is supremely active and we are close held
within it in the depths of eternal love by the virtue of the
Holy Ghost.

Ruysbroeck. (H. 5, p. 50.)

(*f*) " The Father begets the Son, the Second Person of
the Trinity, His everlasting Wisdom, the Word by whom
all was created, in the unity of essence. But the Holy
Ghost, the third Person, proceeds from the Father and the
Son, and is the love of the one for the other ; Their infinite
love by which They are united in an everlasting union.
One God in three Persons enfolds us in the unity of this
same love ; a Unity in Trinity, a Trinity in Unity."

Ruysbroeck. (R. 4, p. 87.)

(*g*) " Now, where the Word is, there is [also] the Virgin
[or Wisdom of God] ; for the Word is in the Wisdom :

and the one is not without the other, or else the Eternity would be *divided.*" Jacob Böhme. (B. 3, Chap. VI, 78.)

(*h*) " And therefore must God, with the heavenly substantiality, *in us become man,* and in the heavenly Virgin and in the earthly, God is become man, and hath put on upon our souls the heavenly substantiality again, *viz.* his heavenly body : yet our earthly must pass away, but the heavenly remaineth standing for ever."
. Jacob Böhme. (B. 3, Chap. XIII, 19.)

(*i*) " And here we must give the Reader (that loveth God) to understand clearly in the great deep, what the pure element is, wherein our body (before the fall of *Adam*) stood, and in the new regeneration now at present standeth also therein. It is the heavenly corporeity, which is not barely and merely a spirit, wherein the clear Deity dwelleth ; it is not the pure Deity itself, but [it is] generated out of the essences of the holy Father (as he continually and eternally goeth in through the eternal gate, in the eternal mind in himself through the recomprehended will) into the eternal habitation, where he generateth his eternal Word."
Jacob Böhme. (B. 2, Chap. XXII, 19.)

(*j*) " Out of the Eternal Nature God hath manifested or revealed His Wisdom ; for in the Divine Wisdom hath the *substance* of the spirits and creatures been from Eternity ; but with the moving of God the Father it passed into a *formed* creation, according to the property of the Essence in the word *fiat,* in the word of power."
Jacob Böhme. (B. 8, Part II, 184.)

(*k*) " This Wisdom of God (which is the Virgin of glory and beauteous ornament, and an image of the Number Three) is the *substantiality* of the Spirit, which the Spirit of God putteth on as a garment, whereby he manifesteth himself, or else ,his form would not be known : for she is the Spirit's corporeity, and though she is not a corporeal palpable substance, like us men, yet she is substantial and visible ; but the Spirit is *not* substantial."

> Jacob Böhme.   (B. 3, Chap. V, 49, 50.)

(*l*) " The triad of things sensible has been begotten, exists, and is maintained only by the Superior Triad, but as their faculties and their actions are evidently distinct, it is not possible to conceive how this triad is indivisible and above time when judged by that which is in time, and as the latter is the one alone which we are permitted to know here below, I can scarcely say anything concerning the other."

> Louis Claud de Saint-Martin.   (W. 2, p. 223.)

(*m*) " The first origin of the concept (of the Holy Ghost) is still enveloped in much uncertainty.   There seems to be something attractive in triads.   We find them in many parts of the world, owing their origin to very different causes.   The trinity of Plato is well known, and in it there is a place for the third person, namely, the World-spirit, of which the human soul was a part. . . .   With the Christian philosophers at Alexandria the concept of the Deity was at first biune rather than triune.   The Supreme Being and the Logos together comprehended the whole of Deity, and we saw that the Logos or the intellectual world was called not only the Son of God, but also the second God (δεύτερος Θεός).   When this distinction between the Divine in its absolute essence, and the Divine as manifested by its own activity, had once been realised, there seemed to be no room for a third phase or person.   Sometimes therefore it looks as if the Third Person was only a repetition of the Second.   Thus the author of the Shepherd and the author of the Acta Archelai both identify the Holy Ghost with the Son of God.   How unsettled the minds of Christian people were with regard to the Holy Ghost, is shown by the fact that in the apocryphal gospel of the Hebrews, Christ speaks of it as His Mother.   When, however, a third place was claimed for the Holy Spirit, as substantially existing by the side of the Father and the Son, it seems quite possible that this thought came, not from Greek, but from a Jewish source."

Max Müller.   (M. 4, p. 440.)

(*n*) " These conceptions concerning the Triune God have come down through the vistas of ages, to the present day, preserved in the works of the philosophers, and are still held sacred by many among Christians and Brahmins. But we do not learn from their sacred books where, when or how the said doctrine originated.   Whatever may have been the source from which it sprang, it is certain that the priests and learned men of Egypt, Chaldea, India, or China, if they still knew the true history of its origin at the time they wrote, kept it a profound secret, and imparted it only to a few select among those initiated in the sacred mysteries.

" We need not seek for information among the fathers of the Christian Church, for they are as silent as the tomb on the subject.   They admitted into their tenets the notion of a Triune God as taught by the pagan philosophers, and appropriated it, as they have many other of their teachings and theories, without knowing, without inquiring, concerning their origin.   The Councils pronounced them revelations from on high ; unfathomable mysteries not to be investigated ; and imposed them as dogmas, to be implicitly believed, with blind faith, as they are to-day, by the followers of the Romish Church."

Augustus le Plongeon.   (P. 6, p. 58.)

(*o*) " This has been sung as the supreme Brahma.
    In it there is a triad.   It is the firm support, the
        Imperishable.

By knowing what is therein, Brahma-knowers
Become merged in Brahma, intent thereon, liberated from the womb of re-birth.

   .   .   .   .   .

' That Eternal should be known as present in the
    self.
Truly there is nothing higher than that to be
    known.
When one recognises the enjoyer, the object of
    enjoyment, and the universal Actuator,
All has been said.   This is the threefold Brahma.''

Svetāsvatara Upanishad.

      I. 7, 12.   (U. 1, p. 395, 396.)

UNION, MYSTICAL SENSE OF

(a) " Becoming wholly absorbed in deity, she [the soul] is one, conjoining as it were centre with centre. For here concurring, they are one ; but they are then two when they are separate. For thus also we now denominate that which is another. Hence this spectacle is a thing difficult to explain by words. For how can any one narrate that as something different from himself, which when he sees he does not behold as different, but as one with himself ? "

Plotinus. Enn. VI. 9, 10. (P. 2, p. 320.)

(b) " According to this union in the depths the spirit meets Christ directly, without intermediary. For this life that we live in the depths of ourselves is in the likeness of our eternal Prototype, and knows not separateness. This is why our spirit in its innermost and holiest life perpetually receives into the purity of its substance the seal and the divine life of its Redeemer. It is the habitation of God Who dwells continually in His temple by a ceaseless advent and a perpetual renewal of His glory. He enters, but this was already His abode ; wherein He dwells there He enters in. Wherein He comes, therein was He already dwelling ; and to that place wherein He never was He never comes. He knows neither chance nor change. When He enters into you you were already His dwelling-place, for He never goes forth from Himself. Thus does the spirit possess God in the nudity of its substance, and God the spirit ; it lives in God and God in it." Ruysbroeck. (H. 5, p. 28.)

" Transcending ourselves, we return towards our origin that we may be absorbed in the abyss, source of every perfection."   (*Ibid.*, p. 31.)

" In this intimate union spiritual perception, that thrice hallowed possession, becomes his (the man's), and plunging into God he is intoxicated by participation in the bliss of essential life. And this participation invokes within the very source and centre of his human powers a plenitude of sensible love that in its penetrating potency flows into the physical life, to the very members of his body."

(*Ibid.*, p. 37.)

" Ceaseless activity and unending rest will meet together in eternity ; for the possession of God demands and exacts perpetual activity, and whoever thinks otherwise deceives and is deceived. Our whole life is in God, immersed in bliss ; our whole life is in ourselves, absorbed in action. And these two movements make but one, self-contradictory in its attributes, rich and poor, hungry, satisfied, active and at rest, sublime, pre-eminent, within time and within eternity, in the midst of His contending glories."

(*Ibid.*, p. 80.)

(*c*) " But when, all forms being detached from the soul, she beholds nothing but the *one alone*, then the naked essence of the soul finds the naked formless essence of the divine unity, the superessential essence, passive (motionless), reposing in itself. O surpassing wonder, what lofty suffering is that, when the essence of the soul experiences nothing but the absolute unity of God."

Eckhart. (E. 1, p. 48.)

(*d*) " If man is not one with the Eternal, in the unity of intuition and feeling which is immediate, he remains, in the unity of consciousness which is derived, for ever apart."

Schleiermacher. (C. 3, p. 266.)

(*e*) " The union of the soul with God is its second birth, and therein consists man's immortality and freedom."

Spinoza. (P. 5, p. 86.)

(*f*) " There is, in sanest hours, a consciousness, a thought that rises, independent, lifted out of all else, calm, like the stars, shining eternal. This is the thought of identity—yours for you, whoever you are, as mine for me. Miracle of miracles, beyond statement, most spiritual and vaguest of earth's dreams, yet hardest basic fact, the only entrance to all ,facts. In such devout hours, in the midst of the significant wonders of heaven and earth (significant only because of the *Me* in the centre), creeds, conventions, fall away and become of no account before this simple idea. Under the luminousness of real vision, it alone takes possession, takes value." Walt Whitman. (W. 6, p. 37.)

UNITY OF THE UNIVERSE

(*a*) " All things are mutually intertwined, and the tie is sacred, and scarcely anything is alien the one to the other. For all things have been ranged side by side, and together help to order one ordered Universe. For there is both one Universe, made up of all things, and one God immanent in all things, and one Substance, and one Law, one reason common to all intelligent creatures, and one Truth, if indeed there is also one perfecting of living creatures that have the same origin and share the same reason."
Marcus Aurelius. (M. 1, VII, 9, p. 169.)

(*b*) " Strange and hard the paradox true I give ;
Objects gross and the unseen Soul are one."
Walt Whitman. (W. 5, p. 87.)

(*c*) " The universe is one in this sense that its differences exist harmoniously within one whole, beyond which there is nothing." F. H. Bradley. (B. 30, p. 144.)
" What we discover is a whole in which distinctions can be made, but in which divisions do not exist."
(*Ibid.*, p. 146.)

(*d*) " It seems more than certain that, as the cells of an immense organism, we are connected with everything that exists by an inextricable network of vibrations, waves, influences, of nameless, numberless and uninterrupted fluids. Nearly always, in nearly all men, everything carried along by these invisible wires falls into the depths of the unconsciousness and passes unperceived, which does not mean that it remains inactive."

Maurice Maeterlinck.   (M. 9, p. 72.)

VEDÂNTA PHILOSOPHY, THE

(a) " THE Vedânta, whether we call it a religion or a philosophy, has completely broken with the effete anthropomorphic conception of God, and of the soul as approaching the throne of God, and has opened vistas which were unknown to the greatest thinkers of Europe."

F. Max Müller. (M. 4, p. 234.)

(b) " We must remember that, like the Eleatic philosophers, the ancient Vedântists also started with that unchangeable conviction that God, or the Supreme Being, or Brahman, as it is called in India, is one and all, and that there can be nothing besides. This is the most absolute Monism. If it is called Pantheism, there is nothing to object, and we shall find the same Pantheism in some of the most perfect religions of the world, in all which hold that God is or will be All, and that if there really exists anything besides, He would no longer be infinite, omnipresent, and omnipotent, He would no longer be God in the highest sense." F. Max Müller. (M. 4, p. 270.)

(c) " The fundamental thought of the Vedânta, most briefly expressed by the Vedic words : *tat tvam asi*, ' that art thou ' (Chând. 6, 8, 7) and *aham brahma asmi*, ' I am Brahmin ' (Brih. 4, 10), is THE IDENTITY OF BRAHMAN AND THE SOUL ; this means that *Brahman, i.e.*, the eternal principle of all Being, the power which creates, sustains and again absorbs into itself all worlds, is identical with the *Atman*, the Self or the Soul, *i.e.*, that in us which we recognise, when we see things rightly, as our very self and true essence. This soul of each one of us is not a part, an emanation of Brahman, but wholly and absolutely the eternal, indivisible Brahman Himself."

Paul Deussen.   (D. 4, p. 453.)

VIRGIN, THE MYSTICAL

(a) " But when I speak of the virgin of the wisdom of God, I mean not a thing, that is (confined, or circumscribed) in a place ; as also when I speak of the Number Three ; but I mean the *whole deep* of the Deity without end and number (or measure)."   Jacob Böhme.   (B. 3, V, 56.)

(b) " Now, where the Word is, there is (also) the virgin (or wisdom of God) ; for the Word is in the wisdom : and the one is not without the other, or else the eternity would be *divided*."   Jacob Böhme.   (B. 3, VI, 78.)

(c) " Eckhart, to quote his *ipsissima verba*, represents the Father as speaking His word into the soul, and when the Son is born, every soul becomes Maria."

F. Max Müller.   (M. 4, p. 520.)

(d) " The declarations of Jesus to Nicodemus are explicit and conclusive as to the purely spiritual nature both of the entity designated ' Son of Man,' and of the process of his generation. Whether incarnate or not, the ' Son of Man ' is of necessity always ' in heaven,'—his own ' kingdom within.' Accordingly the terms describing his parentage are devoid of any physical reference. ' Virgin Maria ' and ' Holy Ghost ' are synonymous, respectively, with ' Water ' and ' the Spirit ' ; and these, again, denote the two constituents of every regenerated selfhood, its purified soul and divine spirit. Wherefore the saying of Jesus,—' Ye must be born again of Water and of the Spirit,' was a declaration, first, that it is necessary to every one to be born in the manner in which he himself is said to have been born ; and, next, that the gospel narrative of his birth is really a presentation, dramatic and symbolical, of the nature of regeneration.

" As the Immaculate Conception is the foundation of the Mysteries, so the Assumption is their crown. For the entire object and end of kosmic evolution is precisely this triumph and apotheosis of the soul. In this Mystery is beheld the consummation of the whole scheme of creation, —the perfectionment, perpetuation, and glorification of the individual human ego. The grave—that is the astral and material consciousness—cannot retain the Mother of God. She rises into heaven ; she assumes its Queenship, and is— to cite the ' Little Office of the Blessed Virgin Mary '— ' taken up into the chamber where the King of kings sits on His starry throne ' ; her festival, therefore, being held at the corresponding season in the astronomical year, when the constellation Virgo reaches the zenith and is lost to view in the solar rays. Thus, from end to end, the mystery of the soul's evolution—the argument, that is, of the kosmic drama and the history of Humanity—is contained and enacted in the cultus of the Blessed Virgin. The Acts and the Glories of the soul as Mary are the one and supreme theme of the sacred Mysteries."

Kingsford and Maitland.   (K. 2, p. 142.)

VISIONS

(a) " Visions are in the powers inferior to the will, and their effect must always terminate at the will, and in the end they must be lost in the experience of what one sees, knows, and hears in these states, otherwise, the soul would never arrive at the perfect union. What she would then have to which she would even give the name of union, would be a mediated union and a flowing of the gifts of God into the powers ; but this is not God himself : so that it is of great importance to prevent souls from relying upon visions and ecstasies, because this retards them almost all

their life.   Besides, these graces are very subject to illusion ,
for that which has form, image and distinction, can be
counterfeited by the devil, as well as sensible delights :
but that which is detached from all forms, images, species,
and above all sensible things, the Devil cannot enter
therein."   Madame Guyon.   (G. 3, p. 82.)

(*b*) " The Soul can never attain to the height of Divine
Union, so far as it is possible in this life through the medium
of any forms or figures. . . .   In the high state of the
union of Love, God does not communicate Himself to the
Soul under the disguise of imaginary Visions, Similitudes,
or Figures, but mouth to mouth ; that is, it is in the pure
and naked essence of God, which is as it were the mouth
of God in love, that he communicates Himself to the pure
and naked essence of the Soul, through the will which is
the mouth of the Soul in the love of God."
St. John of the Cross.   (S. 5, p. 137.)

WILL, NATURE OF IN GOD AND IN MAN

(*a*) " But here ye must consider more particularly, some-what touching the Will. There is an Eternal Will, which is in God a first principle and substance, apart from all works and effects, and the same will is in Man, or the creature, willing certain things, and bringing them to pass. For it belongeth unto the Will, and is its property, that it shall will something. What else is it for ? For it were vain, unless it had some work to do, and this it cannot have without the creature. Therefore there must be creatures, and God will have them, to the end that the Will may be put in exercise by their means, and work, which in God is and must be without work. Therefore the will in the creature, which we call a created will, is as truly God's as the Eternal Will, and is not of the creature.

" And now, since God cannot bring His Will into exercise, working and causing changes, without the creature, there-fore it pleaseth Him to do so in and with the creature. Therefore the will is not given to be exerted by the creature, but only by God, who hath a right to work out His own will by means of the will which is in man, and yet is God's."

Theologia Germanica. (T. I, p. 197.)

(*b*) " In this last proof and trial man becomes the image of God again, for all things become one and the same, and are alike to him. . . . God is as it were dead to all things, and yet himself is the life of all things. He is ONE, and yet NOTHING and ALL. Thus also a man becomes according to his resigned will, when he yields himself wholly to God, and then his will falls again into the unsearchable will of God, out of which he came in the

beginning, and then standeth in the form as an image of the unsearchable will of God, wherein God dwelleth and willeth. . . . And whatsoever willeth in and with God, that is one life with God."
Jacob Böhme. (B. 7, LXVI, 63, 65.)

(c) " Men have led us on in vain images of the essential will, as if the only God did will this or that ; whereas (he) himself is the sole will of the (being of) nature and creature, and the whole creation lieth only and alone in the formation of his expressed Word and will, and the severation of the only will in the expression ; and is understood in the impression of nature."
Jacob Böhme. (B. 7, LX, 41.)

(d) " Never dispute about the will of God. We ourselves are God's will to evil and good : which of them soever is manifested in us, we are that, whether it be Hell or Heaven."
Jacob Böhme. (B. 14, VIII, 287, 288.)

(e) " Our will to live has not an earthly motive, but is a transcendental willing of our Subject ; therefore is it present, even when the contents of the life are not correspondent to our earthly wishes ; this transcendental will of the Subject is for the earthly person an ' ought ' ; therefore is there in the life of ascetic penitence, and in that of Indian and Christian anchorites, as in the daily increasing suicides among civilised peoples, a misconstruction, springing from accentuation of the life here, of our position in the universe, and of our task, an immoral revolt of the person, knowing only the earthly phenomenal form, against the striving of the transcendental Subject for our true good."
Carl Du Prel. (D. 2, Vol. II, p. 304.)
" The whole content of Ethic may be comprehended therein, that the person should be serviceable to the

Subject ; every revolt of the person, in its own favour, against the Subject is immoral." *(Ibid.,* p. 294.)

(*f*) " The will is the *mysterium magnum,* the great mystery of all wonders and secrets, and yet it driveth forth itself, through the *imagination* of the desiring hunger, into substance. It is the original of nature ; its desire maketh a representation ; this *representation* is no other than the will of the desire, yet the desire maketh in the will such a substance as the will in itself is. The true *Magia* is no substance, but the desiring *spirit* of substance ; it is an unsubstantial *matrix,* and revealeth or manifesteth itself in substance. The *Magia* is a spirit, and the substance is its body. The *Magia* is the greatest hidden secret, for it is *above* Nature ; it maketh Nature according to the form of its will." Jacob Böhme. (B. 24, 66–70.)

(*g*)   " Thy will 'tis makes thee damned,
           Thy will that makes thee saved ;
           Thy will that sets thee free,
           Thy will makes thee enslaved."

                    Angelus Silesius. (S. 3, p. 92.)

(*h*) " The *Will-Spirit* in God, is the Beginner or first Cause of all that is in Nature and Creature ; it is that Mysterious, and Abyssal Power of the Deity, which generateth, and bringeth forth Nature with all its Properties, is always in them, and with them, as the Cause of all that they are, and work."

                    Wm. Law. (L. 5, p. 119.)

(*i*) " The Will is not a made Thing, which is made out of something, or that came out of some different State, into a state of Will. But the free Will of Man is a true and real Birth from the free, eternal, uncreated Will of God, which willeth to have a creaturely Offspring of itself, or to see itself in a creaturely state. And therefore the Will of Man hath the Nature of Divine Freedom ; hath the Nature of Eternity, and the Nature of Omnipotence in it ; because it is what it is, and hath what it hath, as a Spark, a Ray, a genuine Birth of the eternal, free, omnipotent Will of God. And therefore, as the Will of God is superior to, and ruleth over, all Nature ; so the Will of Man, derived from the Will of God, is, superior to, and ruleth over, all his own Nature. And thence it is, that as to itself, and so far as its own Nature reacheth, it hath the Freedom and Omnipotence of that Will from which it is descended , and can have or receive nothing but what itself doth, and worketh, in and to itself." Wm. Law. (L. 4, p. 142.)

(j) " Our wills are ours, we know not how ;
Our wills are ours, to make them thine."

Alfred Tennyson.
In Memoriam, Introduction, Stanza 4.

WORKING HYPOTHESES

(a) " A great number of seekers show themselves on their own account perfectly eclectic. They adopt according to their needs, such or such a manner of looking at nature, and do not hesitate to utilize very different images when they appear to them useful and convenient. And, without doubt, they are not wrong, since these images are only symbols convenient for language. They allow facts to be grouped and associated, but only present a fairly distant resemblance with the objective reality. Hence it is not forbidden to multiply and to modify them according to circumstances. The really essential thing is to have, as a guide through the unknown, a map which certainly does not claim to represent all the aspects of nature, but which, having been drawn up according to predetermined rules, allows us to follow an ascertained road in the eternal journey towards the truth." Lucien Poincaré. (P. 4, p. 17.)

WORLD PROCESS, THE

(*a*) " Unceasingly contemplate the generation of all things through change, and accustom thyself to the thought that the Nature of the Universe delights above all in changing the things that exist and making new ones of the same pattern."

Marcus Aurelius. (M. 1, IV, 36, p. 89.)

(*b*) " It is no small matter, this round and delicious globe,
moving so exactly in its orbit for ever and ever, without one jolt, or the untruth of a single second ;
I do not think it was made in six days, nor in ten thousand years, nor in ten billion years,
Nor planned and built one thing after another, as an architect plans and builds a house.
I do not think seventy years is the time of a man or woman,
Nor that seventy millions of years is the time of a man or woman,
Nor that years will ever stop the existence of me, or any one else."

Walt Whitman. (W. 5, p. 210.)

(*c*) " When we have learnt to recognise in history the realisation of a rational purpose, when we have learnt to look upon it as in the truest sense of the word a Divine Drama, the plot revealed in it ought to assume in the eyes of the philosopher also a meaning and a value far beyond the speculations of even the most enlightened and logical theologians." F. Max Müller. (M. 4, p. VI.)

WISDOM IN MAN

(*a*) " Dimensions are limitless ; time is endless. Conditions are not invariable ; terms are not final. Thus, the wise man looks into space, and does not regard the small as too little, nor the great as too much ; for he knows that there is no limit to dimension. He looks back into the past, and does not grieve over what is far off, nor rejoice over what is near ; for he knows that time is without end. He investigates fulness and decay, and does not rejoice if he succeeds, nor lament if he fails ; for he knows that conditions are not invariable. He who clearly apprehends the scheme of existence does not rejoice over life, nor repine at death ; for he knows that terms are not final."

Chuang Tzū. (C. 1, p. 40.)

" The repose of the Sage is not what the world calls repose. His repose is the result of his mental attitude. All creation could not disturb his equilibrium : hence his repose. When water is still, it is like a mirror, reflecting the beard and the eyebrows. It gives the accuracy of the water-level, and the philosopher makes it his model. And if water thus derives lucidity from stillness, how much more the faculties of the mind ! The mind of the Sage, being in repose, becomes the mirror of the universe, the speculum of all creation."   (*Ibid.*, p. 90.)

" The perfect man employs his mind as a mirror. It grasps nothing : it refuses nothing. It receives but does not keep. And thus he can triumph over matter, without injury to himself."   (*Ibid.*, p. 96.)

" A man who knows that he is a fool is not a great fool."

(*Ibid.*, p. 98.)

(*b*) " Happy is he whom the Truth by itself doeth teach, not by figures and words that pass away · but as it is in itself. . . . And what have we to do with *genus* and *species*? He to whom the Eternal Word speaketh is delivered from a world of unnecessary conceptions. From that one Word are all things, and all speak that one ; and this is the Beginning, which also speaketh unto us."

Thomas á Kempis.   (K. 1, Book I, Chap. 3, p. 5.)

(*c*) " The more a man is united within himself, and becometh inwardly single-minded, so much the more and higher things doth he understand without labour, for that he receiveth intellectual light from above."

Thomas à Kempis.   (K. 1, Book I, Chap. 3, p. 6.)

BIBLIOGRAPHY

(1) ARNOLD, Sir EDWIN, M A , K C I E.
"The Song Celestial, or Bhagavad-Gita" Third Edition. By kind permission of the Publishers, Messrs. Kegan Paul, Trench, Trûbner & Co . Ltd., London.

(2) "The Light of Asia" Forty-sixth Edition. By kind permission of the Publishers, Messrs Kegan Paul, Trench, Trûbner & Co., Ltd., London.

(3) ARNOLD, MATTHEW
"Literature and Dogma" 1893 With acknowledgments to the Publishers, Messrs Macmillan & Co , Ltd , London

(4) ATWOOD, MARY ANN.
"A Suggestive Inquiry into the Hermetic Mystery." 1918. By kind permission of the Publisher, Mr. Wm. Tait, Belfast

(5) "A. E." See RUSSELL, GEORGE. (R. 5)

(6) ANGELUS SILESIUS. See SCHEFFLER, JOHAN (S. 3.)

(7) ANONYMOUS.
"Christ in You." An Automatic Writing Script. 1910. By kind permission of the Publisher, Mr. John M. Watkins, London

(8) "The Golden Fountain, or the Soul's Love for God Being some Thoughts and Confessions of one of His Lovers." 1919. By kind permission of the Publisher, Mr. John M. Watkins, London.

(1) BÖHME, JACOB.
"The Aurora."

(2) "The Three Principles of the Divine Essence."

(3) "The Threefold Life of Man."

(4) "Forty Questions of the Soul."

(5) "The Incarnation of Jesus Christ "

(6) "De Signatura Rerum "

(7) "Mysterium Magnum."

(8) "First Apology."

(9) "Second Apology."

(10) "Third Apology."

(11) "Fourth Apology."

(12) "Of True Resignation."

(13) "Of Regeneration."

(14) "Concerning the Election of Grace."

(15) "The Way to Christ Discovered."

(16) "Epistles." (1649.)

(17) "Two Theosophical Epistles." (1645.)

(18) "Of Christ's Testaments, viz.:—Baptisme and the Supper."

(19) "The Knowledge of God and of All Things."

(20) "Of Divine Vision."

(21) "Clavis."

(22) "The 177 Theosophick Questions"

(23) "Great Six Points."

(24) "Small Six Points."

(25) "Of the Earthly and of the Heavenly Mystery."

(26) BERGSON, HENRI.
   "Time and Free Will." Trans. F. L. Pogson. 1912. With acknowledgments to the Publishers, Messrs. George Allen & Unwin, Ltd., London.

(27) "Creative Evolution." Trans. A. Mitchell. 1911. With acknowledgments to the Publishers, Messrs. Macmillan & Co., Ltd., London.

(28) "Matter and Memory." 1890. With acknowledgments to Messrs. Swan, Sonnenschein & Co.'s Successors, Messrs. George Allen & Unwin, Ltd.

(29) BLAKE, WILLIAM.
   Poems.

(30) BRADLEY, F. H.
   "Appearance and Reality." Second Edition. 1902. With acknowledgments to Messrs. Swan, Sonnenschein's Successors, Messrs. George Allen & Unwin, Ltd.

(31) BLAVATSKY, HELENA PETROVNA.
" The Secret Doctrine." First Edition. 1888. Theosophical Publishing Co., Ltd., London.

(32) " The Voice of the Silence." First Edition. 1889. Theosophical Publishing Co , Ltd., London.

(33) " The Key to Theosophy." First Edition. 1889. Theosophical Publishing Co., Ltd., London.

(34) BALL, Sir ROBERT S., LL.D.
" The Story of the Heavens." 1885. By kind permission of the Publishers, Messrs. Cassell & Co , Ltd., London.

(35) BUCKE, Dr. RICHARD MAURICE.
" Cosmic Consciousness : A Study in the Evolution of the Human Mind." 1901. Original Edition. By kind permission of Messrs. E. P. Dutton & Co , New York.

(36) BAILLIE, EARLE.
" Reflections from the Mirror of a Mystic." 1905. By kind permission of the Publisher, Mr. Thomas Baker, London.

(37) *Bhagavad Gita.* (See J. 7.)

(38) BUDDHA, GAUTAMA. (See A. 2, and O. 1.)

(39) BROWNING, ROBERT.
Poetical Works. By kind permission of Mr. John Murray, Publisher, London.

(40) BAILEY, ALICE A.
" Letters on Occult Meditation." " Dedicated to the Tibetan Teacher who wrote these letters and authorised their publication." By kind permission of Mrs Bailey, and the Publishers, Lucis Publishing Co., New York. 1922.

(1) CHUANG TZŪ.
" Musings of a Chinese Mystic." Wisdom of the East Series. 1906. By kind permission of the Publisher, Mr. John Murray, London.

(2) CARPENTER, EDWARD.
" Towards Democracy." Complete Edition. 1911.

With acknowledgments to the Publishers, Messrs. George Allen & Unwin, Ltd.

(3) CALDECOTT & MACKINTOSH.
"Selections from the Literature of Theism." 1904. By kind permission of Professor Caldecott, and the Publishers, Messrs. T. & T. Clark, Edinburgh.

(4) CAIRD, EDWARD
"The Evolution of Religion" 1893. By kind permission of the Publishers, Messrs. Jackson, Wylie & Co , Glasgow.

(5) CAIRD, JOHN, LL.D.
"Spinoza." 1888 By kind permission of the Publishers, Messrs. Wm. Blackwood & Sons, Edinburgh.

(6) CARLYLE, THOMAS.
"Critical and Miscellaneous Essays." 1872. Seven Vols. By kind permission of the Publishers, Messrs. Chapman & Hall, Ltd , London.

(7) "Sartor Resartus." 1871. By kind permission of the Publishers, Messrs Chapman & Hall, Ltd., London.

(8) CAMPBELL, REV. R J., D.D.
"Report of the Proceedings of the Summer School, Penmaenmaer, 1907" By kind permission of the Author.

(9) COLERIDGE, SAMUEL T.
Poetical Works.

(10) "CHRIST IN YOU." (See A. 7.)

(1) DIONYSIUS THE AREOPAGITE.
"The Mystical Theology of Dionysius. By kind permission of the Publishers, "The Shrine of Wisdom," Acton, London. 1923.

(2) DU PREL, CARL.
"The Philosophy of Mysticism." Trans. from the German by C. C. Massey. Two Vols. George Redway, London 1889.

(3) DRUMMOND, HENRY.
"Natural Law in the Spiritual World." Fourteenth

Edition. 1884. By kind permission of the Publishers, Messrs. Hodder & Stoughton, London.

(4) DEUSSEN, PAUL.
" The System of the Vedânta " Trans. by Chas. Johnston. 1912. By kind permission of the Publishers, The Open Court Publishing Co., Chicago.

(5) " Elements of Metaphysics " 1894 With acknowledgments to the Publishers, Messrs. Macmillan and Co , Ltd., London.

(6) DARWIN, CHARLES.
" The Descent of Man." 1871. Two Vols. By kind permission of the Publisher, Mr. John Murray, London.

(1) ECKHART, MEISTER.
" Meister Eckhart." Translation from the German by C. de B. Evans. *The Porch*. Vol. II, No. 2 Sept , 1914. By kind permission of the Publisher, Mr. John M. Watkins, London.

(2) ELIOT, GEORGE.
" The Spanish Gypsy." Warwick Edition. Vol. XI. 1906. By kind permission of the Publishers, Messrs. Wm. Blackwood & Sons, Edinburgh.

(3) EDDINGTON, PROFESSOR A. S.
" Space, Time and Gravitation." 1920. By kind permission of the Author and Publishers, The University Press, Cambridge.

(4) EMERSON, RALPH WALDO.
Complete Works. Bohn's Library. Two Vols. Bell and Daldy, London. 1886.

(1) FABRE D'OLIVET.
" Hermeneutic Interpretation of the Origin of the Social State of Man and of the Destiny of the Adamic Race." Trans. by N. M. Redfield. 1915. By kind permission of the Publishers, Messrs. G. P. Putnam's Sons, Ltd.

(2) FIELDING, H.
" The Hearts of Men." Third Edition. 1904. By

kind permission of the Publishers, Messrs. Hurst and Blackett, Ltd., London.

(1) GOETHE, JOHANN WOLFGANG VON.
    " Faust." Trans. by Bayard Taylor. Two Vols.
    1871. Strahan & Co., London.

(2) GUYON, MADAME JEANNE MARIE.
    " Life of Madame Guyon. ' By Thos. C. Upham.
    1862. Sampson Low, Son & Co., London.

(3)   '" La Vie de Madame J. M. B. de la Mothe-Guyon."
    Libraires Associés. Paris. 1791.

(4) GREEN, T. H.
    " Prolegomena to Ethics." 1883. By kind permission of The Clarendon Press, Oxford.

(5) GASKELL, G. A.
    " A Dictionary of the Sacred Language of all Scriptures
    and Myths." 1923. By kind permission of the
    Author and the Publishers, Messrs. George Allen
    and Unwin, Ltd., London.

(6) " Gnôsis of the Light, The " See LAMPLUGH, REV. F.
    (L. 2.)

(7) " Golden Fountain, The." See ANONYMOUS. (A. 8.)

(1) HATCH, EDWIN, D.D.
    " The Influence of Greek Ideas and Usages upon the
    Christian Church." The Hibbert Lectures, 1888.
    Williams & Norgate, Ltd. 1914. By kind permission of the Hibbert Trustees.

(2) HUXLEY, THOMAS H.
    " Evolution and Ethics, and other Essays." 1903.
    With acknowledgments to the Publishers, Messrs.
    Macmillan & Co., Ltd., London.

(3)   " Essays upon some Controverted Questions." 1892.
    With acknowledgments to the Publishers, Messrs.
    Macmillan & Co., Ltd., London.

(4)   " Collected Essays." 1894. With acknowledgments
    to the Publishers, Messrs. Macmillan & Co., Ltd.,
    London.

(5) HELLO, ERNEST.
" Selected Works of John Ruysbroeck " Translated
from the French by " C.E.S." under the title of
" Flowers of a Mystic Garden." 1912. By kind
permission of the Publisher, Mr. John M. Watkins,
London.

(6) HUME, ROBERT ERNEST, M.A , PH.D.
" The Thirteen Principal Upanishads." 1921 By
kind permission of the Author and the Publishers,
The Oxford University Press, London.

(7) HAECKEL, ERNST.
" The Riddle of the Universe." Sixth Popular
Edition. 1904. By kind permission of the
Rationalistic Press Association, Ltd , London.

(8) HERMES. See MEAD, G. R. S. (M. 6.)

(9) HEGEL, G. W. F.
" Logic." Trans. by Wm. Wallace, M.A. Second
Edition. 1892. By kind permission of the
Publishers, The Clarendon Press, Oxford.

(10) HOLMES, EDMOND G. A.
" The Creed of my Heart and other Poems." By
kind permission of the Author. Constable & Co.
London. 1912.

(11) HOUGHTON, CLAUDE.
" The Kingdoms of the Spirit." 1924. By kind
permission of the Author and the Publishers, The
C. W. Daniel Co., London.

(12) HARTMANN, EDUARD VON.
" Philosophy of the Unconscious."

(13) HUGEL, BARON FREDERICH VON, LL.D., D.D.
" The Mystical Element of Religion as studied in
Saint Catherine of Genoa and her Friends." Two
Vols. 1923. By kind permission of Professor
Edmund Gardner and of the Publishers, Messrs.
J. M. Dent & Sons, Ltd., London.

(1) INGE, WILLIAM RALPH, M.A., DEAN.
" Christian Mysticism." The Bampton Lectures, 1899.
With acknowledgments to the Publishers, Messrs.
Methuen & Co., Ltd., London.

(1) JAMBLICHUS.
  "On the Mysteries." Trans. by Thomas Taylor. B. Dobell. London. 1895.

(2) JALALU'D-DIN RUMI.
  "The Persian Mystics." F. Hadland Davis. Wisdom of the East Series. 1907 By kind permission of the Publisher, Mr. John Murray, London.

(3) JACOPONE DA TODI. See UNDERHILL, E. (U. 3.)

(4) JAMI. See NICHOLSON, R. A. (N. 1.)

(5) JAMES, WILLIAM.
  "A Pluralistic Universe." 1909. By kind permission of the Publishers, Messrs. Longmans, Green & Co., London.

  "The Varieties of Religious Experience." With acknowledgments to the Publishers, Messrs. Longmans, Green & Co., London.

(6) JOHNSTON, CHARLES.
  Bhagavad Gita. Translated by Charles Johnston. By kind permission of the Translator and the Publishers, The Quarterly Book Dept., New York.

(1) KEMPIS, THOMAS λ.
  "Of the Imitation of Christ." The Ancient and Modern Library of Theological Literature. Griffith Farrar & Co. London. 1886.

(2) KINGSFORD AND MAITLAND.
  "The Perfect Way ; or the Finding of Christ." Fifth Edition. 1913. By kind permission of the Publisher, Mr. John M. Watkins, London.

(3) KINGSFORD, ANNA.
  "Clothed with the Sun." Popular Edition. 1912. By kind permission of the Publisher, Mr. John M. Watkins, London.

(4) KING, C. W., M.A.
  "The Gnostics and their Remains." Bell & Daldy. London. 1864.

(5) KEATS, JOHN.
  Poetical Works.

(1) LAO TSZE.
"The Simple Way of Lao Tsze." By kind permission of the Publishers, "The Shrine of Wisdom," Acton, London. 1924.

(2) LAMPLUGH, REV. F.
"The Gnôsis of the Light." 1918. By kind permission of the Publisher, Mr. John M. Watkins, London.

(3) LYTTON, E. BULWER, LORD.
"Zanoni." Chapman & Hall. London. 1853.

(4) LAW, REV. WILLIAM A. M.
"The Way to Divine Knowledge." W. Innys and J. Richardson. London. 1752.

(5) "A Short but Sufficient Confutation of the Rev. Dr. Warburton's projected Defence (as he calls it) of Christianity" J. Richardson. London. 1757.

(6) "An Humble, Earnest and Affectionate Address to the Clergy" J. Richardson. London. 1761.

(1) MARCUS AURELIUS ANTONIUS.
"The Communings with Himself of Marcus Aurelius Antonius." Translated by C. R. Haines, M.A. 1916. By kind permission of the Publishers, Messrs. Wm. Heinemann, Ltd.

(2) MYERS, F. W H.
"Essays Classical and Modern." 1921 With acknowledgments to the Publishers, Messrs. Macmillan & Co., Ltd , London.

(3) "Human Personality and its Survival of Bodily Death." Two Vols. 1903. By kind permission of the Publishers, Messrs. Longmans, Green & Co., London.

(4) MÜLLER, F. MAX.
"Theosophy or Psychological Religion." Gifford Lectures, 1892. With acknowledgments to the Publishers, Messrs. Longmans, Green & Co., London.

(5) MEAD, G. R. S.
"The Doctrine of the Subtle Body in Western

Tradition." 1919. By kind permission of the Author and Publisher, Mr. John M. Watkins, London.

(6) "Thrice Greatest Hermes." Three Vols. Theosophical Publishing Society, London. 1906. By kind permission of the Author.

(7) MacDonald, George, LL.D.
"Phantastes." Smith Elder & Co. London. 1858. By kind permission of Greville MacDonald, Esq.

(8) Mansel, Henry L.
"The Limits of Religious Thought." Fifth Edition. 1867. By kind permission of the Publisher, Mr. John Murray, London.

(9) Maeterlinck, Maurice.
"The Unknown Guest." Third Edition. 1917. With acknowledgments to the Publishers, Messrs. Methuen & Co., Ltd., London.

(1) Nicholson, R. A.
"The Mystics of Islam." 1914. By kind permission of the Publishers, Messrs. G. Bell & Sons, Ltd., London.

(1) Oldenberg, Dr. Hermann.
"Buddha: His Life, His Doctrine, His Order." Translated from the German by Wm. Hay, M.A. 1882. By kind permission of the Publishers, Messrs. Williams & Norgate, Ltd., London.

(1) Plato.
"Philebus." Translated by F. A. Paley. 1873. By kind permission of the Publishers, Messrs. G. Bell & Sons, Ltd., London.

(2) Plotinus.
"Select Works of Plotinus." Translated by Thomas Taylor. New Edition with Preface by G. R. S. Mead. G. Bell & Sons, Ltd., London. 1909.

(3) Picton, J. A.
"The Mystery of Matter." 1873. With acknow-

ledgments to the Publishers, Messrs. Macmillan and Co., Ltd.

(4) POINCARÉ, LUCIEN.

"The New Physics." International Scientific Series, Vol. XC. 1907. By kind permission of the Publishers, Messrs. Kegan Paul, Trench, Trubner and Co., Ltd., London.

(5) POLLOCK, SIR FREDERICK, BART.

"Spinoza's Life and Philosophy." 1899. By kind permission of the Publishers, Messrs. Gerald Duckworth & Co., Ltd., London.

(6) PLONGEON, AUGUSTUS LE.

"Sacred Mysteries among the Mayas and Quiches, 11,500 Years Ago." R. Macroy, New York. 1886.

(1) RUYSBROECK, JAN VAN.

"Œuvres de Ruysbroeck." Trans. par les Benedictines de St. Paul de Wisques. Three Vols. Bruxelles. 1920/21.

(2) See HELLO, E. (H. 5), and BAILLIE, E. (B. 36).

(3) ROYCE, JOSIAH, PH.D.

"The World and the Individual." Two Vols. 1900. With acknowledgments to the Publishers, Messrs. Macmillan & Co., Ltd., London.

(4) RÉCÉJAC, E., D.LIT.

"Essay on the Bases of the Mystic Knowledge." Translated by Sara Carr Upton. 1899. By kind permission of the Publishers, Messrs. Kegan Paul, Trench, Trûbner & Co., Ltd., London.

(5) RUSSELL, GEORGE W. ("A. E.")

"The Candle of Vision." 1918. With acknowledgments to the Publishers, Messrs. Macmillan & Co, Ltd., London.

(6) *Rig Veda.*

Sacred Books of the East.

(1) "SACRED BOOKS OF THE EAST."

Translated by various Oriental Scholars, and Edited

by F. Max Müller. 1879. By kind permission of the Publishers, The Clarendon Press, Oxford.

(2) ST. AUGUSTINE.

"Confessions." Translated by C. Bigge, D.D. The Library of Devotion. Tenth Edition 1919. With acknowledgments to the Publishers, Messrs. Methuen & Co., Ltd., London.

(3) SCHEFFLER, JOHANN. (Angelus Silesius).

"Selections from the Rhyms of a German Mystic." Translated by Paul Carus. 1909. By kind permission of the Publishers, The Open Court Publishing Co, Chicago.

(4)   "The Spiritual Maxims of Angelus Silesius." Translated by Henry Bett. 1914. By kind permission of the Publisher, Mr. C. H. Kelley. London.

(5) ST. JOHN OF THE CROSS.

"The Ascent of Mount Carmel." Translated by David Lewis. 1906. By kind permission of the Publisher, Mr. Thomas Baker, London.

(6) ST. TERESA.

"The Interior Castle." Translated by The Rev. J. Dalton. 1852. T. Jones, London.

(7) ST. CATHERINE OF SIENNA.

"The Dialogue of the Seraphic Virgin Catherine of Sienna." Translated from the Italian by Algar Thorold. 1896. By kind permission of the Publishers, Messrs. Kegan Paul, Trench, Trûbner and Co., Ltd., London.

(8) STERRY, PETER.

"A Sermon preached at the Monthly Fast, before the Right Honourable House of Lords." 1648.

(9) SHAKESPEARE, WILLIAM.

Poetical Works. Sonnets.

(10) SPENCER, HERBERT.

"First Principles." 1862. By kind permission of the Publishers, Messrs. Williams & Norgate, Ltd., London.

(11)   "Autobiography." Two Vols. Williams & Norgate, Ltd., London. By kind permission of Mr Herbert Spencer's Trustees.

(12) SPINOZA, BENEDICT DE.
"The Chief Works of Spinoza" Translated by R. H. M. Elwes. Two Vols. 1883. By kind permission of the Publishers, Messrs. G. Bell and Sons, Ltd., London.

(13) SPENSER, EDMUND.
Poetical Works.

(14) SHELLEY, PERCY BYSSHE.
Poetical Works

(15) SHARPE, A. B.
"Mysticism: Its True Nature and Value" 1911. By kind permission of the Author and the Publishers, Messrs. Sands & Co., London.

(16) SANDAY, DR. WILLIAM, D.D.
"Christologies Ancient and Modern" 1910. By kind permission of the Publishers, The Clarendon Press, Oxford.

(17) SAINT-MARTIN, LOUIS CLAUDE DE. See WAITE, A. E. (W 2.)

(1) *Theologia Germanica.* (*Circa* 1350.)
Authorship unknown. Translated by Susanna Winkworth. Golden Treasury Series. 1913. With acknowledgments to the Publishers, Messrs. Macmillan & Co., Ltd., London.

(2) TAULER, JOHN.
"The Inner Way." 1901. The Library of Devotion. With acknowledgments to the Publishers, Messrs. Methuen & Co., Ltd., London.

(3) TRAHERNE, THOMAS.
"Centuries of Meditation." 1908. By kind permission of the Publishers, Messrs. P. J. & A. E. Dobell. London.

(4) TENNYSON, ALFRED.
Poetical Works.

(5) TUCKWELL, JAMES HENRY.
"Religion and Reality." 1915. With acknowledgments to the Publishers, Messrs. Methuen & Co., Ltd., London.

(6) TRINE, RALPH WALDO.
   "In Tune with the Infinite." Edition 1903. By kind permission of the Publishers, Messrs. G. Bell & Sons, Ltd., London.

(1) *Upanishads*. See HUME, R. E.   (H. 6.)

(2) UNDERHILL, EVELYN.
   "Mysticism. A Study in the Nature and Development of Man's Spiritual Consciousness." First Edition. 1910. With acknowledgments to the Author and Publishers, Messrs. Methuen & Co., Ltd., London.

(3)   "Jacopone da Todi." Translated by Mrs. Theodore Beck. By kind permission of the Translator and Editor. Published by Messrs. J. M. Dent and Sons, Ltd., London.

(1) VAUGHAN, ROBERT ALFRED, B.A.
   "Hours with the Mystics." Two Vols. John W. Parker & Son. London. 1856.

(2) VIVEKANÂNDA, SWAMI.
   "Râja Yoga." 1896. By kind permission of the Publishers, Messrs Kegan Paul, Trench, Trûbner and Co., Ltd., London.

(1) WORDSWORTH, WILLIAM.
   Poetical Works.

(2) WAITE, ARTHUR EDWARD.
   "The Life of LOUIS CLAUDE DE SAINT-MARTIN." William Rider & Sons, Ltd., London. By kind permission of the Author and Publishers.

(3)   "Strange Houses of Sleep." 1906. P. S. Wellby, London. By kind permission of the Author.

(4) WHITMAN, WALT.
   "Leaves of Grass." New York. 1855.

(5)   Poems, Selected and Edited by W. M. Rosetti. 1908. By kind permission of the Publishers, Messrs. Chattq & Windus, London.

(6)   " Democratic Vistas." Washington, D. C. 1871.

(7) WILBERFORCE, THE VEN. ARCHDEACON BASIL, D.D.
" Mystic Immanence." Third Impress. 1919. By
kind permission of the Publisher, Mr. Elliot Stock,
7, Paternoster Row, London, E.C.

BIOGRAPHICAL NOTES
AND INDEX

PRINTED BY
JARROLD AND SONS LTD.
NORWICH

A SELECTION OF

MESSRS. METHUEN'S PUBLICATIONS

This Catalogue contains only a selection of the more important books published by Messrs. Methuen. A complete catalogue of their publications may be obtained on application.

PART I. GENERAL LITERATURE

Allen (R. Wilberforce)
METHODISM AND MODERN WORLD PROBLEMS. *Crown 8vo.* 7s 6d. *net.*

Bain (F. W.)
A DIGIT OF THE MOON THE DESCENT OF THE SUN. A HEIFER OF THE DAWN. IN THE GREAT GOD'S HAIR A DRAUGHT OF THE BLUE. AN ESSENCE OF THE DUSK. AN INCARNATION OF THE SNOW. A MINE OF FAULTS. THE ASHES OF A GOD. BUBBLES OF THE FOAM A SYRUP OF THE BEES. THE LIVERY OF EVE THE SUBSTANCE OF A DREAM *All Fcap. 8vo* 5s. *net.* AN ECHO OF THE SPHERES. *Wide Demy 8vo.* 10s. 6d *net.*

Balfour (Sir Graham)
THE LIFE OF ROBERT LOUIS STEVENSON *Twentieth Edition. In one Volume. Cr. 8vo. Buckram,* 7s. 6d. *net.*

Barker (Ernest)
NATIONAL CHARACTER. *Demy 8vo.* 12s. 6d *net.*

Belfield (Reginald)
FROM LANDSCAPE TO STUDIO. Illustrated. *Fcap. 4to.* 12s. 6d. *net.*

Belloc (Hilaire)
PARIS THE PYRENEES. *Each 8s 6d net.* ON NOTHING. HILLS AND THE SEA. ON SOMETHING. FIRST AND LAST THIS AND THAT AND THE OTHER. ON. ON EVERYTHING ON ANYTHING EMMANUEL BURDEN. *Each 3s. 6d. net* MARIE ANTOINETTE 18s. *net.* A HISTORY OF ENGLAND In 4 vols Vols I and II. 15s. net each.

Birmingham (George A.)
A WAYFARER IN HUNGARY Illustrated. 8s 6d. *net* A WAYFARER IN IRELAND. Illustrated 7s. 6d *net* SPILLIKINS a Book of Essays. 5s. *net* SHIPS AND SEALING WAX · a Book of Essays 5s. *net.*

Bowles (George F. S.)
THE STRENGTH OF ENGLAND. *Demy 8vo.* 8s. 6d. *net.*

Bryden (H. A.)
HORN AND HOUND : Memories of Hunting. Illustrated. *Demy 8vo.* 15s. *net.*

Bulley (M. H.)
ART AND COUNTERFEIT. Illustrated.
15s. net ANCIENT AND MEDIEVAL ART
A SHORT HISTORY. *Second Edition,
Revised. Crown 8vo.* 10s. 6d. net.

Burns (Robert)
THE POEMS AND SONGS Edited by
ANDREW LANG. *Fourth Edition. Wide
Demy 8vo.* 10s. 6d net.

Chandler (Arthur), D.D.
ARA CŒLI. 5s. net. FAITH AND EXPERI-
ENCE. 5s. net. THE CULT OF THE PASS-
ING MOMENT. 6s. net. THE ENGLISH
CHURCH AND REUNION. 5s. net. SCALA
MUNDI. 4s. 6d. net.

Chesterton (G. K.)
THE BALLAD OF THE WHITE HORSE.
ALL THINGS CONSIDERED TREMEN-
DOUS TRIFLES. FANCIES VERSUS FADS.
CHARLES DICKENS. *Each Fcap. 8vo.*
3s 6d net. ALARMS AND DISCURSIONS.
A MISCELLANY OF MEN. THE USES OF
DIVERSITY. THE OUTLINE OF SANITY.
Each Fcap. 8vo. 6s. net A GLEAMING
COHORT. *Fcap 8vo.* 2s 6d. net. WINE,
WATER, AND SONG. *Fcap. 8vo* 1s 6d. net.

Clutton-Brock (A.)
WHAT IS THE KINGDOM OF HEAVEN?
ESSAYS ON ART. SHAKESPEARE'S HAM-
LET. *Each 5s. net.* ESSAYS ON BOOKS.
MORE ESSAYS ON BOOKS ESSAYS ON
LIFE. ESSAYS ON RELIGION. ESSAYS
ON LITERATURE AND LIFE. *Each 6s
net.* SHELLEY, THE MAN AND THE POET.
7s. 6d. net.

Cowling (George H.)
A PREFACE TO SHAKESPEARE. Illustrated.
5s. net. CHAUCER. Illustrated. 6s. net.

Crawley (Ernest)
THE MYSTIC ROSE Revised and En-
larged by THEODORE BESTERMAN. Two
Vols. *Demy 8vo.* £1 10s. net.

Cromer (Countess of)
LAMURIAC and other Sketches. *Small
Demy 8vo.* 6s. net.

Dolls' House (The Queen's)
THE BOOK OF THE QUEEN'S DOLLS'
HOUSE. Vol. I. THE HOUSE, Edited
by A. C. BENSON, C.V.O., and Sir
LAWRENCE WEAVER, K.B.E. Vol. II.
THE LIBRARY, Edited by E. V. LUCAS.
Profusely Illustrated. A Limited Edi-
tion. *Crown 4to.* £6 6s. net.
EVERYBODY'S BOOK OF THE QUEEN'S
DOLLS' HOUSE. An abridged edition
of the above. Illustrated. *Crown 4to.*
5s. net.

Edwardes (Tickner)
THE LORE OF THE HONEYBEE. *Thir-
teenth Edition* 7s 6d net. BEEKEEPING
FOR ALL. 3s. 6d. net. THE BEE-
MASTER OF WARRILOW. *Third Edition*
7s 6d. net All Illustrated. BEE-
KEEPING DO'S AND DON'TS 2s. 6d. net.

Einstein (Albert)
RELATIVITY : THE SPECIAL AND GEN-
ERAL THEORY 5s. net. SIDELIGHTS
ON RELATIVITY. 3s. 6d. net. THE
MEANING OF RELATIVITY. 5s. net
THE BROWNIAN MOVEMENT 5s net.
Other books on the Einstein Theory.
AN INTRODUCTION TO THE THEORY OF
RELATIVITY. By LYNDON BOLTON.
5s. net.
THE PRINCIPLE OF RELATIVITY By
A. EINSTEIN, H. A. LORENTZ, H.
MINKOWSKI and H. WEYL. With
Notes by A. SOMMERFELD. 12s. 6d. net.
Write for Complete List

Erman (Adolph)
THE LITERATURE OF THE ANCIENT
EGYPTIANS. Translated by Dr A. M.
BLACKMAN *Demy 8vo.* £1 1s. net.

Fouquet (Jean)
THE LIFE OF CHRIST AND HIS MOTHER
From Fouquet's "Book of Hours"
Edited by FLORENCE HEYWOOD, B A
With 24 Plates in Colours. *Wide
Royal 8vo.* £3 3s net.

Fyleman (Rose)
FAIRIES AND CHIMNEYS. THE FAIRY
GREEN. THE FAIRY FLUTE. THE
RAINBOW CAT. EIGHT LITTLE PLAYS
FOR CHILDREN. FORTY GOOD-NIGHT
TALES FAIRIES AND FRIENDS. THE
ADVENTURE CLUB. FORTY GOOD-MOR-
NING TALES. *Each 3s 6d net.* A SMALL
CRUSE, 4s 6d. net. THE ROSE FYLEMAN
FAIRY BOOK. Illustrated. 10s. 6d.
net. LETTY. Illustrated. 6s. net. A
LITTLE CHRISTMAS BOOK. Illustrated.
2s. net.

Gibbon (Edward)
THE DECLINE AND FALL OF THE ROMAN
EMPIRE. With Notes, Appendixes, and
Maps, by J. B. BURY. Illustrated.
Seven volumes. *Demy 8vo.* 15s. net
each volume. Also, unillustrated.
Crown 8vo. 7s. 6d. net each volume.

Glover (T. R.)
THE CONFLICT OF RELIGIONS IN THE
EARLY ROMAN EMPIRE. POETS AND
PURITANS. VIRGIL. *Each 10s. 6d. net.*
FROM PERICLES TO PHILIP. 12s. 6d. net.

Graham (Harry)

THE WORLD WE LAUGH IN: More Deportmental Ditties. Illustrated by "FISH." *Sixth Edition. Fcap. 8vo.* 5s. net. STRAINED RELATIONS. Illustrated by H. STUART MENZIES and HENDY. *Royal 16mo.* 6s. net.

Grahame (Kenneth)

THE WIND IN THE WILLOWS. *Nineteenth Edition. Crown 8vo.* 7s. 6d. net. Also, Illustrated by NANCY BARNHART. *Small 4to.* 10s. 6d. net. Also unillustrated *Fcap. 8vo.* 3s. 6d net

Hadfield (J. A.)

PSYCHOLOGY AND MORALS. *Sixth Edition Crown 8vo.* 6s. net.

Hall (H. R.)

THE ANCIENT HISTORY OF THE NEAR EAST. *Sixth Edition, Revised. Demy 8vo.* £1 1s. net. THE CIVILIZATION OF GREECE IN THE BRONZE AGE. Illustrated. *Wide Royal 8vo.* £1 10s. net.

Hamer (Sir W. H.), and Hutt (C. W.)

A MANUAL OF HYGIENE Illustrated *Demy 8vo.* £1 10s. net.

Hewlett (Maurice)

THE LETTERS OF MAURICE HEWLETT. Edited by LAURENCE BINYON. Illustrated. *Demy 8vo.* 18s. net.

Hind (A. M.)

A CATALOGUE OF REMBRANDT'S ETCHINGS. Two Vols. Profusely Illustrated. *Wide Royal 8vo.* £1 15s. net.

Holdsworth (W. S.)

A HISTORY OF ENGLISH LAW. Nine Volumes. *Demy 8vo* £1 5s. net each.

Hudson (W. H.)

A SHEPHERD'S LIFE. Illustrated. *Demy 8vo.* 10s. 6d net. Also, unillustrated *Fcap. 8vo.* 3s. 6d. net.

Hutton (Edward)

CITIES OF SICILY. Illustrated. 10s. 6d. net. MILAN AND LOMBARDY. THE CITIES OF ROMAGNA AND THE MARCHES. SIENA AND SOUTHERN TUSCANY. VENICE AND VENETIA. THE CITIES OF SPAIN NAPLES AND SOUTHERN ITALY. Illustrated. *Each,* 8s. 6d. net. A WAYFARER IN UNKNOWN TUSCANY. THE CITIES OF UMBRIA. COUNTRY WALKS ABOUT FLORENCE. ROME. FLORENCE AND NORTHERN TUSCANY. Illustrated. *Each,* 7s. 6d. net.

Imms (A. D.)

A GENERAL TEXTBOOK OF ENTOMOLOGY Illustrated. *Royal 8vo.* £1 16s. net.

Inge (W. R.), D.D., Dean of St. Paul's

CHRISTIAN MYSTICISM. (The Bampton Lectures of 1899.) *Sixth Edition. Crown 8vo.* 7s. 6d. net.

Jackson (H. C.)

OSMAN DIGNA. *Demy 8vo.* 12s. 6d. net.

Kipling (Rudyard)

BARRACK-ROOM BALLADS. *241st Thousand.*

THE SEVEN SEAS. *180th Thousand.*

THE FIVE NATIONS. *139th Thousand.*

DEPARTMENTAL DITTIES. *111th Thousand*

THE YEARS BETWEEN. *95th Thousand.* Four Editions of these famous volumes of poems are now published, viz.:— *Crown 8vo.* Buckram, 7s. 6d. net. *Fcap 8vo.* Cloth, 6s. net. Leather, 7s. 6d. net. Service Edition. Two volumes each book. *Square Fcap. 8vo.* 3s. net each volume.

A KIPLING ANTHOLOGY—Verse. *Fcap 8vo.* Cloth, 6s. net. Leather, 7s. 6d net.

TWENTY POEMS FROM RUDYARD KIPLING. *447th Thousand. Fcap. 8vo.* 1s. net.

A CHOICE OF SONGS. *Second Edition. Fcap. 8vo.* 2s. net.

Lamb (Charles and Mary)

THE COMPLETE WORKS. Edited by E. V. LUCAS A New and Revised Edition in Six Volumes. With Frontispieces *Fcap. 8vo* 6s. net each. The volumes are: I. MISCELLANEOUS PROSE. II. ELIA AND THE LAST ESSAYS OF ELIA. III. BOOKS FOR CHILDREN. IV PLAYS AND POEMS V. and VI LETTERS.

SELECTED LETTERS. Chosen and Edited by G. T. CLAPTON. *Fcap. 8vo.* 3s. 6d. net.

THE CHARLES LAMB DAY BOOK. Compiled by E. V. LUCAS. *Fcap. 8vo.* 6s. net.

Lankester (Sir Ray)

SCIENCE FROM AN EASY CHAIR. SCIENCE FROM AN EASY CHAIR · Second Series. DIVERSIONS OF A NATURALIST. GREAT AND SMALL THINGS. Illustrated. *Crown 8vo.* 7s. 6d. net. SECRETS OF EARTH AND SEA. Illustrated. *Crown 8vo.* 8s. 6d. net.

Lodge (Sir Oliver)

MAN AND THE UNIVERSE (*Twentieth Edition*). THE SURVIVAL OF MAN (*Seventh Edition*). *Each Crown 8vo. 7s. 6d. net.* RAYMOND (*Thirteenth Edition*). *Demy 8vo. 10s. 6d. net.* RAYMOND REVISED. *Crown 8vo. 6s. net.* RELATIVITY (*Fourth Edition*). *Fcap. 8vo. 1s. net.*

Lucas (E. V.)

THE LIFE OF CHARLES LAMB. 2 Vols. £1 1s *net.* EDWIN AUSTIN ABBEY, R.A. 2 Vols. £6 6s. *net.* VERMEER OF DELFT. 10s 6d. *net.* A WANDERER IN ROME. A WANDERER IN HOLLAND A WANDERER IN LONDON. LONDON REVISITED (Revised). A WANDERER IN PARIS. A WANDERER IN FLORENCE. A WANDERER IN VENICE. *Each 10s. 6d. net.* A WANDERER AMONG PICTURES. 8s. 6d. *net.* E. V. LUCAS'S LONDON £1 *net.* INTRODUCING LONDON. 2s. 6d. *net.* THE OPEN ROAD. 6s. *net.* Also, illustrated. 10s. 6d. *net* Also, India Paper. *Leather, 7s. 6d. net.* THE FRIENDLY TOWN. FIRESIDE AND SUNSHINE. CHARACTER AND COMEDY. *Each 6s. net.* THE GENTLEST ART. 6s. 6d. *net* And THE SECOND POST 6s. *net* Also, together in one volume 7s. 6d. *net.* HER INFINITE VARIETY. GOOD COMPANY. ONE DAY AND ANOTHER. OLD LAMPS FOR NEW. LOITERER'S HARVEST. CLOUD AND SILVER. A BOSWELL OF BAGHDAD. 'TWIXT EAGLE AND DOVE. THE PHANTOM JOURNAL. GIVING AND RECEIVING. LUCK OF THE YEAR. ENCOUNTERS AND DIVERSIONS. ZIGZAGS IN FRANCE. EVENTS AND EMBROIDERIES. 365 DAYS (AND ONE MORE) *Each 6s. net.* SPECIALLY SELECTED. 5s. *net.* URBANITIES, 7s. 6d. *net. Each* illustrated by G. L. STAMPA. YOU KNOW WHAT PEOPLE ARE. Illustrated by GEORGE MORROW. 5s. *net.* THE SAME STAR : A Comedy in Three Acts. 3s. 6d. *net.* THE BRITISH SCHOOL. 6s. *net.* LITTLE BOOKS ON GREAT MASTERS. *Each 5s net.* ROVING EAST AND ROVING WEST. 5s. *net.* PLAYTIME AND COMPANY. 7s 6d *net* See also **Dolls' House** (The Queen's) and **Lamb (Charles)**

Lynd (Robert)

THE MONEY BOX. THE ORANGE TREE. THE LITTLE ANGEL. *Each Fcap. 8vo. 6s. net.* THE BLUE LION. THE PEAL OF BELLS. *Each Fcap. 8vo. 3s. 6d. net.*

Marie Louise (H.H. Princess)

A CHOICE OF CAROLS. *Fcap. 4to. 2s. 6d. net.* LETTERS FROM THE GOLD COAST. Illustrated. *Demy 8vo. 16s net.*

McDougall (William)

AN INTRODUCTION TO SOCIAL PSYCHOLOGY (*Twentieth Edition, Revised*). 10s. 6d *net.* NATIONAL WELFARE AND NATIONAL DECAY 6s. *net.* AN OUTLINE OF PSYCHOLOGY *Third Edition*). 12s. *net.* AN OUTLINE OF ABNORMAL PSYCHOLOGY. 15s *net.* BODY AND MIND (*Fifth Edition*). THE CONDUCT OF LIFE. *Each 12s. 6d. net.* ETHICS AND SOME MODERN WORLD PROBLEMS (*Second Edition*) 7s 6d net.

Mackenzie-Rogan (Lt.-Col. J.)

FIFTY YEARS OF ARMY MUSIC. Illustrated. *Demy 8vo. 15s. net.*

Maeterlinck (Maurice)

THE BLUE BIRD. 6s. *net.* Also, illustrated by F. CAYLEY ROBINSON. 10s. 6d. *net.* MARY MAGDALENE. 2s. *net.* DEATH. 3s. 6d. *net.* OUR ETERNITY. 6s. *net.* THE UNKNOWN GUEST. 6s. *net* POEMS. 5s. *net* THE WRACK OF THE STORM. 6s. *net.* THE MIRACLE OF ST. ANTHONY 3s. 6d. *net.* THE BURGOMASTER OF STILEMONDE. 5s *net.* THE BETROTHAL. 6s. *net.* MOUNTAIN PATHS. 6s. *net.* THE STORY OF TYLTYL. £1 1s. *net.* THE GREAT SECRET. 7s. 6d. *net* THE CLOUD THAT LIFTED and THE POWER OF THE DEAD. 7s. 6d. *net.*

Masefield (John)

ON THE SPANISH MAIN. 8s. 6d *net* A SAILOR'S GARLAND. 6s *net. and* 3s. 6d. *net.* SEA LIFE IN NELSON'S TIME. 5s. *net.*

Methuen (Sir A.)

AN ANTHOLOGY OF MODERN VERSE. 122nd *Thousand.*

SHAKESPEARE TO HARDY : An Anthology of English Lyrics. 19th *Thousand. Each Fcap. 8vo. Cloth, 6s. net. Leather, 7s. 6d. net.*

Milne (A. A.)

NOT THAT IT MATTERS. IF I MAY. THE SUNNY SIDE THE RED HOUSE MYSTERY ONCE A WEEK. THE HOLIDAY ROUND. THE DAY'S PLAY. *Each 3s 6d. net.* WHEN WE WERE VERY YOUNG. *Fourteenth Edition.* 139th *Thousand.* WINNIE-THE-POOH *Fourth Edition.* 70th *Thousand. Each* Illustrated by E H. SHEPARD. 7s. 6d. *net.* Leather, 10s. 6d. *net.* FOR THE LUNCHEON INTERVAL. 1s. 6d. *net.*

Milne (A. A.) and Fraser-Simson (H.)
FOURTEEN SONGS FROM " WHEN WE WERE VERY YOUNG." (*Tenth Edition.* 7s 6d net.) TEDDY BEAR AND OTHER SONGS FROM " WHEN WE WERE VERY YOUNG " (7s. 6d net) THE KING'S BREAKFAST. (*Second Edition* 3s 6d net.) Words by A. A. Milne. Music by H. Fraser-Simson.

Montague (C. E.)
DRAMATIC VALUES. *Cr. 8vo.* 7s 6d. net.

Morton (H. V.)
THE HEART OF LONDON. 3s. 6d. net. (Also illustrated, 7s. 6d. net.) THE SPELL OF LONDON. THE NIGHTS OF LONDON. *Each* 3s. 6d. net. THE LONDON YEAR. IN SEARCH OF ENGLAND. Each Illustrated. 7s. 6d. net.

Newman (Tom)
HOW TO PLAY BILLIARDS. *Second Edition.* Illustrated. *Cr. 8vo.* 8s. 6d net BILLIARD DO'S AND DON'TS. 2s. 6d. net.

Oman (Sir Charles)
A HISTORY OF THE ART OF WAR IN THE MIDDLE AGES, A.D. 378-1485. *Second Edition*, Revised and Enlarged. 2 Vols. Illustrated. *Demy 8vo.* £1 16s. net.

Oxenham (John)
BEES IN AMBER. *Small Pott 8vo.* 2s. net. ALL'S WELL. THE KING'S HIGHWAY. THE VISION SPLENDID. THE FIERY CROSS. HIGH ALTARS. HEARTS COURAGEOUS. ALL CLEAR ! *Each Small Pott 8vo. Paper*, 1s. 3d. net. *Cloth*, 2s. net. WINDS OF THE DAWN. 2s. net.

Perry (W. J.)
THE ORIGIN OF MAGIC AND RELIGION THE GROWTH OF CIVILIZATION (*Second Edition*). *Each* 6s. net. THE CHILDREN OF THE SUN. 18s. net.

Petrie (Sir Flinders)
A HISTORY OF EGYPT. In 6 Volumes
Vol. I. FROM THE 1ST TO THE XVIth DYNASTY. *Eleventh Edition, Revised.* 12s. net.
Vol. II. THE XVIIth AND XVIIIth DYNASTIES. *Seventh Edition, Revised.* 9s. net.
Vol. III. XIXth TO XXXth DYNASTIES *Third Edition.* 12s. net.
Vol. IV. PTOLEMAIC EGYPT. By EDWYN BEVAN. 10s. 6d. net.
Vol. V. EGYPT UNDER ROMAN RULE. By J. G. MILNE. *Third Edition, Revised.* 12s. net.
Vol. VI. EGYPT IN THE MIDDLE AGES. By STANLEY LANE POOLE. *Fourth Edition.* 10s. net.

Raleigh (Sir Walter)
THE LETTERS OF SIR WALTER RALEIGH. Edited by LADY RALEIGH Two Vols. Illustrated. *Second Edition Demy 8vo.* £1 10s. net.

Ridge (W. Pett) and Hoppé (E. O.)
LONDON TYPES : TAKEN FROM LIFE. The text by W PETT RIDGE and the 25 Pictures by E. O. HOPPÉ. *Large Crown 8vo.* 10s. 6d. net.

Smith (Adam)
THE WEALTH OF NATIONS. Edited by EDWIN CANNAN. 2 Vols. *Demy 8vo.* £1 5s. net.

Smith (C. Fox)
SAILOR TOWN DAYS. SEA SONGS AND BALLADS. A BOOK OF FAMOUS SHIPS. SHIP ALLEY. *Each, illustrated,* 6s. net. FULL SAIL. Illustrated. 5s. net. TALES OF THE CLIPPER SHIPS. 5s. net. THE RETURN OF THE " CUTTY SARK." Illustrated. 3s. 6d. net. A BOOK OF SHANTIES. 6s. net.

Sommerfeld (Arnold)
ATOMIC STRUCTURE AND SPECTRAL LINES. £1 12s. net. THREE LECTURES ON ATOMIC PHYSICS 2s. 6d. net.

Stevenson (R. L.)
THE LETTERS. Edited by Sir SIDNEY COLVIN. 4 Vols. *Fcap. 8vo. Each* 6s. net.

Surtees (R. S.)
HANDLEY CROSS. MR. SPONGE'S SPORTING TOUR. ASK MAMMA. MR. FACEY ROMFORD'S HOUNDS. PLAIN OR RINGLETS ? HILLINGDON HALL. *Each illustrated*, 7s. 6d. net. JORROCKS'S JAUNTS AND JOLLITIES. HAWBUCK GRANGE. *Each, illustrated*, 6s. net.

Taylor (A. E.)
PLATO : THE MAN AND HIS WORK. *Demy 8vo.* £1 1s. net.

Tilden (W. T.)
THE ART OF LAWN TENNIS. SINGLES AND DOUBLES. *Each, illustrated*, 6s. net. THE COMMON SENSE OF LAWN TENNIS. Illustrated. 5s. net.

Tileston (Mary W.)
DAILY STRENGTH FOR DAILY NEEDS. 32nd Edition. 3s. 6d. net. *India Paper, Leather*, 6s. net.

Underhill (Evelyn)
MYSTICISM (*Eleventh Edition*) 15s. net. THE LIFE OF THE SPIRIT AND THE LIFE OF TO-DAY (*Sixth Edition*). 7s. 6d. net. CONCERNING THE INNER LIFE (*Fourth Edition*). 2s. net.

Vardon (Harry)
HOW TO PLAY GOLF. Illustrated.
19th Edition. Crown 8vo. 5s. net.

Waterhouse (Elizabeth)
A LITTLE BOOK OF LIFE AND DEATH.
22nd Edition. Small Pott 8vo. 2s. 6d.
net.

Wilde (Oscar).
THE WORKS. In 16 Vols. Each 6s. 6d.
net.

I. LORD ARTHUR SAVILE'S CRIME AND
THE PORTRAIT OF MR W. H. II. THE
DUCHESS OF PADUA. III. POEMS IV
LADY WINDERMERE'S FAN. V. A
WOMAN OF NO IMPORTANCE. VI AN
IDEAL HUSBAND. VII. THE IMPOR-
TANCE OF BEING EARNEST. VIII. A
HOUSE OF POMEGRANATES. IX. IN-
TENTIONS. X. DE PROFUNDIS AND
PRISON LETTERS. XI ESSAYS. XII
SALOME, A FLORENTINE TRAGEDY, and
LA SAINTE COURTISANE XIII. A
CRITIC IN PALL MALL. XIV. SELECTED
PROSE OF OSCAR WILDE. XV. ART AND
DECORATION XVI. FOR LOVE OF THE
KING (5s net)

William II. (Ex-German Emperor)
MY EARLY LIFE. Illustrated. Demy
8vo £1 10s. net.

Williamson (G. C.)
THE BOOK OF FAMILLE ROSE. Richly
Illustrated. Demy 4to. £8 8s. net.

PART II.   A SELECTION OF SERIES

The Antiquary's Books
Each, illustrated, Demy 8vo. 10s. 6d. net.
A series of volumes dealing with various
branches of English Antiquities, comprehensive and popular, as well as
accurate and scholarly.

The Arden Shakespeare
Edited by W. J. CRAIG and R. H. CASE
Each, wide Demy 8vo. 6s. net.
The Ideal Library Edition, in single
plays, each edited with a full Introduction, Textual Notes and a Commentary
at the foot of the page. Now complete
in 39 Vols.

Classics of Art
Edited by J. H. W. LAING. Each, pro-
fusely illustrated, wide Royal 8vo. 15s.
net to £3 3s net
A Library of Art dealing with Great
Artists and with branches of Art.

The "Complete" Series
Demy 8vo. Fully illustrated 5s net
to 18s. net each.
A series of books on various sports and
pastimes, all written by acknowledged
authorities.

The Connoisseur's Library
With numerous Illustrations. Wide
Royal 8vo £1 11s. 6d. net each vol.
EUROPEAN ENAMELS FINE BOOKS.
GLASS. GOLDSMITHS' AND SILVER-
SMITHS' WORK. IVORIES. JEWELLERY.
MEZZOTINTS. PORCELAIN. SEALS.

The Do's and Dont's Series
Fcap. 8vo. 2s. 6d. net each.
This series, although only in its infancy, is already famous. In due course
it will comprise clear, crisp, informative
volumes on all the activities of life.
Write for full list

The Faiths : VARIETIES OF CHRISTIAN
EXPRESSION Edited by L. P. JACKS,
M A, D.D., LL.D. Crown 8vo. 5s. net
each volume The first volumes are :
THE ANGLO-CATHOLIC FAITH (Rev.
Canon T. A LACEY), MODERNISM IN
THE ENGLISH CHURCH (Prof. P GARD-
NER) ; THE FAITH AND PRACTICE OF THE
QUAKERS (Prof R. M JONES);
CONGREGATIONALISM (Rev. Princ W. B
SELBIE) ; THE FAITH OF THE ROMAN
CHURCH(Father C.C MARTINDALE, S.J.).

The Library of Devotion
Handy editions of the great Devotional
books, well edited. Small Pott 8vo.
3s. net and 3s. 6d net.

Little Books on Art
Well Illustrated Demy 16mo. Each
5s. net.

Modern Masterpieces
Fcap. 8vo 3s 6d each volume.
Pocketable Editions of Works by
HILAIRE BELLOC, ARNOLD BENNETT,
E F BENSON, G. K. CHESTERTON,
JOSEPH CONRAD, GEORGE GISSING,
KENNETH GRAHAME, W H HUDSON,
E V KNOX, JACK LONDON, E V.
LUCAS, ROBERT LYND, JOHN MASEFIELD,
A A MILNE, ARTHUR MORRISON, EDEN
PHILLPOTTS, AND R L STEVENSON

Sport Series
Mostly Illustrated. Fcap. 8vo 2s net
to 5s net each
Handy books on all branches of sport by
experts.

Methuen's Half-Crown Library
Crown 8vo and Fcap. 8vo.

Methuen's Two Shilling Library
Fcap. 8vo.

Two series of cheap editions of popular books.
Write for complete lists

The Wayfarer Series of Books for Travellers
Crown 8vo. 7s. 6d. net each. Well illustrated and with maps. The volumes are :—Alsace, Czecho-Slovakia, 6

The Dolomites, Egypt, Hungary, Ireland, The Loire, Provence, Spain, Sweden, Switzerland, Unfamiliar Japan, Unknown Tuscany.

The Westminster Commentaries
Demy 8vo. 8s 6d. net to 16s. net.
Edited by W. Lock, D.D., and D. C. Simpson, D.D.
The object of these commentaries is primarily to interpret the author's meaning to the present generation, taking the English text in the Revised Version as their basis.

THE LITTLE GUIDES

Small Pott 8vo.   Illustrated and with Maps

THE 62 VOLUMES IN THE SERIES ARE :—

Bedfordshire and Huntingdonshire 4s net.
Berkshire 4s net
Brittany 4s net
Buckinghamshire 4s net
Cambridge and Colleges 4s. net.
Cambridgeshire 4s. net.
Cathedral Cities of England and Wales 6s. net
Channel Islands 5s. net
Cheshire 5s. net
Cornwall 4s. net.
Cumberland and Westmorland 6s. net
Derbyshire 4s net.
Devon 4s net.
Dorset 5s. 6d. net
Durham 6s. net
English Lakes 6s. net
Essex 5s. net
Gloucestershire 4s net
Gray's Inn and Lincoln's Inn 6s net
Hampshire 4s net.
Herefordshire 4s 6d. net
Hertfordshire 4s net
Isle of Man 6s. net
Isle of Wight 4s. net.
Kent 5s. net
Kerry 4s net
Lancashire 6s. net
Leicestershire and Rutland 5s net
Lincolnshire 6s. net
London 5s. net

Malvern Country 4s. net.
Middlesex 4s net.
Monmouthshire 6s. net
Norfolk 5s net
Normandy 5s. net
Northamptonshire 4s net.
Northumberland 7s 6d. net
North Wales 6s. net
Nottinghamshire 4s net
Oxford and Colleges 4s. net.
Oxfordshire 4s net
Rome 5s. net
St. Paul's Cathedral 4s net
Shakespeare's Country 4s net
Shropshire 5s. net.
Sicily 4s net
Snowdonia 6s. net
Somerset 4s net.
South Wales 4s net.
Staffordshire 5s net
Suffolk 4s net.
Surrey 5s. net
Sussex 4s. net
Temple 4s net
Warwickshire 5s. net
Westminster Abbey 5s. net
Wiltshire 6s. net
Worcestershire 6s. net
Yorkshire East Riding 5s. net
Yorkshire North Riding 4s. net.
Yorkshire West Riding 7s. 6d net
York 6s. net

METHUEN & CO. LTD., 36 ESSEX STREET, LONDON. W.C.2.

CPSIA information can be obtained at www.ICGtesting.com
Printed in the USA
BVOW081732080312

284750BV00003B/512/P

9 781174 784668